Books by JOHN SIMON

ACID TEST

PRIVATE SCREENINGS

FILM 67/68 *(coeditor with Richard Schickel)*

FOURTEEN FOR NOW *(editor)*

MOVIES INTO FILM

INGMAR BERGMAN DIRECTS

UNEASY STAGES

SINGULARITIES

SINGULARITIES

SINGULARITIES

Essays on the Theater / *1964~ 1973*

by JOHN Ivan SIMON

RANDOM HOUSE *New York*

All rights reserved under International and Pan-American Copyright Conventions. Published in the United States by Random House, Inc., New York, and simultaneously in Canada by Random House of Canada Limited, Toronto.

Library of Congress Cataloging in Publication Data

Simon, John Ivan.
  Singularities: essays on the theater, 1964-1974.

  1. Theater—Addresses, essays, lectures. I. Title.
PN2038.S5   792'.09'046   75-10260
ISBN 0-394-49804-6
ISBN 0-394-73118-2 pbk.

PN
2038
S5
1975

Most of these selections were originally published in *New York* magazine. Other sources of first publication include: *The New York Times, Commonweal, The New Leader, The Hudson Review, The Nation,* the Chicago *Sun-Times* and *Cultural Affairs.*

Acknowledgment is made to the following publishers for permission to reprint other selections by Mr. Simon:
Chicago *Tribune:* For "Theatrical Disorder of the Day," "Grope, Grapple, Fulminate, Lament—Don't Just Sit There!" and "A Roller-coaster Ride with Kenneth Tynan" by John Simon.

Caedmon Records, Inc.: For the Note by John Simon from the record album cover of *Cyrano de Bergerac.*

AHM Publishing Corp.: For the Introduction by John Simon to the play *Peer Gynt* by Henrik Ibsen and the Introduction by John Simon to the play The Wild Duck by Henrik Ibsen. Both trans. and ed. by Kai Jurgensen and Robert Schenken. Copyright © 1966 by AHM Publishing Corp.

Avon Books: For the Introduction by John Simon to the play *Danton's Death* by Georg Büchner, translated by Henry J. Schmidt. Copyright © 1971 by Avon Books.

To Karen
who unlike most of us
who merely know some of the answers
knew all of the questions

No two on earth in one thing can agree,
All have some darling singularity.

CHARLES CHURCHILL
(from *The Apology*, 1761)

CONTENTS

xii

INTRODUCTION

COLLECTED in this volume are most of the pieces I wrote about theatrical matters between 1964 and 1974. Not being reviews or critiques, they are, I suppose, essays. This should not sound pretentious, when you consider that all *essay* means is an attempt or undertaking. A very distinguished scholar once objected to my calling him, in a review of a book of his, a critic rather than an essayist. But all such distinctions are somewhat artificial. The specific critiques by a writer could be translated, in painterly terms, into portraits; his more general critical writings could then be considered anything from formal portraits through group portraitures to landscapes with figures. Yet in all genres he is—is condemned to be—himself.

Here, then, is a collection of my formal portraits and landscapes, along with a few historical subjects, still lifes and caricatures. It would be useless to pretend that there is an overarching theme other than *Theater* and, implicitly, the personality of the critic-essayist. Yet something, I believe, does emerge more clearly from such a collection: what the critic is like when he is a little freer than usual—when he picks his own subject, or is given one that he could turn down if he wanted to (as he cannot the plays that regularly present themselves for review), or has more time or space than usual (as was sometimes, though not always, the case here). In short, these pieces approximate what I might do for a hobby, as against what I do in the line of duty. But approximate only; a critic is wholly untrammeled only when he writes a much longer work.

What, then, is gained by collecting such shorter pieces? There are those who claim that random articles never deserve such enshrining, either because they have been read before or because they have only immediate interest. Not so. Many of them escape notice until they are available in book form, and if they were worth reading individually, they are worth rereading as a group. The principle is the same as with a painter's retrospective: single works are illuminated by juxtaposition, themes and developments emerge, and one is afforded an overview of the painter's cumulative achievement. Of course, if the pieces were worthless individually, they will remain so as a group. In that case, however, blame the publisher for gathering them, and yourself for picking them off a bookstore counter. The only innocents then are the author, who is naturally and guilelessly eager to have his scattered limbs collected into a whole; and the professional critic who, reviewing the book for a living, rightfully vents his indignation upon it.

SINGULARITIES

APPRECIATIONS

There exists a popular misconception that critics relish writing negative reviews much more than they do laudatory ones. Tougher critics are supposed to be particularly guilty of this character deficiency. The truth of the matter is that no one who spends his working life at a certain occupation wants to hate it, or is happy if it bores or angers him, as repeated sitting through and writing about bad plays surely must. But, we are told, isn't it so much easier to write a clever putdown than a persuasive encomium? Maybe so, but what serious writer in any field enjoys an easy success as much as a more difficult and challenging one? Actually, the only reviews one enjoys writing less than others are the lukewarm ones of routine mediocrities.

The "appreciations" that follow demonstrate, I hope, that enthusiastic approbation is as good a spur as anything to the critic—probably the best. One only wishes there were more occasions to experience and express it. There are many great theatrical works and artists I would like to write about; but the professional, nonacademic critic tends to write, like certain professional composers, only on commission. As a student, I could never understand why such magnificent composers as Bartók and Stravinsky, from whom I hungered for more and more works, wrote almost always on commission. Now that I have one thing in common with them, the fact of living by my pen, I understand, alas. But at least I was asked or called upon to write the following pieces in which, I trust, my grateful admiration, whether pure or slightly alloyed, does not in any way cramp my style.

PEER GYNT

A NUMBER OF YEARS AGO, members of the Comparative
Literature Society at Harvard received post cards announcing
a talk by Professor Francis Bull of the University of Oslo "On
Henry Gibson." After the initial shock ("those damned Scandi-
navians always know more about our literature than we do—
who ever heard of Henry Gibson?"), it became apparent that a
typist's error had transmogrified Henrik Ibsen into Henry
Gibson. Now, as any artist knows, a slip of the brush or pen can
be most felicitous for the work being created; here, however,
was that rare error from which a critic could benefit. For were
not those profound plays written, in fact, by two men: Henrik
Ibsen, a mage from the North, an exotic, quixotic heir of the
Vikings and child of the fjords; and Henry Gibson, some eminently sensible scion of the nation of shopkeepers, a trenchant
and acerbic son of Albion? Was there not behind, say, *Peer
Gynt*, an author who poetically exulted in his hero's adventures,
and a coauthor who critically deplored and mocked his misadventures?

Surely that is why Ibsen's drama in general, and this play
in particular, could give rise to such diversity of interpretations,
and, indeed, beyond diversity, to perplexity. Thus Una Ellis-
Fermor could remark of *Peer Gynt* that "few plays have be-
wildered more critics or led to more discussion," whereas Alfred Jarry declared that "the public does not understand *Peer
Gynt*, which is one of the most lucid plays imaginable." But
perhaps this cockiness of Jarry's can be explained by the fact
that he was himself a fantast and a *fumiste*, a visionary and

3

a practical joker, and that nothing could be plainer to him than what is utterly complex, if not contradictory.

For complex *Peer Gynt* certainly is. In a memorable scene of the play, the hero picks up an onion and peels away its layers, each of which he identifies with a phase of his life, in the hope of discovering what is at the core. The reader, too, may consider *Peer Gynt* an onion, with many layers to scrutinize in the pursuit of its full significance. The outermost layer might, then, be the verse form, which is no mean achievement in itself. *Peer Gynt,* written in 1867 by the thirty-nine-year-old Ibsen, is, along with its counterpart, *Brand,* written the preceding year, the high point of Norwegian verse drama. But whereas *Brand* depended almost exclusively on a somewhat doggerel-like trochaic measure, in *Peer Gynt* there is knowing alternation between trochees and—for more casual moods, more conversational effects—anapests. Even though Ibsen was to abandon verse drama after *Gynt,* he could justly pride himself on having erected a landmark both for poetic drama and poetry itself: "My book is poetry," he wrote to his fellow-dramatist Bjørnson. "The conception of poetry . . . in Norway shall be made to conform to my book." And so it was to be; but since we are dealing here with the play in translation, we might as well proceed to the next layer of the onion.

Peer Gynt, like *Brand,* was born out of Ibsen's indignation at his country's behavior. He wrote these plays in Italy, for to Italy and Germany he had exiled himself; for twenty-seven years he was scarcely to set foot among his countrymen again. One reason for his bitterness was that they had not recognized his ability and were cheerfully letting him starve. Ibsen, his wife and their little son were living off the charity of friends. But what hurt more was the political fiasco of Norway. For when Bismarck's Germany declared war on Denmark over Schleswig-Holstein in 1864, despite all the fine "Scandinavianism" that had been in the air, the Kingdom of Sweden-Norway under Charles XV neatly left Denmark in the lurch. Though students and intellectuals might be for Scandinavian solidarity and support of the Danes, the Swedish and Norwegian majority, and especially the peasants, suddenly cultivated their own gardens as never before. To Ibsen's despair and disgust, Moltke's army overran a Denmark abandoned by all the great powers.

In the sociopolitical sense, then, *Peer Gynt* is a satire on Norwegian pettiness, cowardice and lack of vision. These selfish, inhuman trolls and loutish but craven peasants are potent political satires—especially when the borderline between man and troll is shown to be as fluid as that between Denmark and Germany. Here are savage jokes at the expense of those who live in the past—whether the military past of good King Charles XII's iron days (the mad Fellah who wants to be King Apis); or the cultural past of the Old Norse language and themes to which the scholar A. O. Vinje and his followers would return (the madman Huhu who wants to reinstate the gibbering of orangutans), instead of moving forward with the present. Similarly, the insane counselor Hussein, who thinks he is a pen, is a takeoff on the Swedish foreign secretary, Count Manderström, who had believed the pen to be mightier than the sword when it came to averting Prussian aggression, but who found out otherwise—though this did not prevent Ibsen from skewering him quite adequately with *his* pen.

But the chief attack on the Norwegian social and political temper is the characterization of Peer himself, with his trollish notions of unearned and unrewarding self-sufficiency. When the down-at-heel King of the Trolls, whose own grandchildren have proclaimed him a myth, declares that he will go into the theater, which is looking for folk types, and the aged Peer, with death awaiting him at the next crossroads, opines that he will join him there, Norwegian culture, folklore and character—Norwegian everything—has been pretty well reduced to a pulp. Except that the satire is so precise and cogent that it transcends national boundaries. Ibsen was taking too glum a view when he tried to dissuade Ludwig Passarge, a German translator, with the warning, "Of all my works I consider *Peer Gynt* the least likely to be understood outside Scandinavia." Actually, it was not all that well understood inside Scandinavia, and soon Ibsen had to protest that the satire was being overemphasized at the expense of the poetic values.

The next layer of *Peer Gynt* is autobiographical. For here, more than in any other of his plays perhaps, Ibsen has included —or, more properly, transmuted—many elements of his own present and past. Aase has a good many of the features of his mother, and the grandiosely swaggering, then bankrupt and boozy Jon Gynt is modeled on Ibsen *père*. Ibsen's own bankruptcy, his ambivalences and tergiversations, his irascibility and any number of autobiographical details can be traced in the play, though all this is of minor interest compared to what the play offers by way of—shall we call it autopsychography?— the account of the movements of Ibsen's soul. "Everything that I have written," Ibsen informed Passarge apropos of *Gynt*, "has the closest possible connection with what I have lived through *inwardly*—even if I have not experienced it outwardly." Thus it matters comparatively little that Fru Marichen may have played at elaborate fairy-tale games with her boy Henrik; what does matter is that Ibsen clearly sees Aase as making her son into a flibbertigibbet and ne'er-do-well by blowing hot and cold: alternately threatening and cajoling, all set to take a stick to him, yet ready to defend him against the righteous ire of the whole world. And, indeed, Ibsen's real-life relationship with his mother lacked anything like that final loving kindness Peer shows Aase—though it should be noted that Ibsen makes it very plain that this is loving kindness, not love.

We now reach the layer that is most rewarding to examine: the imagery, construction and meaning of the play. Far more could be said about these than I have room for here, though to some, what follows will still seem overmuch. *Peer Gynt* is one of those rare poems or plays—or poem-plays—that attempt to see the life of man whole. Great as *Oedipus Rex* is, great as are the plays of Shakespeare, Racine and whatever masters before Ibsen you care to adduce, almost none of them dared to grapple with human existence in its totality. Those that did, like *Faust* (especially the second part), the Pole Krasiński's *Undivine Comedy*, the Hungarian Madách's *Tragedy of Man*, are not very effective on the stage. *Peer Gynt*, though not intended for the stage, succeeds admirably on it.

What makes *Peer Gynt* a great human document is that it

manages to squeeze almost every basic aspect of life into its comparatively narrow scope, and that however supernatural some of its elements may be, the play is finally closer to ordinary experience than are such poetically superior works as *King Lear* or *Life Is a Dream*. Its achievement lies to some extent in its underlying relevance to unextraordinary lives.

How does Ibsen manage to encompass so much in so little? He does it largely by means of two devices: ambiguity and counterparts. Let us consider the ambiguity first. *Peer Gynt* begins with Peer's account to his mother of a marvelous ride on a reindeer's back across mountains and into the sea. Now, we know that *Gynt* is both a fairy tale and a realistic work (just as the hero's personality and exploits are based to some extent on Asbjørnsen and Moe's *Norwegian Fairy Tales*, but also on what appears to have been a real person who lived in the romantic Gudbrandsdal in which the scene is set), and so we are as apt to believe as to disbelieve his story: it might be a *donnée* of the fairy-tale world of the play and meant to establish the fabulous nature of the protagonist; or it might be a mockingly realistic comment on Peer, a shiftless teller of tall tales. Which is it? Aase's reaction might provide the clue; but she first scoffs, then gets involved and credits, then rejects again—until one realizes that the unstable Aase cannot serve as a touchstone. In the wedding episode, we see Peer as an inept local Münchhausen, and this would seem to clinch the case against him. But forthwith he almost literally flies away with Ingrid, and thereafter literally encounters the Mountain King and his trolls. Or does he? In II, iv, Peer imagines that the crags around him are his father's house in its former splendor, and tries to enter, only to bang his nose on hard reality and fall down senseless. But a scene or two later the rocks *do* open to admit him to the hall of the Mountain King. Does this mean that in the former scene the dreamer's (or, if you prefer, liar's) imagination was not up to its peak form, whereas in the latter it was? Or does it mean that attempting to relive the past is impossible, whereas to sink into impish bestiality in the present is possible? Or does it imply that trolls actually do exist, and that though their appearance varies from fair to foul according to the spirit in which they are contemplated, their presence is real enough?

This ambiguity is a part, an important part, of the play's structure, and is not to be resolved. Accordingly, it is possible to view *Peer Gynt* as an allegory (despite Ibsen's not necessarily ingenuous protests); as a fairy tale with symbolic overtones but to be taken at face value for all that; or as a psychodrama in which the various supernatural manifestations are merely projections of Peer's greed, lust and fear. I believe that a correct reading of the play requires acceptance of it on all three levels, as an expression of Ibsen's own uncertainty about the meaning of life—and let him who is certain cast the first critical stone. It seems to me that this very threefoldness of the play is the source of its overpowering three-dimensionality.

Ibsenian ambiguity has the further fascination of operating like a set of Chinese boxes, the biggest of which is nothing less than Ibsen's *oeuvre*. Take the ending of *Gynt*. Does Peer die with his head in Solveig's lap as dawn breaks for the last time? Or is he merely being put to sleep by her lullaby? In other words, does Peer—or Everyman—find peace at the end of his restless journeys in loving senescent quietude? Or is there rest only when all journeying is done, in death? But this ambiguity is embedded in a greater one: is Peer saved in the end by Solveig's love, or can it be only a grace note before the Button-moulder's *coup de grâce*? What, in fact, does the latter's "We'll meet at the final crossroads, Peer!/ And then we'll see if—" mean? Is Peer damned or redeemed? From the facts that dawn is breaking, that Solveig is given the last word, and that Ibsen in his instructions to Grieg about the musical setting writes, "While the curtain is falling, the psalm singing will be heard again, nearer and louder," one assumes that Peer is saved. But F. L. Lucas has quite rightly raised the question of what being saved could mean in this context, since Ibsen did not believe in a Christian afterlife. And yet, in this scene, can we be quite sure even about that?

But if we now look at *Peer Gynt* in conjunction with the other panel of the diptych, *Brand*, the ending takes on deeper significance. *Brand* concerns an ice-cold, intransigent idealist who, having sacrificed everything to his uncompromising faith, ends up alone on a mountaintop, swallowed up by an avalanche out of which a voice proclaims, "He is the God of Love." This ending would seem to mean that Brand, magnificently moral being though he was, lacked Christian charity and is being punished by death. But it may also mean that God, forgiving Brand for a minor flaw in spite of which he was still too good for the world, now charitably gathers him to his bosom. However, the endings of the two plays appear to be complementary. The essentially noble Brand (Ibsen saw in him his own better self) is still, up to a point, condemned in the end; whereas Peer (in whom Ibsen incorporated his errant self) is almost certainly pardoned. And there is the ultimate ambiguity: Brand's altruism may not receive its full due, nor Peer's egoism its just punishment, which would be submersion in the ladle of anonymity. Ibsen's "deepest quarrel" may be, as Robert Brustein has suggested, "with the supreme authority figure, God himself," and the injustice of his universe. Still, I think we are not so much supposed to reconcile these antinomies as to recognize their existence—in Ibsen and in human destiny itself.

And what of the counterparts, the other device that Ibsen makes ample and rewarding use of? Well, the endings of *Brand* and *Gynt* constitute one example. Throughout Ibsen's individual works, as throughout his work as a whole, themes, figures, situations echo, complement or contradict one another. In *A Doll's House,* a woman suffocates in her husband's constricting world and leaves it through the front door. In *Hedda Gabler,* a woman similarly confined, but neurotic as well, leaves the world through the muzzle of a pistol. In *The Lady from the Sea,* a romantic past lover comes to claim the heroine, but she opts for a more conventional marital happiness. In *When We Dead Awaken,* the hero is lured out of a mundane marriage by a lover from the past and released through her to a higher, though tragic, destiny. Such counterparts crisscross Ibsen's work, and are particularly important constituents of the individual plays.

The counterparts may be thematic. Thus Aase's death, assuaged by Peer's soothing lies, contrasts with what may be Peer's own death, sweetened by Solveig's loving truth. More often, personal history seems to repeat itself: Peer's adventure among the trolls is echoed by the episode with the baboons (IV, iv), and again by the madhouse sequence. Does this mean simply that life is cyclical, or that there are various but related ways in which Peer—or man—loses his humanity? Inasmuch as in these episodes Peer tends to quote himself (often, ironically, ascribing the words to some great thinker), I would agree with Rolf Fjelde, who feels that Ibsen in this way "suggests that experience takes its shape primarily from the set of the personality, and that the world we never made is, often to a surprising extent, an outgrowth of our human powers or a denial thereof . . ." The lesson of the truth-hating trolls is that every single thing can be seen in two ways; the lesson of Peer's narrowness of understanding is that every different thing can be seen as merely more of the same.

The counterparts may be characters of the play through whose opposition certain fundamental views are revealed. Reviewing Brian Downs's *Ibsen, The Intellectual Background* for *Scrutiny*, R. G. Cox went so far as to conclude that "the plays show a pathological abhorrence of physical passion," and some ambiguity or unease about sex does emerge from *Peer Gynt* when we consider its contrasting pairs of women. To Ingrid, whom Peer uses and abandons, corresponds Anitra, who plucks and forsakes Peer. Though there is sex in both relationships, it merely contributes to their shabbiness; ultimately, moreover, both Ingrid and Anitra are sluts—though, to be sure, men's treatment of them may be to blame. Conversely, the Troll Princess (the Greenclad) and Solveig represent the dangers of the absence of a full relationship. Peer begets a monstrous imp on the Princess merely by lustful thoughts; scarcely less disastrous is his inability to confess to Solveig and receive absolution for his shady past. Abstinence permeated by carnal thoughts (a kind of lechery *de tête*) and abstinence out of guilt feelings and fear of commitment prove equally deleterious. Both put Peer to flight and play him into the hands of the Boyg by making him swerve from the straight path and direct action. Peer can come to grips neither with the Princess's swinishness nor with Solveig's purity. His untrammeled escapade with the three cowgirls is only a brief interlude: this game of Lucky Peer is an erotic tour de force, not emotional fulfillment. The happy medium between abstinence and indulgence, the counterparts seem to say, is hard, if not impossible, to achieve.

Peer himself has a counterpart in the play: the nameless boy who cuts off his finger to stay out of the army and remain with his girl and child, and who, fiercely loyal to his family and farm, toils away in the teeth of calamities that destroy his property from without, and amid filial ingratitude that poisons his happiness from within. Shunned by the community and shunning it, he nevertheless earns some grudging respect and a promise of heaven in his pastor's eulogy. In public, the fellow always hid the hand with the missing finger as his shame; at home, he was as active with nine fingers as others with ten. Was he a coward to avoid the army? Or was the sacrifice of a finger a brave act, enabling him to marry the mother of his child and live up to his private responsibilities? Certainly Peer is his opposite. He could not cut off a finger because, as he says, he would never do the irrevocable. He is more at ease in an alien world full of indifferent, even hostile, people to whom, however, he is unbound, than alone in a cottage with a loving woman to whom he would be obligated. His life is all irresponsible movement, whereas the young peasant's is all sedentary commitment. But—and this is where the techniques of counterparts and ambiguity combine—which of them is right? Nothing is certain: the pastor merely hopes that the peasant has been redeemed; besides, there may be no afterlife, in which case Peer, at least, lived a life of intense variety. It may even be that both were wrong, though both perhaps are forgiven. In any case, this counterpart serves as the point of departure for the questioning of Peer's life. And the great dramatist, as modern criticism has become progressively more aware, is not there to provide answers—only to ask the right questions.

Yet another kind of counterpart in the play is that elicited by refrains or incremental repetition: a catch phrase of the play recurs, identical or slightly modified, in a different context,

to take on new meaning and shed new light. Consider the Troll
King's ghastly motto—which puts the trolls into the same category as Dante's trimmers: "*che non furon ribelli/ nè fur fedeli
a Dio, ma per sè foro*" (neither rebels, nor faithful to God, but
for themselves). Men, according to the Troll King, say, "Man,
be yourself!" whereas trolls say, "Troll, be to yourself—
enough!" * The phrase pops up again from time to time in Peer's
mind, and never more dramatically than when he observes a
toad in the desert sandstone:

> *All petrified round—just his head sticking out*
> *He's sitting and staring, as if through a window,*
> *At life, and he is to himself—enough.*
> *Enough? To himself? Where was it I saw—?*
> *I read as a boy in a so-called "great book"—*
> *Was it the Good Book . . . ?*

What once repelled Peer has now come to seem so admirable—
as a saying and as a way of life—that he attributes it to the
Bible.

And just as verbal images recur throughout the play, physical images are resurrected. Thus the statue of Memnon reminds
Peer of the Troll King on his throne, though the Dawn God's
message is as different as could be: song and strife, effort and
creation. But to the superficial Peer, surface similarities, real
or imagined, are all that matter.

This brings us to the innermost layer of the onion, which
is Peer himself—a nothing, too, just like the core of the onion
in V, v, but an important nothing, a nothing that speaks to us.
"*Peer Gynt,*" wrote Kenneth Tynan, "remains unrivaled as a
study of the fallacy that is inherent in total dedication to self-
fulfillment." Indeed Peer's ideal is self-fulfillment; as he declares
to the foreign businessmen in IV, i, a man should be "*Himself./
Should love only himself and his./ But can he if he, like a
camel,/ Is burdened down with others' woes?*" Now put this
statement beside a beautiful bit of symbolism from III, iii,
where Peer, deciding to run away from Solveig waiting for

* In Norwegian, this antithesis is much more lapidary: "*Mand, vaer
dig selv!—Trold, vaer dig selv—nok!*"

him at the cabin door, calls out, "You must wait./ It's dark and I've got something heavy to fetch"; to which she replies, "Wait; let me help; we'll share the burden." The little white lie turns into a great black truth: Peer is going out into the world forever, or almost forever; he has to fetch the heavy realization that happiness does not lie out there; and Solveig must truly wait at the cottage door till it becomes death's doorway. And all because Peer cannot accept her offer to share his burden. To the self-deluding Peer, that which comes from another is a "woe," and sharing itself is a burden; whereas exclusive possession is ipso facto a prize. Peer's tragedy (and comic or tragicomic figures do have their tragedies) is that he thinks his problem to be *where* to find fulfillment rather than to understand *what* fulfillment is. Let us briefly examine some of his errors and trials, which unfortunately never become a trial-and-error method of self-discovery. If Peer is saved, he stumbles upon his salvation; if he dies happy, his happiness is thrust upon him while he is still, to the very end, trying to elude it.

It is Peer's besetting sin that he cannot give himself wholly to anything—he cannot even abide the word "completely" or the phrase "once and for all"—and that he must always feel behind him a bridge to take him back. Yet self-realization is commitment to something and someone to the point where, in the Lean One's expression, one slays oneself. But Peer can feel himself a part of the community only in a negative sense: when the ship he is on seems doomed and he may have to drown because the boatswain's number is up. With a woman he can experience communion only when he can take away something from her or wheedle it out of her: the woman is always an inferior or a superior from whom one gets things, never an equal with whom one shares. As for dedication to a calling or an idea—to being a prophet or scholar or emperor or whatnot—there is none of this in him; only opportunistic impulses—sometimes practical, sometimes not—and vague, infantile longing. From Solveig, the Ideal, he is always running away, except when she runs away from him; even at the end he barely has the courage to come to her, and then only for a list of his sins with which to sway the Button-moulder.

With sovereign dramatic sense, Ibsen establishes Peer's character in a series of correlated confrontations, some of which I have already mentioned, and some of which I shall rapidly sketch in here. There is, for instance, the mysterious Boyg. It is most likely that just as the trolls stood for that "damned compact liberal majority" Ibsen despised for its mediocrity, so the Boyg stands for some inner, psychological weakness, the pusillanimity that is the individual's invisible flaw. Now, though Peer is ostensibly rescued by bells and women's love from both trolls and Boyg, both encounters infect him. Even if he succeeded in protecting his front (his eyes) from the trolls, he did not defend his rear: their tail was affixed to him, and, years later, the Troll King reveals to Peer that he has remained a secret troll all his life. So, too, the Boyg's insidious command to go around, to rationalize and compromise and avoid direct-ness, has stuck.

Some encounters, like that with Memnon, are totally lost on Peer; others give rise to misinterpretation. The Sphinx, who is neither fish nor fowl, characteristically seems "himself" to Peer; and this misconception promptly leads to a vaster one: in the confrontation with the lunatics and their no less lunatic keeper, Peer finally emerges as Caesar, Emperor of Self. It is in the madhouse that, as Robert Brustein puts it, "Peer unwit-tingly discovers his most appropriate Kingdom of Self, for there illusion reigns supreme, madness being the triumph of the ego over external reality." Self-realization, as Peer practices it, is being beside the point, beside oneself.

The meeting with the Strange Passenger, who seems to represent a *memento mori*, the need to come to one's senses at the last, proves wasted on Peer. Even the minister's words about the dead peasant, "And he was great—because he was *himself*," fail to produce more than a lame nostalgia. The But-ton-moulder's effect is something else again: the threat of certain death and submersion in the nameless mass of the uni-verse hits home. Rather than give up his precious albeit abused self, Peer would prove himself a great sinner; he would rather preserve his identity even in painful, though not irrevocable damnation than lose it in painless but complete dissolution.

It is worth noting here what an effective symbol the Button-moulder is. For it was Peer himself who as a child played at button-moulding, and his ladle reappears to haunt him at Ingrid's funeral, where it has been acquired for a pittance by a strange youth. First the ladle was a symbol of waste: Peer's prodigal father encouraged the child to make buttons of silver and gold; now it is a symbol of mutability and transience. Thus death appears to Peer's psyche as an appropriately personalized image of waste and loss. By contrast, the Lean Figure is not so apt a vision of the devil: it is not clear why he should not recognize Peer when they meet, mistake him for the great sinner he is not, and be outwitted by a cheap trick of Peer's. He does, however, provide Peer with the opportunity of remaining himself to the last: although it is Peer's desperate need to paint himself to the devil blacker than he is, he still cannot help portraying his sins as grayer, smaller, more mediocre than they were. And, as mentioned earlier, he goes to his final encounter with Solveig barely able to conquer his hesitancy and for the wrong reason—trying to ward off redemption to the end.

Why, then, is Peer saved, if he is; why was Brand damned, if he was? Probably because of the dual authorship of the plays I mentioned at the beginning. Because no matter how much the idealistic Henrik Ibsen might condemn Peer, the common-sensical "Henry Gibson" recognized that such, at best, are today's heroes. "In his admirable theatre," André Gide wrote, "[Ibsen] presents . . . bankruptcies of heroism. How could he have done otherwise without drawing too far away from [contemporary] reality . . . ?"

Consider the richness of *Peer Gynt:* from antiquity it inherits the master image of the quest, and handles it, like the ancients, both rationally and, at times, with stunning irrationality; from the medieval morality it derives the supreme theme of man between salvation and damnation, and like the Middle Ages, treats it both with deadly seriousness and with broad comedy; from our own times it is imbued with that spirit of ambiguity and complexity that we feel, rightly or wrongly, to be the hallmark of us "moderns." And all this is cast into one magisterial metaphor: the restless voyaging of Peer Gynt.

Be it noticed that in Ibsen—in *Brand, The Master Builder, When We Dead Awaken*—the road to heroic truth leads upward into the heights of summits and towers; and so here, in the earlier parts of the play, Peer's path takes him first into the mountains and to that cabin he might have shared with Solveig. Then, however, the road begins to lead down and pointlessly across—across oceans, flatlands, deserts. But in the end it is up again: to the cabin and Solveig. With what mastery the outermost form of the play becomes identical with its innermost meaning.

CYRANO DE BERGERAC

(1965)

Cyrano de Bergerac is not a great play, merely a perfect one. The distinction is worth noting. Great plays struggle with materials so intractable, explore terrain so uncharted, attempt things so truly impossible, that parts of them inevitably resist encompassing by the author, let alone by the audience. In *Cyrano*, however, the playwright is always in full control. The profile of every act is a swiftly rising action, a succession of ever more resounding climaxes, ending with a perfect punch line. The contour of the whole play, on the other hand, is a parabola reaching its peak with the fourth act, then falling away into the bittersweet denouement of the quietly heart-rending fifth act.

But that is only part of the perfection. Almost every action in *Cyrano* is a gesture, a *beau geste;* almost every utterance a tirade of remarkable bravura or an epigram scintillant with irony. This to the accompaniment of the alexandrine handled with self-assured ease and elasticity, the verse never ceasing to further the dramatic development while maintaining many of the graces of intimate lyric poetry. (Unfortunately, the Hooker translation, though the most serviceable we have, loses—perhaps unavoidably—much of the marvelously punning wit and —avoidably—a good deal of the pointed concision and syntactical symmetry of the French.) Riposte after riposte hits relentlessly though charmingly home. In short, the play has, like its hero, a little too much panache, which proves, however gallantly, the undoing of both.

Yet if *Cyrano* falls short of the highest literary standards—

indeed, Rostand's last plays, *Chanticleer* and *Don Juan's Last Night,* are superior as literature—it is nevertheless a masterpiece of the theatrical. Consider the characters: a hero who is a delicious mixture of Romeo and Falstaff, Mercutio and Hotspur; a heroine who is brave, beautiful, pure, faithful, and even literate; a young soldier of overwhelming handsomeness who, though lacking the gift of words, can at crucial points find the right insight and even the right remark; a villain who in the end proves intrepid and chivalrous, devoted to the woman who spurned him and generous to an old enemy; a friend to the hero at least as appealing as Horatio; a poetic clown who on a humbler level is not unworthy of the fools in Shakespeare. Altogether, Cyrano at its worst is rather like Shakespeare rewritten by Dumas *père;* at its best, like Dumas adapted by the young Shakespeare.

And what pure theater there is in the various scenes: an uproarious play-within-a-play scene, a duel as good as any on the stage, a balcony scene second only to *Romeo* and well ahead of *Pelléas,* a battle sequence as rousing as anything this side of the movies—and any number of scenes full of moonstruck foolhardiness, heroic self-abnegation or noble dying. But for all this unabashed theatricality, *Cyrano* is not a mere escapist *divertissement.* In escapism, the good, or most of them, emerge triumphant and happy, while the villains are punished. Here, however, everybody suffers, every longing remains unfulfilled, and success, such as De Guiche's, scarcely differs from failure, such as Cyrano's.

This underlying melancholy is redeemed by incomparable verve, pluck and wit. Like Ragueneau, Rostand is a master poet-confectioner, magisterially blending pathos and humor, absurdity and common sense, abstention from felicity and affirmation of life. Everyone can find something in *Cyrano:* there is enough romance for the sentimentalist, enough wit and worldly wisdom for the unsentimental, and enough exemplary construction for those capable of apprehending form with their fingertips.

Cyrano offers splendid opportunities for the actors to shine, for set and costume designers to dazzle, and for audiences to empathize with characters rich in delightful virtues and no less delightful flaws. It is rather more theater than literature, but in that honorably second category the play has not been surpassed; its popularity continues undimmed since its first performance in 1897. In fact, *Cyrano* can be said to finish ahead of many more ambitious efforts by a nose, a long nose. I think it will always be as much a part of the life of our theater as it is of the imaginary theater of our inner life.

DANTON'S DEATH

(1971)

At a dinner party, W. H. Auden once expounded the idea that such is the wisdom of Divine Providence that people die when they have fulfilled themselves; that however short an artist's life may seem, he would not have added appreciably to his life's work by living on. James Merrill raised the name of Mozart, but Auden insisted that Mozart had nothing to add to his accomplishment. I ventured to name Georg Büchner, but to the best of my recollection Auden ignored the remark; perhaps, in the heat of discussion, he had not even heard it. That Georg Büchner should have died at the age of twenty-three is to me almost sufficient proof in itself of the nonexistence of God.*

* Georg Büchner (1813–1837) distinguished himself as a scientist (his doctoral thesis on the cranial nerves was a genuine contribution to contemporary medicine); as a political writer and activist (he edited *Der Hessische Landbote*—a journal later suppressed, and Büchner forced to flee Germany—and was the only littérateur of his time to move from theory to political action); as a fiction writer (the brilliant but fragmentary novella, *Lenz*) and, above all, as a dramatist of genius. His three plays are *Danton's Death* (1835), the only one published during his lifetime; the comedy *Leonce and Lena;* and his unfinished masterpiece, *Woyzeck,* not published till 1879. Hailed by Hauptmann and the naturalists as a precursor, Büchner has finally come into his own, and is now regarded as the first "modernist" playwright of Germany, if not indeed of the world. He died of an illness in Zurich, well before his twenty-fourth birthday. To compound our loss, his puritanical family destroyed many of his papers, among them, apparently, a play about Aretino, which they considered pornographic. His letters testify to a spirit as humane and loving as his art was profound and ahead of its day.

I can think of no greater loss to world drama, indeed to world literature, than this untimely decease. Think of what would have remained of Shakespeare had he died at twenty-three: probably not even the first part of *Henry VI*. Of Ibsen, only the melodramatic *Catiline* and *The Warrior's Barrow,* on the strength of which Ibsen himself would not remain. Shaw did not start to write plays till he was almost thirty. Brecht would have left behind unfinished versions of *Baal, Drums in the Night* and *In the Jungle of Cities,* three obviously gifted and equally obviously immature plays, as inferior to Büchner as they are plainly influenced by him. Pirandello came to the theater in middle life; O'Neill was twenty-four when he started out, in a sanitarium, on his first tentative little plays.

This is not intended as a brief for precocity; the play, not the date of its composition, is the thing. My point, in fact, is how unprecocious, how finished the writings of the young Büchner were: how different, for example, from those of that other youthful genius of the German-speaking theater, Hugo von Hofmannsthal, whose early plays (the first of them written when he was only sixteen or seventeen) are intensely lyrical, to be sure, but divorced from reality except in its most poetic transpositions. The works of a *Wunderkind* who came to art through art rather than life, Hofmannsthal's plays were, even later on, more readable than actable. Despite extensive experience in the theater, the Viennese poet-dramatist was never to achieve the instinctive, immediate stageworthiness of Büchner, who never had any experience in the playhouse.

To repeat, the point is not Büchner's precocity but his genius. Precocity and brilliance can perhaps replace existential experience, but only genius can triumph over total theatrical inexperience. Büchner could not even have *seen* much theater; his school was his politically and otherwise active life, and of course his reading. The influence on him of Shakespeare and Goethe is manifest, and he clearly knew the work of the gifted *Sturm und Drang* dramatist Lenz, about whom he wrote his one superb novelistic fragment. He may also have learned something from Victor Hugo, a brace of whose plays he ably translated, and something else (though this applies chiefly to his comedy, *Leonce and Lena*) from Musset. Yet these influences are already digested by the time Büchner writes his first play at the age of twenty-one: *Danton's Death* is no more like one of Shakespeare's histories or tragedies than *Hamlet* is like *The Spanish Tragedy*.

In the case of Büchner, moreover, the negative influences, the works and ideas he did not allow to affect him, are probably as important as the positive ones. Thus he managed to ignore the powerful suasion of Kant and Schiller, and to eschew high-flown idealism, a puritanical sense of right and wrong, the somewhat facile elevated style couched in strictly metrical verse—models to be avoided if one was to create the theater of the future, which Büchner so spontaneously and unprogrammatically did.

The objections most often raised against *Danton's Death* are that it is much too sprawling and episodic a play; that its hero is a passive victim, doomed from the outset and accepting it without truly fighting back; that the play is one long, depressing downward movement without reversals to speak of; and that there is not even a major confrontation between Danton and Robespierre. To the first objection the answer is that the hero of the play is not so much Danton as humanity in a moment of eye-opening crisis, and that the broad canvas is the most suitable one. In an *Athenaeum* fragment of 1798, after dismissing other interpretations of the French Revolution as commonplace, Friedrich Schlegel wrote: "One can, however, consider it as the center and pinnacle of French national character, where all of its paradoxes are crowded together; as the most fearful grotesquerie of the age, where its most deep-seated prejudices and most powerful intuitions, commingling in a dread chaos, are as bizarrely as possible woven into a tragicomedy of mankind." The emphasis in Schlegel's observation correctly shifts from "French" to "mankind," for the Revolution begged for, and elicited from Büchner, nothing less than a tragic view of life itself. Hans Mayer does not go far enough when he speaks of *Danton's Death* as "the expression of a whole foundered revolution, not just of the foundering of one revolutionary." Büchner does everything in his power to raise the action to the heights of timelessness and universality: Danton's predicament is manifestly not tied to revolutionary circumstances alone, and a protean despair, or at least clammy malaise, seems to envelop all the characters of the play except the crassest and vilest.

Indeed, the play is about human suffering and about the feverish, ludicrous, passionate ways in which people try to elude it, and about how all, whether gallant or ignoble, prove unsuccessful. Almost all the dramatis personae, certainly all the main ones, die in the course of the play, or are predictably not much longer for this world. But what makes the atmosphere so tragic lies elsewhere: in the pervasive sense of the vanity and sheer waste of it all. As Wolfgang Kayser expressed it (in *The Grotesque in Art and Literature*), there is an increasing awareness of "the aimlessness not only of man's action but also of his suffering." A good part of tragedy, in life as on the stage, is mitigated by the sense of purification, redemption or furthering of the cause of humanity by the example set. To take an obvious instance, the ordeals of a Romeo and Juliet or the sufferings of a Hamlet have an ultimately beneficial effect on their respective societies, and even the heroic victims themselves may have a sense of tragic dignity, indeed exultation, as they rise to the loftiness of their deaths. But there is another kind of suffering—that of a Lear, for example—which does not purify, fulfill or improve anyone or anything. In fact, before Lear knew the meaning of suffering, which alone could teach him humanity, he was considerably better off. Acquaintance with injustice, grief and suffering makes him aware of the abundance of causes for suffering, open him up to it, invite suffering upon his head.

So, too, with Danton. He was once a great warrior for the cause, later a great butcher for it; now he has become conscious of the futility of it all, and life has become a burden to him. He can afford to be, he has to be, a passive hero, being a man who has been granted—or been punished with—a glimpse of the ultimate emptiness of the universe. Clearly he expresses the disillusion with politics and people of Büchner himself: for this sensitive, magnanimous young man to learn that you couldn't help the lower orders against their oppressors, not so much because of the political power of the latter as because of the moral weakness of the former, must have been a soul-shaking blow. Büchner's statement to August Becker that the masses were accessible by almost no other route than the purse, and his words to Gutzkow that there were only two levers for the large majority, material misery and religious fanaticism, are in part what is dramatized in *Danton's Death*. It must have struck Büchner as a significant coincidence that both Danton and he were named George, and this, along with the identical disenchantment in revolutionary activity (however different in scope and significance), must have encouraged Büchner to project himself into that much larger but coarser figure. And this is what makes the figure of Danton in the play less passive on closer inspection: his revulsion, fed by Büchner's youthful ardor, becomes cosmic; the wit, poetic passion and intemperateness with which he gives himself over to it add up to something almost like an affirmation.

Karl Viëtor is certainly right when he observes that "Danton's rejection of the world and life does not stem from a stoically resigned disposition. To damn so vehemently, one has to be a disappointed lover, a deceived friend . . . one who in all his inconsolable desperation feels that it is a pity about life." What also makes Danton's passivity less gray is the sense of something splendid being discarded, of the grandeur of this downfall even in its predictability. If there is no resounding final confrontation between Danton and Robespierre, it is because there was none in history, and because, in this play at least, the enemy is not so much Robespierre as the *condition humaine*, which Danton confronts throughout—with sardonic wit, with exquisite sadness, with brilliance of perception and utterance.

It is worth noting that the very first context in which we encounter Danton's existential dissatisfaction is the conjugal one. Julie, the simple, loving wife who gives evidence of supreme devotion and courage in the course of the action, clearly does not satisfy Danton. What lies behind her words of love? What hides beneath her beautiful exterior? The problem is both emotional and epistemological: can there be true love, and also can there be mutual understanding between two people? Our senses are too crude both for loving and for understanding. The superb and painful images in which these doubts are couched are enhanced by those two curious little "no's" with which two of Danton's most affectionate speeches to Julie begin: no's of impatience, restlessness, sheer exasperation. And the final image of Danton's loving Julie as he loves the grave magisterially compresses into itself all the themes of the play: the transience and inadequacy of life and love, the exhaustion from living and struggling, the maw of death gaping for these people basking in the last embers of their existence.

Danton is an exacerbated perfectionist. When Lacroix describes him as trying to piece together the Venus of Medici from the best features of the various grisettes of the Palais Royal, we are to understand that he is speaking the truth, for the next scene shows Danton precisely so engaged with the lovely Marion. We hear him bemoaning that he cannot encompass and absorb her entire beauty—which ironically echoes his complaint to his wife about not being able to possess her innermost thoughts. And yet he strives: "Danton, your lips have eyes," Marion tells him, for like eyes, his lips have been gliding over and enveloping her entire body. But if Danton is in pursuit of the Whole, so is Marion—another one of those wistful, shadowy female figures, like Rosetta in *Leonce and Lena,* whom Büchner drew so well. Marion, the girl of easy virtue, is a somewhat cruder replica of Danton: she reaches incessantly after all men, convinced that whoever enjoys the most prays the most. She embodies an uninterrupted yearning and clasping in much the same way Danton does, except that in her the hunger for quality is translated into an itch for quantity. We feel that Danton is after the "All," whereas Marion craves the "Every." Most remarkably, however, Marion starts her two first speeches to Danton, whom she momentarily loves, with the same intemperate no's with which Danton parried his wife's lovingly importunate questioning.

"Multiplicity of episode," Max Spalter writes (in *Brecht's Tradition*) in defense of the play's much-carped-at episodic structure, "allows Büchner to make the content of one scene footnote the content of another." He observes that the playwright translates his realization "that all human activity is equally senseless" into "the very manner in which the drama unfolds. Robespierre pontificates, Danton philosophizes, and Simon curses—it all comes down to the same thing." By his episodism, Büchner not only sketches in a larger canvas of the Terror, but also does "his reporting in a context of meaningful cross-reference." Episodism "also makes for an exceedingly varied mixture of tonalities as Büchner alternates vulgar dialogue with political oratory as well as nihilistic lyricism." This is true enough but stops short of explaining how the scenes of the play interpenetrate and dramatically reinforce one another. The principal device is parody. Just as the major revolutionaries in their scenes earnestly emulate or ironically compare themselves to ancient Romans, so the little men in the street scenes consciously or unconsciously ape old and new heroes. But travesty can be nonpolitical too, like Marion's insatiability, which is a distortion and vulgarization of Danton's.

There are, to be sure, simple contrasts as well: the successful Moderates enjoying the fruits of *embourgeoisement* at the gaming table and in drawing-room badinage in Act I, Scene 1; in Scene 2 the impoverished masses venting their frustrations on daughters and wives reduced to whoring, or on some unlucky passer-by who for the mere possession of so aristocratic a luxury as a handkerchief is thought worthy of hanging. But consider now the two last scenes of Act III. In the first of these, Danton by his oratory manages to swing the spectators at his trial to his side. In the following scene the Second Citizen, vulgarizing oratory into mere demagoguery, makes the fickle crowd revert to Robespierre merely because he lives austerely, whereas Danton indulges in various pleasures. But Danton's hedonism at least has style; a few scenes before, Collot, Billaud and Barère evoked Clichy. There those among the Ultras who do not share Robespierre's asceticism revel in orgies that are a gross distortion of Danton's epicureanism.

For Danton is, above all, an epicurean. "There are only epicureans," he says, "either crude or refined. Christ was the most refined of all. That's the only difference I can discern among men." Later, awaiting execution at the Conciergerie, Danton reiterates this sentiment. In the hour of death Hérault declares, "Greeks and gods cried out, Romans and Stoics put on a heroic front." To which Danton replies, "But they were just as good epicureans as the Greeks. They worked out for themselves a very comfortable feeling of self-satisfaction." In that last, histrionic moment it is "not such a bad idea to drape yourself in a toga and look around to see if you throw a long shadow." From life to death, from sinner to savior, the motive is epicureanism.

But this homage to the pleasure principle is not gratuitous self-indulgence on Danton's part. Rather it is a strategy in the all-out war on boredom (we find it again in *Leonce and Lena,* and even Marie's unfaithfulness in *Woyzeck* is largely motivated by it), a boredom which, as Michael Hamburger notes in *Contraries,* "is not the result of idleness, but its cause; and behind this cause there is another, the demoralization induced by the experience of the abyss." We might call this a heroic epicureanism, a placebo to allay one's despair, to thwart the suicidal urge—thus not only a heroic but also a tragic epicureanism.

Corresponding to this bitter laughing all the way to the guillotine is the style, the language of most of the play. I say "most" because one-sixth, as Viëtor estimates, is taken over almost verbatim from Büchner's three historical sources. Such, however, is the young dramatist's artistry that quotations blend seamlessly into the fabric of his own poetic invention. Often it is almost disappointing to discover that a superb piece of dialogue (and not only, more predictably, the major political harangues) is transcribed from one of these sources. For example, Danton's remark that life is not worth the effort expended to maintain it ought really to be Büchner but is in fact Danton. Yet the slight tarnish this realization gives our pleasure is promptly swept away by our appreciation of how smoothly the passage fits into its context, which is from no other source than the wellspring of Büchner's imagination.

But to return to the correspondence of the style to the acrid, bittersweet, and finally wormwoodlike laughter that is the true subject, the dramatic vision of *Danton's Death*. To this underlying mood of gallows—or, in more up-to-date terms, black—humor the stylistic unit most appropriate is the epigram. Let us remember that "epigram" has two meanings, both of them relevant to the play's construction. *Danton's Death* is first epigrammatic in the sense of aphoristic, witty and compactly pregnant utterances. Characters, even some of the lowest, tend to express themselves in maxims, boutades, epigrams. This heightened, compressed wit—at times admittedly somewhat grating—is the nonobjective, the linguistic correlative of teetering on the brink, of trying to get off a good one before one topples, of feeling that every sentence may prove one's last and had better be memorable. Through such bons mots one keeps one's spirits up, one's fear or hopelessness amused. Yet these rounded, self-contained clevernesses are kept by their very rounding off, their smooth and hard sculpturedness, from fully latching onto and meshing with what the previous speaker said: there is something solipsistic about epigrams. They are part of what Spalter reminds us is the *Aneinandervorbeisprechen* ("talking past one another") that characterizes this play, which "is . . . Büchner's point, that most dialogue is really monologue."

But "epigram" has another meaning in classical prosody. The epigrams of the *Greek Anthology*, for example, are not necessarily witty; quite often they are simply lyrics characterized by concision and elegance. In this sense of a short, pithy poem, the epigram, or its prose-poetic equivalent, abounds in *Danton's Death*. Sometimes its lyricism approaches the laughter of the witty epigrams by its heightened, desperate cleverness; at other times it is the witty epigrams that become so fierce as to be a kind of savage poetry. But frequently the epigrams are sheer poignant lyricism. Let me give four examples of these shadings of the epigram and, to make the relationship and differences perspicuous, I choose them from among the specimens of the cosmic imagery that runs through the play and so powerfully contributes to lifting it above its time and place into transcendent poetry. "Nothingness has killed itself," says Danton. "Creation is its wound, we are its drops of blood,

the world is the grave in which it rots." This is the witty epigram approaching the poetic one. The purely poetic is exempli-
fied by Danton's *de profundis* as he looks at the night sky on
the eve of his execution: "The stars are scattered over the sky
like shimmering tears. There must be deep sorrow in the eye
from which they trickled." The straight witty epigram appears
in Danton's rebuke of Robespierre, set against a cosmic back-
drop: "I'd be ashamed to walk around between heaven and
earth for thirty years with that righteous face just for the
miserable pleasure of finding others worse than I." Finally a
poetic epigram, but with a wryness, a black nihilism that brings
it back into the ambience of the bon mot: "The world is chaos.
Nothingness is the world-god yet to be born." It should be
noted that this image turns the first one in our series inside out.
Why not? The play lurches and reverses itself, circles despair-
ingly, guffawingly, weepingly, howlingly around that center
that should be inhabited by the divine but remains empty—
unless, worse yet, it is inhabited by the gods of *King Lear,* who
kill us for their sport.

I SAID EARLIER that in *Danton's Death,* scene comments
on scene, often by way of travesty. The Second Gentleman,
who is afraid of puddles because he sees them as holes in the
thin crust of the earth through which he might fall, crudely en-
acts the predicament of Danton and the Moderates, for whom
the puddles of sensual indulgence, indolence and easy living
prove indeed to be fatal holes through which they drop into
their graves. But the grossly, bizarrely, vulgarly, even cruelly
comic scenes involving the populace are meant as more than
parodies: they are the unvarnished expression of Büchner's
disenchantment with the masses. Still, even here there are
not infrequent reversals, the mood flapping over into intense
understanding, in the spirit of those beautiful lines from *Lenz:*
"You must love mankind in order to penetrate into the essential identity of each individual; there must be no one too lowly,
no one too unsightly, only then can you understand them all."
It is this humaneness that acts as a softening echo of the shrill,
anguished or sardonic, outcries of the play and lets them re-

verberate with softened edges, without however making the play less tragic—more tragic, in fact.

Michael Hamburger seems to me absolutely right when he says about Büchner's *oeuvre:* "What is so remarkable about all these works is their fusion of fact and imagination, verisimilitude, and passion made possible by Büchner's extraordinary gift of empathy." Very often it is this empathy that takes over in *Danton's Death,* displacing that much lesser artistic stance, sympathy. Büchner infiltrates all his characters; rather than feeling for them, he simply becomes Danton or Lucile or Simon or Marion, or even the contemptible yet fully apprehended and realized Laflotte. Even those ghoulish harridans, the *tricoteuses* of the Place de la Révolution, are so penetrated and comprehended by him that we cannot cast stones at them without hitting ourselves—or at least some ugly part within us. Having realized this, thanks to Büchner's empathy with them—and with other monsters, high and low, from Robespierre and St. Just to the venal carters—we may still cast those stones, but we cast them more in sorrow than in anger.

Finally there is the great, unalloyed beauty that weaves its way through the action in the figures of the two wives faithful unto death, Julie and Lucile—the former an out-and-out invention of Büchner's (the real wife was nothing like this), the latter a poetization of the historic Lucile. "The two feminine figures," writes Karl Viëtor, "are the poet's offering of thanks to the one pure happiness in his precarious, problematic existence." The reference is to Büchner's loving and forever true fiancée, who, without being fully able to understand his genius, remained faithful to his memory and never married another. This tribute to women—even to fallen ones, like Marion or Simon's daughter—is a strand of loveliness that becomes visible at crucial points of the play and makes its last scene almost unbearably moving. And with what terseness! In a few last words Büchner transports us to the summit of tragedy. That Lucile Desmoulins should have to cheer the king, the lord of misrule against whom she and her husband fought, in order to be able to buy herself the death that alone can unite her with her beloved husband Camille! Unite? Everything in the play denies the afterlife. And in whose name will she be slaughtered? "In the name of the Republic," that wise and righteous state for which she and Camille toiled and struggled. What a laugh! What horrible sadness!

Irony and sadness: a twenty-one-year-old youth writes a play from which he wants to make enough money to escape to political asylum, and has to leave before he can collect the measly honorarium. In exile he sees the play published, but with certain changes that deeply pain him. It is, needless to say, not performed during his lifetime—not until sixty-seven years after its publication. Yet it is a play that, along with its sister masterpiece *Woyzeck*, anticipates, as the literary historian Ernst Alker pointed out, the essential elements of realism, poetic realism, naturalism, impressionism, expressionism, *Sachlichkeit* and magic realism. And to these we might add black humor and the theater of the absurd.

Reviewing an unfortunate production of *Danton's Death* by the Lincoln Center Repertory Company, I wrote in *The Hudson Review* (Winter 1965–66) something about the language of the play that strikes me as worth repeating here: "The language, from the outset, catches hold of poetry, and, though dragged through the mire of history and morass of hopelessness, never lets go. There is, if anything, an overdose of poetry . . . simile, metaphor, symbol are not so much its utterance as its very breath; yet the imagery is handled with such integrity and tact that the personal flavor of each character is sovereignly preserved." Today, however, what might strike us as even more important about the play is its warning to young revolutionaries, not from an old fogy, but from an ex-revolutionary as young as, or younger than, most of today's radicals and, unlike them, a genius. The danger of a just revolution, runs the warning, is not only its failure; it is also its success.

HAM OF GENIUS

(1974)

I'VE NEVER SEEN an actual Max Reinhardt stage production, although, like everybody, I saw his 1935 movie version of *A Midsummer Night's Dream*. I have seen the Salzburg *Jedermann*, a Reinhardt staging preserved in formaldehyde, and probably bearing no more resemblance to the real thing than an embryo so preserved does to a living baby. Yet I have formed a syncretic, secondhand image of a Reinhardt production that can be summarized in the words of Hugo von Hofmannsthal to Count Harry Kessler about Richard Strauss, with whom the poet was then collaborating on *Der Rosenkavalier*: "A curiously mixed nature, in which crassness is stirred up with the dangerous ease of a groundswell. He won't butcher [the opera], but it'll be as far removed from Beardsley as a Bavarian cow from dancing a minuet."

Some artists are impure. This is what the fascinating exhibition *The Theater of Max Reinhardt*, now at The New York Cultural Center, makes abundantly clear. Take the huge photomurals of the producer-director: the face—which started out as that of an actor specializing in old men's roles—runs the gamut of grimaces from the simian to the sublime. It is the mug of a plucky little Jewish shopkeeper haggling with fate; also the serene aspect of a *châtelain* posing before his castle, Leopoldskron. Here it is the face of a man being toasted at an international banquet covering a square mile with tablecloths; there the visage of a canny artist, its eyes amused and bemused by all they have encompassed, penetrated, seen through. And the faces of a director who acted out all of his actors' roles for them—magisterially, as many have testified.

"The acquaintance with Reinhardt aroused me in the way that my childish head is always aroused by personal contact with a man with a mission," wrote Thomas Mann in 1909, when his childish head was thirty-four. There was a boundless energy about Reinhardt, which neither the success of running concurrently three theaters, ranging from intimate to elephantine, and influencing the whole course of theatrical history, nor the sadness of running from the Nazis could in any way abate. A thorough megalomaniac ("he finds it intolerable to watch a play as an ordinary spectator," Kessler noted in his diaries), Reinhardt labored steadfastly, nevertheless, to make his theater truly popular. "He transformed the art of listening," Hofmannsthal wrote in the foreword to a book by Ernst Stern, one of the gifted designers Reinhardt employed; "he strove to draw the listener to another plane."

This is at least suggested in the present show by the remarkable set and costume designs on display. The number of Reinhardt's productions was legion—some, apparently, rather vulgar; others, it would seem, marvelous—as even these color sketches, photographs and slides indicate. At sixty-two, already an exile and making one of his last appearances at the Salzburg Festival he co-founded with Hofmannsthal, Reinhardt gave the impression of inexhaustibility to Annette Kolb, who observed him at the end of a dinner party at Schloss Leopoldskron: "No shadow of tiredness emanated from him," she wrote; "did he ever lie down to sleep at all?" And inexhaustible, too, is the range and diversity of the scenic artists represented in this exhibition, from Lovis Corinth to Norman Bel Geddes. A p.a. system dispenses the recollections of performers who worked under Reinhardt; it would be even nicer if these voices announced to us to whom they belong.

Most impressive is a documentary film by Reinhardt's son, Gottfried (shown on Sunday afternoons), in which we see Max in moving and still pictures, often in the company of famous writers and theater people, directing, making speeches, conversing. There are precious glimpses of his productions, and

interviews with some major actors, singers and composers of
the Austro-German theater, opera and cinema talking about
what Reinhardt taught them and meant to them. It is indescrib-
ably moving to see these venerable figures, first glamorous as
they were in youth, then commanding as they still are in old
age; they have a nobility, we come to feel, that working in a
theater such as Reinhardt's engraved on their countenances, in-
stilled in their voices and bearing.

Yet Reinhardt's achievements were ambiguous, even if we
dismiss the attacks of so fanatical a genius as Karl Kraus, e.g.,
"Formerly, the sets were made of cardboard and the actors
were genuine. Now the sets are indubitably real, and the actors
are made of cardboard." It is harder to disbelieve so eminent
a director and cogent an essayist as Berthold Viertel, summing
up the Reinhardtian theater: "The actor became more histrionic—in both the good sense and the bad—and more exquisite.
The director became—in every sense of the word—too luxuri-
ous." Reinhardt gave the audience "often intoxicating nerve
food" but "not sustenance for the soul."

Our own master critic Stark Young observed apropos *The
Miracle* (1924) that it ended up as "mere multiplication" and
"theatrical exhibitionism"; that later Reinhardtian super-produc-
tion, *The Eternal Road* (1937), he called "half vision, half
vulgarity." And he continued: "This elaboration and pretentious profusion only serve to remind me of what Cicero wrote
of Accius and his efforts to gild the classic pill with spectacle:
quid enim delectationis habent sescenti muli in Clytemnestra—
what do I care for six hundred mules in *Clytemnestra?*" Yet it
was of this ham of genius that Gordon Craig, the touchiest,
most self-centered of giants, wrote: "Reinhardt, who promised
me *Hamlet,* is a first-class man, whether he lets me do it or not."

THE WILD DUCK

(1966)

"It is hardly possible to criticize *The Wild Duck*," declared the eighteen-year-old James Joyce in a lecture; "one can only brood upon it as upon a personal woe." That was a daringly advanced view for 1900, but it came to be the accepted one. By 1934, however, Bertolt Brecht was telling an interviewer, "Works by such people as Ibsen and Strindberg remain important historical documents, but they no longer move anybody. A modern spectator can't learn anything from them." This was meant to be a deliberate provocation, but it, too, has come to be more or less accepted—if only by default of dissenting voices.

A young person confronting Ibsen for the first time nowadays may be more than a little unsure about what he is in for. After Shakespeare, Ibsen may well be the most frequently invoked dramatic presence, but whereas everyone more or less knows what he thinks—or is supposed to think—about Shakespeare, about Ibsen one is far less certain. His plays, in this country at least, are not often enough performed, and when they are, are performed poorly. Not much of interest is being written about him, and what notions about him linger in the ambient air have something to do with his being the first modern dramatist, his having ensconced the stage action firmly among the four (or three) walls of the living room, and his having been a "great realist"—a worthy accomplishment but no longer of burning interest.

Such half-truths and commonplaces are of little use, but neither can the problem of Ibsen be resolved by saying that after a while every great literary reputation suffers a temporary eclipse, only to be reinstated later as a classic. To begin with, there are too many exceptions to this so-called rule: Chekhov, for example, shows no sign of being relegated to oblivion, and even Strindberg, who was indeed buried, as in Brecht's remark, in the same grave with the Ibsen he hated and was hated by, is beginning to be busily resurrected, while Ibsen is allowed to molder. Moreover, to become a firmly established classic is no guarantee of anything; it may mean no more than being exhumed and reburied in a massive mausoleum, there to be somewhat more respectfully ignored.

If the neglect of Ibsen cannot be explained simply in terms of generations reacting excessively to one another, it also cannot be accounted for even by that somewhat more pertinent generalization that Ibsen has been confused in our minds with the Ibsenites, his various disciples and imitators, and that the sins of the children have been visited upon the father. All one can say for certain is that, for whatever reason, critics and scholars (with some honorable exceptions) have tended to misunderstand or oversimplify him, so that it is no surprise to find a reputable academician summarizing Ibsen's alleged message as "the necessity of clinging to the maximal ideal, however futile." Even if this were substantially true—as, except for one of the major plays, it is not—it would still be crudely condescending: can one sentence ever encapsulate a major artist's meanings?

But it is significant that even distinguished fellow-artists have been prone not to recognize Ibsen's worth. Thus Valéry and Cocteau once intensely irritated Gide by proclaiming the lively but mediocre Octave Feuillet far superior to Ibsen, whom Valéry dismissed as *assommant,* a crashing bore. D'Annunzio rejected Ibsen because of his "lack of beauty," but Ibsen himself indirectly answered that charge in a letter to Georg Brandes: "The Latin's aesthetic principles are quite different from ours: he wants absolute formal beauty, while to us conventional ugliness may be beautiful by virtue of its inherent truth." For D. H. Lawrence, Ibsen was, like Strindberg, "a bit wooden . . . a bit skin-erupty." For Yeats, he was "the chosen author of very clever young journalists, who, condemned to their treadmill of abstraction, hated music and style"; in *Rosmersholm,* Yeats saw "symbolism and a stale odour of spilt poetry." Max Beerbohm, for whom, as for many critics, Ibsen fell into the ambiguous category of "dramatist of ideas," wrote: "That is the dangerous thing about new ideas: they are old so soon." Ibsen's characters, Max carped, had a way of being mouthpieces for ideas that, if accepted, became truisms; if rejected, "irritating little old paradoxes." But at least Max foresaw that by the end of our century Ibsen's characters, having gradually grown younger again, would make their creator much admired.

In Austria and Germany, countries friendly to Ibsen's theater, there was again no lack of imperception. That master critic, Karl Kraus, while esteeming the plays up to *Emperor and Galilean,* deplored Ibsen's desertion of poetry to become "a rationalist of the miraculous who yet made out of the soberest thing in the world, out of social criticism, a dramatic abracadabra." "We younger ones," Kraus went on to say, "do not grasp much more of the Ibsen of the bourgeois dramas than that he has become the apostle of lady candidates for the schoolteacher's licence." Even Gerhart Hauptmann, much as he had loved and learned from Ibsen, was to note, "Ibsen's dramas are shadow plays." But perhaps the most unfair comment, because it is couched in the ostensible form of judiciously circumscribed praise, occurs in a letter of Henry James's: "Yes, Ibsen is ugly, common, hard, prosaic, bottomlessly bourgeois—and with his distinction so far in, as it were, so behind doors and beyond vestibules, that one is excusable for not pushing one's way to it. And yet of his art he's a master—and I feel in him, to the pitch of almost intolerable boredom, the presence and the insistence of life." But James hastens to add that if genius in the contemporary theater were "otherwise represented," Ibsen's mastery, "so bare and so lean," wouldn't count for nearly so much.

I have dwelt at such length on these censures and strictures because they sum up compactly the various objections through which we must today fight our way to Ibsen, which we must answer to our full satisfaction before genuine appreciation can begin. It would be a pity indeed not to bring off this rebuttal, for we should then have to forfeit the rewards of a playwright about whom Pirandello, so different an artistic temperament, was to say, "After Shakespeare, without hesitation, I put Ibsen first."

IBSEN, it would seem to emerge from the attacks, is a writer of problem plays concerned with ideas of interest to his particular time; also, he is the purveyor of a slightly rancid symbolism. He is preoccupied with the dreariest bourgeois realities to the point of becoming a bore, yet he is somehow unreal and shadowy. He turns the simplest things into a complicated mystique, but then again, he is as bare and lean and literal as (if I understand Lawrence's "skin-erupty" correctly) a pimply youth. These rather contradictory charges appear to be referring to at least two different authors, but that in itself does not invalidate them. For Ibsen wrote at least three different kinds of drama, as he himself indicated when he made his allegorically autobiographical Master Builder Solness tell about the three kinds of buildings he erected in three phases of his life. In accord with Solness' description of his structures (churches, plain dwellings, and a combination of the two), it has become customary to view Ibsen's career as a kind of Hegelian process: the early romantic plays and metaphysical verse dramas (thesis); the sober, socially concerned plays, prosaic and dialectical, of the middle period (antithesis); and, last, works introducing symbolic and visionary elements into realistic situations and dialogue (synthesis). Although there is obvious justification for this schematization of Ibsen's development, there are reasons for not swallowing it whole. For one thing, the division is not that rigid: one can find individual scenes within almost any play of Ibsen's that hark backward or look forward. For another, the danger of this view is the implication that the last phase, because it blends the principal strains of the two preceding ones, must needs surpass them in quality. Now, though I would agree that one of these last plays, The Master Builder, is probably Ibsen's best, this does not mean that Little Eyolf is better than Peer Gynt, or that John Gabriel Borkman is to be preferred to Ghosts.

However, once we recognize the variety within Ibsen's work, we realize that none of the cited charges can bear on more than one aspect of it, and that sweeping condemnations are likely to mean insufficient acquaintance with the writings as a whole. But the objections might still be valid at least as far as some part or aspect of Ibsen's creation is concerned, and so need to be examined one by one. Let us begin with the charge of excessive bourgeois realism, and its apparent complement, that of mistily vague symbolism, as they might apply to *The Wild Duck.*

That Ibsen's sympathies were not with the bourgeoisie—or, for that matter, with the lower classes—he was at no pains to hide. It was in a speech to, of all people, the workingmen of Trondhjem, that Ibsen declared "real liberty" to be "beyond the power of the present democracy" to achieve. "An element of aristocracy," he continued, "must enter into our national life, our administration, our representative bodies, and our press." "Of course," he added, "I am thinking of an aristocracy of character, of mind, and will." The fact remains that an aristocracy (or nobility), even if of mind rather than birth, is not a bourgeois concept, and Ibsen made it plain in all his plays that he had little sympathy with the bourgeois way of life. True, Hjalmar Ekdal is patently bourgeois, not the least so in his spurious aspirations to be something else, but Hjalmar is very clearly an antihero. Ibsen may write his publisher that "long daily association with the characters of this play has endeared them to me, despite their manifold failings," but this shows only that, like any true artist, he gets inside his creations, not that he shares their values.

If we look for Ibsen's sympathies in the play, they lie chiefly with Hedvig and Dr. Relling, and perhaps to some extent also with Gina. But Gina is definitely plebeian, whereas Relling, whatever his origins and in spite of his calling, has become a bohemian. As for Hedvig, in her capacity for love and her love of beauty, she is patently a member of Ibsen's nobility, as her Viking name further suggests.

So much for the "bourgeois." But what about the realism? I should think that in itself realism is hardly a pejorative label. It has not harmed Balzac or Dickens, Tolstoy or Thomas Mann.

The question is merely whether the naturalistic detail is re-deemed by sufficient resonance, whether it does not exhaust it-self—and us—in simple enumeration. Here it is relevant to examine Ibsen's language, and it is only fitting to pick the very passage Karl Kraus contemned: Hedvig has just said of the wild duck that "nobody knows who she is, and nobody knows where she comes from even."

> GREGERS: And she's been down in the depths of the sea.
> HEDVIG (*looks quickly at him, suppresses a smile and asks*): Why do you say "depths of the sea"?
> GREGERS: What else should I say?
> HEDVIG: You could have said "the sea bed" or "the bottom of the sea."
> GREGERS: Can't I just as well say "the depths of the sea"?
> HEDVIG: Yes, but it sounds so strange to me when someone else says "the depths of the sea."

It will be noticed immediately that there is something poetic, or, at the very least, hypnotic in the way Ibsen uses repetition here. It becomes more than a mere incantatory refrain, more even than the evocation of a trancelike state in which every reiteration transports the speakers farther down toward the depths of the sea. It conveys, above all, Hedvig's rapt astonish-ment at the fact that someone else uses the romantic, idealistic vocabulary of her fairy-tale vision; it explains why and how Gregers gains his baleful ascendancy over the girl; and finally it establishes for us the tragicomic kinship between the deleteri-ously foolish idealism of the adult and the touching, perilous idealism of the child.

Throughout this play, Ibsen manages to use his "realistic" dialogue very much in the manner of a poet, which he had been and never quite ceased to be, whatever he might say, and even though he gave up writing plays in verse. It is with a poet's care that Ibsen, in the Norwegian, attuned his ear to each character's particular diction; as he warned a translator, "each person in the play has his own special, individual way of speaking, by means of which his degree of education or learn-ing can be noted." But the control of language goes much further. When, for instance, Hjalmar, overdramatizing things in his customary fashion, refers to Hedvig as an intruder, and the unhappy girl, trembling, asks barely audibly, "Is that me?" * the use of these three tiny, incredulous, anguished monosyllables is infinitely more moving and poetic than any longer, more deliberately pathetic utterance could be. Again, Hjalmar's grandiloquent periphrases and euphuisms—like the references to his father as "that poor old silver-haired man," when in fact he is bald and wears a dirty reddish wig—have a way of achieving heights of the antipoetic accessible only to the true poet. Moreover, as I shall try to show later, Ibsen is a virtuoso of imagery, a talent hardly consistent with prosaism. For the moment, consider only Hjalmar's histrionic description of Hedvig to Gregers: "She's as happy and carefree as a little bird—flying straight into a life of endless night." He is, of course, referring to her approaching loss of sight, but the phrase-making clearly suggests how insensitive Hjalmar is to the true meaning of his daughter's impending blindness. However, the trashy sentimentality of "little bird" and "a life of endless night" contains a harrowing, prophetic truth undreamt of by the speaker: Hedvig ends up taking the little bird's place as sacrificial victim, and she does fly straight—not into a life of endless night, but, more dreadfully, into the endless night of death.

This brings us to the matter of Ibsen's symbolism, and the shadowy or "spilt" poetry of which he has likewise been accused. As in the case of realism, there is nothing wrong with symbolism per se, unless (as with Maeterlinck and certain *fin-de-siècle* writers) it ceases to be grounded in reality, so that the symbols, having no longer any recognizable life in them, become shadows, shadows not even cast by human bodies. But consider now the central symbol of the wild duck. She is, first, a very real bird, serving as a mirror for the various characters' attitudes toward life: old Ekdal, for example, dodderingly relives in her his past as a great hunter; Hjalmar relishes her as "the aristocrat of the attic" endowing him with status. To Gregers, she is that illusion he is determined to uproot; to Gina, a

---

* The translators have correctly translated the three Norwegian monosyllables, "*Er det mig?*," with the tersest English equivalent.

harmless whim in which a wise woman indulges her family; to Hedvig, the promise of all that beauty of which her impoverished childhood is deprived. As such, the duck is entirely believable and a thoroughly functional dramatic device.

But the duck is also a complex and multilaterally operative symbol. She lives, wounded yet almost normal, in a make-believe natural habitat, an attic that postures as sea and woods. She survives well enough, and yet she does not belong among these tame, insipid pigeons and hens. In this sense, she stands for beings like Hjalmar and Hedvig, who live in imaginary worlds: Hjalmar in that of his own "genius," Hedvig in that of her egotistical father's love, a love that she has to invent for herself. Hjalmar is wounded by his weakness, his megalomania; Hedvig by her dimming eyesight, the drabness of her present and future, the very fragility of puberty. Yet the illusion of forest, sky, sea—of greatness, freedom, beauty—keeps them going. Would it have been better for the duck to die of its wounds in the depths of the sea?

Gradually the duck absorbs into herself that illusion, or life-lie, that Gregers is out to destroy. Thus Hedvig's last act takes on an intensely symbolic significance. But the act is, first of all, psychologically right and true to life. Hedvig does not go into the attic to immolate herself, as Mary McCarthy and some others extravagantly suppose. A girl in the difficult phase of puberty, Hedvig is, besides being intelligent and charming, what the French call *une petite exaltée*—or rather she becomes one, goaded by Gregers' malefic hints and by Hjalmar's rejection of her. Very plainly she exclaims, as she leaves the stage, "The wild duck!"—she will now shoot her dearest possession to regain her father's love. Suicide is not at all on her mind, nor any grand, symbolic self-identification with the duck. But confronted with the deed (note how much time elapses before the shot is heard), she cannot do it. Rather than kill the beloved creature, and profoundly miserable as she already is, she prefers to kill herself. It is at this point only that the symbolism takes over: man cannot slay the illusion, the life-lie, he lives by; if he tries to, he kills himself.

This does not yet exhaust the wild duck's symbolic value.

She is also an emissary of the mystery that surrounds life; as Hedvig puts it, one knows neither who the duck is, nor whence she comes. In that sense, her very presence, so incongruous and somehow provocative in that attic, embodies the incursion of the natural world, of forces beyond man's control or ken, into his everyday life. When the duck is mentioned, the persons of the play seem to become more passionately alive, the dialogue quickens and takes on overtones not entirely canny. And for this reason, too, it is fitting that Hedvig should be unable to shoot and extinguish a being that represents something bigger than man and unconquerable by him.

When one assesses how much this symbol concentrates, deepens and sums up the action and meaning of the play, and with what insight, assurance and naturalness Ibsen handles it, one is amazed that anyone should have questioned Ibsen's right to his symbolism. Thus it is incomprehensible how Brian W. Downs, after making some cogent remarks about the duck, can still consider her a "detachable" part of the play, "a grace note," merely because Ibsen did not have her in his first draft and because the plot does not absolutely require her presence. Surely the fact that a drama would have validity even were it less powerful, or the circumstance that the poet-playwright found his perfect expression only after some groping, cannot be sufficient cause for doubting the germaneness of a triumph of the imagination.

What, next, of Beerbohm's charge, that Ibsen is essentially a playwright of new ideas, of problem plays with topical interest—in short, a polemist? It is true that polemic, unlike realism or symbolism, is likely to be artistically limiting. As Max pointed out, specific social issues cease to matter. One or two lesser plays of Ibsen's, *The League of Youth*, for example, do fall into the problem-play category, and can indeed be dismissed today. It is even true that a much better work, *An Enemy of the People*, has elements of the problem play about it (though the propagandistic aspects became underlined only in Arthur Miller's adaptation—a telling example of the difference between Ibsen and one of the Ibsenites); it is also true that *The Wild Duck*, written in part as an answer to *An Enemy of the People*, to show the other side of the coin, might seem in part polemical. In the earlier play, intransigent, heroic idealism is shown as the only honorable way of life, however fraught with peril; whereas in *The Wild Duck*, Ibsen reveals how impractical, obtuse and disastrous idealism can be in the wrong hands, wrongly applied. Even *An Enemy of the People*, however, is far from being a mere tract: for one thing, the polluted water and the unmasking of the corruption that fosters it function as symbols for the state of society and for Ibsen's dramatic fight for truth; for another, the issues are so basic, the conflicts so timeless, the characters so gripping, that the play has the same kind of eternal artistic validity that, say, *Coriolanus* has.

But as for *The Wild Duck*, if it has any polemical character, the polemic is strictly against Ibsen himself: in Dr. Stockmann, he had shown himself in a highly idealized light; in Gregers Werle, he caricatures himself relentlessly. Beyond that, in what possible sense can *The Wild Duck* be considered time-bound? The issue is clearly between those who believe in "the claim of the ideal" and the partisans of "the life-lie," and this battle is not to be localized in space any more than in time. Eric Bentley is very right when he observes in his *In Search of Theater* that Ibsen "is less interested in 'modern ideas' themselves than in certain ideas that go behind them. In Ibsen one must always look for the idea behind the idea."

And the charge of "lack of beauty," as voiced by d'Annunzio, what of that? What of James's all too willing concession that Ibsen is "ugly, common, hard, prosaic"? The fact is that the mere handling of various kinds of imagery in *The Wild Duck* should dispel any such notions: poet's images, for Ibsen in his lyrics and verse dramas was very much the poet; and painter's images, for Ibsen was also a not ungifted painter, and might have developed further in this direction had not his wife insisted that he stick to drama.

Take, first of all, the lighting of each act, to which Ibsen urged producers to pay careful attention. In the first act, in Werle's well-appointed study, there are those green-shielded lamps that shed a muted, viridescent light. Northam and other critics have recognized in this a reminder of the forests and their revenge, about which old Ekdal keeps babbling; as well as of the sea-deep from which the wild duck was dragged. Certainly this light is also a reminder of the blindness that is settling on Haakon Werle, and that directly or indirectly is to infect the Ekdal household. At the Ekdals', the second act is moonlit, to underscore the romantic illusions being nurtured there; the third takes place on a bright morning, in the kind of light equally suited to false cheerfulness and rude awakenings; the fourth, in the growing darkness of descending evening as misery progressively enwraps the family; the fifth, on a gray, snowy, disconsolate day almost inviting disaster. Again, the bipartite division of both sets, with a front room for the facts of life, so to speak, and another in back, for the feasts money can buy or the dreams poverty can feed on, is conceived along splendidly painterly lines. So too are such striking individual images as when Gregers complains of the dark in which the Ekdals live, and Gina, with touching innocence, removes the shade from the lamp.

But Ibsen does not excel merely in such visual imagery; his verbal-intellectual images are no less commanding. Take the whole series of references to eyes and seeing. We hear from Werle, Sr., that his wife's eyes had been "befogged," presently we see Werle's guests and wife-to-be playing blindman's buff, and we have already learned that Werle is losing his sight. So the unfortunate Gregers seems to have blindness of one kind or another on both sides of his family, and in his social class as well. Hjalmar, too, is a non-seer. As the first act concludes with the symbolic game of blindman's buff, the second ends with Hjalmar's dozing off even as he gibbers about his great forthcoming invention in the field of photography—itself a form of seeing—but an invention that will never come about. Thus Gina's words that end the act, "Shh! Don't wake him up," take on added, poignant meaning. Gregers' ailment (and how modern Ibsen is in having Dr. Relling observe that we are all crazy or sick) is his befogged vision of reality; Hjalmar's is being asleep and not seeing at all. But to shut one's eyes to life is less catastrophic than to see distortedly and distortingly; still, Gregers announces to his father that he will "open Hjalmar Ekdal's eyes." Marvel of marvels: the purblind shall lead the sleeper!

The image takes on darker hues. The jealous and outraged Hjalmar, characteristically forgetting that his own daughter is going blind, exults in Werle's approaching affliction. When he declaims about retribution for what he calls Werle's blinding of an innocent fellow-creature—which is his grandiloquent way of referring to his father's imprisonment (as much the old man's fault as Werle's, by the way)—Gina is rightly terrified: Hedvig, as Hjalmar doesn't know and mustn't find out, is the fruit of Gina's affair with Werle; if there is to be retribution as well as heredity, what chance has poor Hedvig got? Echoes of the Biblical eye for an eye further contribute to the somber ludicrousness of Hjalmar's rhetoric. Later, when Hjalmar, in connection with Werle's deed of gift to Hedvig, exclaims, "Now I'm beginning to see!" and still later, as unbeknown to him Hedvig is about to shoot herself, reiterates, "My eyes have been opened," the eye-image grows into something enormous and outrageous and not the less tragic for being absurd. In The Life of the Drama, Eric Bentley properly insists that "Hjalmar Ekdal is the classical instance . . . of tragedy intensified, instead of lightened, by comedy." How fearfully appropriate this tragicomic master-image is to a play in which neither of the co-perpetrators comes to see anything in the tragedy: Gregers will go on being the thirteenth at table, and Hjalmar will make pretty speeches at Hedvig's grave.

Ibsen's imagery aptly subserves the bitter irony and jarring comedy that make The Wild Duck one of the finest tragicomedies in all dramatic literature. So Gregers' mishap with the stove is a masterly example of the use of a symbolic incident to epitomize a character with concision and wit. Gregers makes a mess of trying to start a fire (kindle a passion for the ideal) and of putting the damper on the stove (or on his victims' life-giving illusions). To rescue the situation, he throws his dirty water on the stove (projects his own sickness onto other people), and when he has smelled up and flooded everything, walks out on the debacle, leaving it to the others to clean up after him if they can.

Similarly, the scenes between Hjalmar and his father are exemplary comic revelations of character—which needless to say does not mean that they must elicit loud laughter. Yet this is clearly a very long way from "the intolerable boredom" that James, whose plays could never hold an audience, attributed to Ibsen. Granted, the ironic comedy of the play is, if not black, mostly charcoal gray, but the harrowing inner laughter it begets is laughter all the same, emotionally and intellectually stimulating. It was the poet-dramatist Hugo von Hofmannsthal who described the characters in Ibsen's plays as living "in unbearable, painful, depressing little yellowish-gray relationships," and nothing could be more yellowish-gray than the manner in which the Ekdals indulge one another's whims and foibles. But the irony is susceptible of heightening to the point of horror, a horror to which the grotesque undertone adds the stridently discordant note that makes us wince even as we would weep. I am thinking of the Hjalmar-Hedvig scenes: the thoughtless cruelty of Hjalmar, bringing a Hedvig starved alike for affection and good food, not the tidbit he promised, but a menu from the rich man's table. Adding insult to injury, he decries the quality of the delicacies he ate, while promising to give the girl a description of exactly how each one tasted. Not only does this episode evoke, with the economy of superior comic insight, the egotistic hypocrisy and heedless hurtfulness of Hjalmar, but it also shows up his supposed kindnesses for the envenomed darts they are. I do not think that the massacre of Lady Macduff and her children or the spectacle of the blinded and abject Oedipus can affect us more painfully than this scene, or that subsequent one in which, after rationalizations about his health, the perfectly well Hjalmar allows the wretched Hedvig with her fading eyesight to toil in poor light at his job of retouching photographs. And then, cruelest of all, his warning: "But don't ruin your eyes! Do you hear me? I'm not going to be responsible."

Yet the most overpowering example of this brutal irony is still to come: the scene in which, while Hedvig is about to shoot herself through the fault and for the sake of Hjalmar, that fool is blaming Relling and Molvik for his having lost his hat, and shouts about how *he* will not lose *his* life by going out hatless into the cold. And it is while he is orating about how Hedvig would not give up a rich life with the Werles that the shot with which Hedvig gives up her poor life is heard. Finally, and no less horribly, what hurts Hjalmar most about Hedvig's death is that he will now be unable to tell her how much he loved her. Egocentricity could not be carried to greater heights, and yet, for all the man's hideousness, Ibsen manages to make his failed artist, inventor, husband and father—this human being *manqué*—above all a pitiful oaf. The comic incompetence that dogs him through life, as Gregers hounds him with his claim of the ideal, makes the story more gruesome; but it also enables us the better to recognize Hjalmar's kinship with our own unheroic selves, and so to forgive this hypocrite actor, our fellow, our brother.

Humor is omnipresent in this grim play. It is there in Gregers' deflation of Hjalmar's high-flown sophistry about the courage he showed in choosing life over suicide with the devastating understatement, "Well, that depends on how you look at it." It is there, doubly, in Hjalmar's sublime response to Gina's question whether she should prepare for his departure or his staying on, with the Pythian "Pack—and fix the room," wherein the absurdity of contradiction is heightened by Hjalmar's grand refusal to perform either task himself. And what of the marvelous triple irony in Relling's remark about righteousness being the Norwegian national disease, but that it appears only sporadically; not only is this a joke at the expense of both righteousness and Norway, but also, what kind of an endemic is one that hardly ever occurs? With these samples of Ibsen's humor, I conclude my debate with his sundry detractors.

There remains the sovereign question: why has *The Wild Duck*—original yet universal, poetic yet witty, savage yet humane, symbolic yet earthy—survived as an acknowledged, but not a beloved and popular, masterpiece? Does it perhaps lack something, after all? Two things, to be sure, are patently missing: a love interest and a hero. It would seem that the public can forgive one or the other of these omissions, but not both.

That there is no love interest in the play is plain enough; indeed, what may be the cause of the worthy Relling's alcoholism is the loss of Mrs. Sörby's love, but was ever a lover's disappointment more laconically expressed—in just one line! And is there truly no hero? There is none: Gina and Hedvig, though good people, are too passive; Relling, though he is the nearest thing to a hero, is kept out of sight all too much, perhaps for that very reason. In the new drama of which Ibsen is the fountainhead, "there are no villains and no heroes," as Bernard Shaw (who was so often wrong about Ibsen) rightly remarked. We can be equally sorry for Gregers and Hjalmar, and we can also despise them equally. Rather than heroes or villains, they are clever dogs or wounded, submerged ducks; but what they resemble most are the unhappy rabbits in the attic of an old duffer who kills them for his sport.

"In tragic life," wrote George Meredith, "no villain need be! Passions spin the plot." But passions are precisely what is most lacking in *The Wild Duck;* at the utmost there is Hjalmar's sickly love for himself, or Gregers' no less sickly fixation on ideals wholly inappropriate to the mediocre bourgeois who could as easily handle a lance or a rapier. But if there are no passions to spin the tragicomic plot, is there not perhaps something else?

Ibsen, it should be noted, is the dramatist of depth psychology; not for nothing was Freud to use the heroine of *Rosmersholm* as the most pronounced specimen of a certain kind of neurosis he wished to describe. It has been cogently argued that Ibsen's plays are profoundly autobiographical in the sense of an interior autobiography: "these divers human beings are nothing but the one Ibsenian human being in the various phases of development"; they are "merely stages of the selfsame inner experience," as Hofmannsthal observed. And in Robert Brustein's words, "Unable to master his contradictions, [Ibsen] dramatizes them in his plays, grateful for a form in which tensions do not have to be resolved." Hjalmar, Gregers, Relling—all of them are but isolations of certain impulses, tendencies, stirrings within the playwright, but a playwright rich enough in inner experience to subsume us all.

Ibsen's drama delves and descends; from the point of view

of the untrained eye, it even recedes. No one has described this process better than Rilke, in that splendid passage of *The Notebooks of Malte Laurids Brigge* which conjures up and salutes Ibsen, and which reads in part:

> You measured the scarcely measurable: a feeling that rose by half a degree, the angle of deflection of a will weighted with hardly anything which you read off from very near by, the slight clouding in a drop of yearning and that wisp of discoloration in an atom of confidence: these you had to track down and preserve, for in such occurrences was life to be found now, our life, which had slipped into us, which had withdrawn inward, so deep that there were barely any surmises left concerning it.
>
> Such as you were, inclined toward pointing up, a timelessly tragic poet, you were obliged to convert with one swoop these capillary processes into the most compelling gestures, into the most available matters. So you proceeded to the unexampled deed of violence that was your work, your work that searched ever more desperately among the visible for the equivalents of the inwardly perceived.

It is in this inward vision and the ability to find external equivalents for it that Ibsen's achievement lies. Dramatists of all times have had to cope with similar problems, but in a world of drab burgherdom, incrustated with layers upon layers of philistinism, it was hard indeed to find the deep-buried roots of idiosyncratic motivation, and no less hard to present actions and events dramatic enough, yet also credibly the outgrowth of those roots. The drama in Ibsen is spun by discrepancies, tensions and contradictions: the war of conflicting passions has shrunk to a tug-of-war of floundering uncertainties. Juliet Capulet was fourteen years old when she died; so was Hedvig Ekdal. Both died by their own hands, but how different the causes of their deaths! The clash that results in Hedvig's suicide takes place between two small men, Hjalmar and Gregers, themselves divided against themselves, and never even cognizant of their clash. Gregers is aware of his ugliness and the ugliness of his background, but would combat it not by making himself finer, but by cravenly trying to foist incommensurate nobility on another weak vessel. Hjalmar has intimations of his weakness, as when he momentarily admits that his great invention is a figment, but he cannot combat his faults with actions—only with acting, acting the part of the gallant paterfamilias. And it is out of the petty division of these two self-divided creatures that suddenly, for reasons that are almost no reason at all, a young girl loses her life. It is not passions that spin the plot but the tug of discrepancies.

Or we might call it the struggle between illusion and reality —a warfare, however, in which the combatants have switched uniforms. For the real truth of Gregers is unreal among a bourgeoisie unable to live it, and in a world unwilling to house it; the illusions of Hjalmar, on the other hand, contemptible as they may be, are viable, and might with luck tender genuine survival. Yet when neither illusion nor reality can any longer be made to stand and be recognized, what is left but ignorant armies shadowboxing by night?

Ibsen's perceptions and language function on appropriately submerged levels; "his distinction," in James's words, "is far in," but rightly so. Yet the drama surfaces wherever it justifiably can. It is "in the imaginative use of unimaginative language," as Bentley has said, that Ibsen's great realism lies; or, to quote F. L. Lucas on *The Wild Duck*, in "blend[ing] so perfectly together reality, irony, pity, and poetry." So, far from agreeing with Brecht's contention that Ibsen no longer can teach us anything, I believe that we are only today beginning to get at his true meanings, meanings so manifold and self-renewing that there is no danger of their ever being exhausted.

PROPOSALS

Readers are always clamoring for something they like to call "constructive criticism." Why that belongs to the there-ain't-no-such-animal category, along with the unicorn and chimera, should emerge from various passages of this book. Nevertheless, in the following pieces I have made proposals— some modest, and some immodest—that are as close as I can decently come to what goes by that mythical appellation "constructive criticism."

To be sure, some of the suggestions made are seemingly negative rather than positive—but only seemingly. Do not drive when you've had too much to drink, do not smoke in bed (or, better yet, do not smoke at all) are, I would say, supremely positive, constructive suggestions.

CAN DRAMA BE SAVED?

(1970)

The American people in general, and Broadway theater-goers in particular, do not want drama. The number of dramas just having the nerve to open during a Broadway season has decreased to a baby's handful, for they know that the number of survivors rarely exceeds that of the fingers on a baby's mitten. The playgoers want comedy, farce or musicals. In fact, when this last-named great new American genre was invented, they had to name it "musical comedy" in order to sell it to the American public. If they had called it musical anything else (tragedy, drama, chairs), it would never have made it.

Oddly enough, it's different at the movies, where all kinds of dramatic stuff—mostly bad, but dramatic with a vengeance—sells like hotcakes, or even like comedy. The reason for this would appear to be that the movies cost, say, three dollars, whereas a good seat at the theater, if you include the musical theater, will cost you anywhere from nine to fifteen. For three dollars, an American customer will buy a drama, even if it's only on screen, but for twelve dollars, which is no laughing matter, he wants a comedy. And if it's absolutely free of charge, on television, he will even sit and watch the tragedy of Vietnam.

What is the solution? Since calling it musical comedy worked so well for the musical—even though, God knows, most musicals aren't funny, except as attempts at a book, score and lyrics—perhaps the solution is nomenclature. Maybe drama has to change its image by changing its name to Dramatic, or Tragic, Comedy. It may well be that people would actually go to see The Tragic Comedy of *King Lear,* or The Dramatic

55

Farce of *Dr. Faustus*. One could always get Gerald Freedman or Tom O'Horgan to direct those plays, and their very authors wouldn't know them from a comedy.

The other option, of course, would be to lower box-office prices. But what with the unions, the space program, the war and inflation, this seems to be out of the question. Still, in theory, there is the possibility of government subsidy. Thus we are lucky enough to have a President with a taste for drama, who loudly expressed his admiration for such dramatic fare as *Patton*, starring George C. Scott, and *Chisum*, starring John Wayne. Perhaps if we assured him that our National Theater would star Scott as Coriolanus, a Roman general, and John Wayne as Macbeth, a Scottish general, the project might stand a chance. But Mr. Nixon's laudatory criticism came for filmed drama; the live-action kind he prefers to review and judge in the courtroom rather than onstage, so we may have to look for help elsewhere.

There are a few harbingers of hope. For instance, next season Broadway will offer a new drama—yes, drama—by Neil Simon. The assumption must be that anyone who has been able to make us laugh so heartily at his farces will undoubtedly succeed in making us laugh at his drama as well. Then there is Dame Judith Anderson, who will be playing Hamlet. The title part, you understand, not Gertrude or the Ghost. After all, Sarah Bernhardt played Hamlet in France. But, then, in France the basic word for actor is *comédien*, regardless of whether the actor or actress is not particularly funny in comedy, and not that much of a joke in drama. Still, Dame Judith probably figured that if boys could play women in Shakespeare's time, in these days of Women's Liberation women certainly could, and do, play men. The only trouble with this *Hamlet*, which could give drama a shot in the arm—or in the head, to put it out of its misery—is that it is scheduled to be seen in New York for one performance only at Carnegie Hall. But such is the magic of Miss Anderson's name that she could undoubtedly make the Dane an unmelancholy Broadway best-seller.

And in stars might lie the drama's real hope. For example, the public will gladly pay fifteen dollars to see Helen Hayes act in anything, for it is well known that Miss Hayes will always be adorable, no matter what the part. Miss Hayes could make Medea truly lovable, funny and cute. She could also make Hedda Gabler shoot herself with a blank, and smile the sting out of Cleopatra's asp. And the reviews would be money reviews, irrespective of the performance.

But if none of these cures proves practicable, is the drama doomed to slow, lingering extinction? Yes, unless the public acquires some taste, education and culture, which is easily the most utopian of all my suggestions. The lowbrow or middlebrow resents drama and tragedy. This has nothing to do with the widespread assumption that his life may be so tough—his earnings low, his milieu gloomy—that he must laugh to forget his woes. Not so. As everyone knows, it is only the highbrow whose livelihood is precarious in our society; yet he is quite willing to see anything if it is good and done well. No, the problem is one of detachment, which the lower-brows lack. The civilized playgoer can suffer for and with the Trojan women and still preserve a core of intellectual detachment. This permits him to experience drama aesthetically as well as emotionally, to recognize the poetry beneath the pathos, the art beyond the life of the play.

Moreover, the thinking person is aware of the fact that he is a man condemned to a sooner or later death, and that an even better solace than to laugh and forget is to feel one's kinship with all those doomed and dying heroes and heroines and their dying or dead authors, and to achieve a tragic joy in the courage with which one faces the pity of it all. Onstage, that is. Anyone can watch drama on a screen, which manages to screen the ultimate reality from most people.

SHOULD ALBEE
HAVE SAID "NO, THANKS"?

(1967)

THERE ARE TWO KINDS of prizes in literature (and it behooves the theater to remember that it is a branch of literature): those that are necessary evils and those that are unnecessary goods. The unnecessary goods are the ones that come to already established, prosperous writers, who do not need them any more; the necessary evils are those that come to talented, struggling authors who need the money, but whom this sudden recognition, this unexpected accolade of the Establishment, may well corrupt. There is also a third kind of prize, such as the Pulitzer. It is an unnecessary evil.

I am not talking here, of course, of the Pulitzer prizes in journalism, though this year in particular it became apparent that these, too, are dubious commodities. I am speaking of the drama prize, although, *mutatis mutandis*, much the same applies to other Pulitzer prizes in the arts. And here my point is (it is so simple and obvious that I would be ashamed to make it, were it not that the simple and obvious is usually far from universally apparent) that journalists are the last people qualified to bestow literary awards.

The sad truth is that the literary spirit and the journalistic mode (I do not think that journalism can be said to have anything so close to a soul as a spirit) are fundamentally antipathetic and inimical. The journalistic mind is always geared to the now, to making things as simple as possible, and buttonholing the largest number of breakfasting people. The literary sensibility is geared to the timeless—that is, to the now only as an avenue by which all time can be reached. It is willing and solicitous to allow things their complexity, and to respect the irreducibility of much of the best art to anything like simple statements or basic English; and it is really concerned with pleasing one reader only: its owner, with his uncompromising demands on his abilities.

Though no journalist, with the possible exception of Hemingway, has ever become a major writer, writers, even the best, have often been driven into, or reduced to, journalism. (I am not speaking of "literary journalism"—articles and criticism published by serious writers in more or less respectable periodicals, and often of considerable literary value—but of journalism of the common, unweeded garden variety, as written by those, for example, who adjudge the Pulitzer prizes.) When this reduction occurs, the writer will, if he has a stomach for it, turn out journalism with the best of them. If he is less gastrically athletic, he will prefer anything from teaching to driving a taxi. But in no case will he be able to raise journalism to the level of literature, any more than literature will descend to the level of journalism, except parodistically, as in the newspaper-office sequence of Joyce's *Ulysses*, which, characteristically, corresponds to the Homeric Cave of the Winds.

In "The Teats of Tiresias," the great French poet Guillaume Apollinaire (who also pokes fun there at the Nobel Prize: "a literary award consisting of twenty crates of dynamite"— Alfred Nobel having been the inventor of that explosive) describes satirically how a journalist is made. You take an empty cradle, and toss into it finely shredded newsprint ("He must be a maid of all work,/ Able to write for all sides"), the contents of an ink bottle for blood, a penholder for a spine, the gluepot for a brain ("A brain for not thinking"), and a pair of scissors by way of "A tongue the better to drool with." It is not by journalists that the literary artist wants to be recognized; he profoundly mistrusts those who, perhaps quite honorably, wish to use the word for the conveying of facts. For the artist, the truth lies in the way in which words are put together, in the form they find with which to impress themselves on the consciousness, rather than in mere neat expression of cleverly accumulated data—in short, not in the spelling out of something but in the casting of a spell.

Not that journalism, or for that matter, Pulitzer journalism, is all that factually reliable. In 1963 the advisers on drama to the Pulitzer Committee, John Mason Brown and the late John Gassner, resigned because their recommendation to give the prize to Edward Albee was ignored: very few of the Pulitzer arbiters had even bothered to see the play, *Who's Afraid of Virginia Woolf?*; those who did declared it obscene or unsavory, and that was that. No prize for drama was given in 1962–63. This was one of several such hassles, sometimes involving the resignation of advisers—thus the musical advisers once resigned when their recommendation of a mere citation to Duke Ellington was not honored. The St. Louis *Post-Dispatch,* a paper owned by the Pulitzer family, sent up to New York a young reporter to write up not only what was behind these incidents, but also how people in the arts felt about them and about the Pulitzer prizes in general. The journalist wanted to get Dwight Macdonald's views on the matter, but Macdonald, about to leave town, recommended me as a replacement.

I remember having a very pleasant session with the reporter, an intelligent young man, though I cannot recall exactly what I told him. The gist of it was that the Pulitzer is, among the civilized, more honored in the refusal than in the acceptance (Sinclair Lewis and William Saroyan turned it down), and that if a play, for example, received a Pulitzer, the tendency among the cultivated was to regard it, not always justly, with suspicion, and to reckon its author forthwith as a confirmed middlebrow. Later, I received a copy of the printed article, along with a letter in which the reporter sardonically commented on how all the quotations from me had somehow been omitted by the editor. True enough, the article had been reduced to pap; but at least it did not—as far as I know—win a Pulitzer Prize.

It is instructive to look back upon what has won Pulitzer prizes, since their inception in 1918. There are among the drama awards some incontestably good ones; indeed, two of the best

American plays, *Long Day's Journey Into Night* and *A Streetcar Named Desire* are on the list, and one may approve also of finding there such items as *Craig's Wife* and, though the years have not been kind to it, as a revival demonstrated, *Of Thee I Sing*. But one also finds, cheek by jowl with greatness and solid workmanship, the flimsy, the cute and the trashy: doubtful concoctions by Paul Green, Marc Connelly, Maxwell Anderson, Sidney Kingsley, and numerous other overinflated and, since then, generally collapsed reputations. There are even things like *Miss Lulu Bett, The Old Maid* and *Hell-bent for Heaven*, which even the scholarly may have some difficulty placing, though one might remember that the movie version of *The Old Maid* kept dozens of Bette Davis impersonators off the streets.

But I suppose the only useful test of a prize is to examine it in context, in terms of what the winner was running against—though it should be recalled that the option not to award a prize exists and has been made liberal, and sometimes unjust, use of. Why, under any circumstances, give an award to a medical soap opera like *Men in White* or to a pseudodaring, tuneless musical like *How to Succeed in Business* . . . ? Let us look more closely, however, at some of the awards of the last dozen years.

In 1945 the Pulitzer went to *Harvey*, a play about a sweet, ineffectual drunk who conjures up for a companion a giant white rabbit. Needless to say, our hare-raising hero is hounded by the dour, greedy, sober folk, and even less needful of saying, he finally gets the better of them. This piece of fluff by Mary Chase, who was never again able to turn out anything even of commercial value, won out over *The Glass Menagerie*, which, dated as it is, is still one of our finest plays. In 1949, the prize went to that perfect piece of mock-tragedy and pseudoliterary inflation, *Death of a Salesman*, anybody's dream Pulitzer. Next year, it was given to *South Pacific*, an adroit enough musical if you can swallow a certain pretentiousness in the book and the moral uplift of some of its lyrics. What was by-passed in its favor, however, was *The Member of the Wedding*, probably Carson McCullers' best novel, preserving even in the stage adaptation an authenticity and intensity of insight that *South Pacific*, based on the subliterary work of James A. Michener, could not begin to match.

No award was given in 1951, although *Darkness at Noon* and *Guys and Dolls* were available to the judges, either of which could, except for a lack of wholesomeness of the most factitious sort, make claims as good as those of *Picnic*, which won in 1952. In 1954 the prize went to *The Teahouse of the August Moon*, an amusing piece of tomfoolery, and not to *The Golden Apple*, one of the most original musicals this country has produced—somewhat uneven, perhaps, but having a canny, unostentatious pointedness that, backed by a musical idiom with a personality of its own, places the show not far below *Street Scene*. Other recent Pulitzers went to *The Diary of Anne Frank*, as slippery a piece of prettification as one could ask for (and if one happens to be the Broadway audience, one asks), and to *J.B.*, which surpasses any recent play in bloated, grandiose hollowness. In 1965 the award went to *The Subject Was Roses*, a conventional family drama about which more anon, and not to Saul Bellow's *The Last Analysis*, which, even in a vulgar, uncomprehending production, cut, funnily and frighteningly, a good bit deeper.

And here we are in 1967: *A Delicate Balance*, one of Albee's weakest plays, gets the Pulitzer, and Albee accepts the award that was denied *Virginia Woolf*. Here was a chance for a playwright who is independent of spirit and pocket to tell the Pulitzers to go soak their heads. Indeed, he seriously considered so doing. Instead, he called a press conference to justify his reasons for accepting. These, as Ross Wetzsteon reported in the *Village Voice*, were 1) that though the Pulitzer was "in danger of losing its position of honor" and may "cease to be an honor at all," accepting it allows one to criticize the awards, whereas refusing it does not; 2) that by accepting one spares other recipients possible embarrassment; and 3) that an honor in decline is still an honor.

As Wetzsteon quite rightly pointed out at the press conference, Sartre refused the Nobel Prize precisely in order to be able to criticize it. Surely refusing a prize is the only proper way of criticizing it so that neither the judges nor the public can ignore the criticism. As for concern for other recipients, this is totally inconsistent with Albee's cult of the private conscience, of the individual's right and need to make up his mind for himself. The characters in his plays are castigated for bowing down to convention or prejudice—yet now, out of mere conviviality, one is to go along with the crowd? Reason number 3 alone strikes me as not disingenuous.

But here Albee's ambition blinds him, for he must surely know that *Virginia Woolf* is a far better play than *A Delicate Balance*. By accepting this award, Albee is not only kissing the hand that pats him belatedly and stupidly after having stupidly and undeservedly slapped him, he is doing worse: he is encouraging that philistine stratagem of almost all prize-givers, editors, reviewers and foundations—the bestowal of largesse on a later and feeble work of an author who has "arrived" while the supposed arbiters were taking their customary nap. Out of innumerable examples, one should suffice. Frank Gilroy's excellent first play, *Who'll Save the Plowboy?*, went relatively unnoticed by the powers that be. Meanwhile Gilroy's reputation among the cognoscenti grew so steadily that his next play, *The Subject Was Roses*, well-meaning but paltry TV fare, had all the mass media flipping over it, and in due time garnered both the Pulitzer Prize and the Drama Critics' Circle Award. Thus one atones for previous obtuseness and proves how knowing one is. All that gets proved is the opposite.

IT WOULD HAVE BEEN a splendid gesture on Albee's part to refuse this creaky prize that he must know could have been given him only as blood money. For *A Delicate Balance* was neither a critical nor an audience success, and never before has a Pulitzer been given to such a play. Even the 1961 winner, *All the Way Home*, a rather flatfooted adaptation of Agee's *A Death in the Family*, got somewhat better audience response and rather better notices; besides, Agee was considered a genius untimely snatched away and deserving of posthumous laurels despite the manifold vulgarizations of the stage version—or perhaps because of them.

But I suppose it may be asking too much of an author not to accept something that he may consider belated penance on the part of the unwashed. What one might certainly have hoped for is that he would not indulge himself in public equivocation and prevarication that can only emphasize the lack of independence and courage in those few quarters of the American theater establishment where one was still looking for them.

TOWARD THE CONQUEST
OF INNER SPACE

(1969)

THE COMMON BELIEF TODAY—it has, in fact, been enshrined as a platitude—is that the theater is inferior to the movies. On a superficial level, this is true. There are usually more good films around than there are decent plays. A controversial film engenders more discussion, especially among young people, than its theatrical equivalent—assuming that one can be found. More people go to the cinema, ever fewer to the theater. Wherever you look there are film festivals, film courses, film grants and awards. The only way the theater can match the excitement is by desperate stratagems: nudity, onstage copulation, anarchic rituals uniting the performers and audience, love-ins. But moviemaking and moviegoing complacently and undesperately keep mushrooming all around.

Yet in another sense the comparison is deceptive and unfair. Of course there are more good films around than plays because films are imported from all over, whereas theatrical productions are, for the most part, home-grown. Film is a more accessible, newer, less explored medium than the drama, so naturally it appeals to the pioneer spirit of the youth of America. It is also easier on the pocketbook.

There is even a sociocultural reason for the flowering of movies at the expense of drama. We live in an age that can at best be called that of science; at worse, that of gadgetry. On the initial levels of involvement with theater you don't get to play around with gadgets. Rather, you and your friends get

together and read *Volpone* or *Ah, Wilderness!* Your only gadget
is a paperback. How different when you buy your basic movie
equipment! Not just the 8 mm. camera and film; before long,
you are also projecting, cutting, splicing, making titles, acquir-
ing additional lenses . . . there is no end to it. Then come the
experiments with sound—your first tape recorder—and you are
really on your way into The Age We Live In.

Far be it from me to knock movies. For years now I've been
writing film criticism, and my second book was all about film.
I am able to praise many more films than plays in the course
of a year, but it does not make me despair of theater or
proclaim it secondary and inferior. Precisely because it is
older, the theater has a stock of treasures that the movies do
not yet possess. And there is even a way in which the theater
can equal what is, in the last analysis, the great but unearned
advantage of the film: I mean the ability of the lens to see
more than the average human being can—and the average
film maker is average with a vengeance. But he has that camera
that catches things—faces in the throng, shapes of things, odd
corners, relationships between people and objects—which the
naked eye is too slow or clouded or lethargic to perceive unaided. The playwright continues to depend on his bare eyesight
and hearing, on his merely human gestures and words. When
used greatly, however, these words can penetrate deeper than
any lens ever will.

What the theater needs is an extensive national, state and
private endowment. We must have a National Theater like
Britain's, but even more than that, we need a true theatrical
culture. I think the solution lies in accepting that, until the
novelty of film wears off and another great wave of playwriting
hits the world, the theater must be—predominantly, not exclusively—a minority art. Rather than trying to bring commercial
plays to the masses, or putting on masterpieces like *Peer Gynt*
in vulgarized versions presumed to be accessible to hoi polloi,
the larger universities should develop, with government support, advanced institutes in theater research. These would include such disciplines as the translation and study of plays

as yet un- or mistranslated, and the development of actors, directors and technicians who could do them justice.

The world abounds in important twentieth-century playwrights who might never have immense popular appeal, but whose works, intelligently produced, could start an upsurge of domestic playwriting. Imagine, for example, an advanced center for Scandinavian drama at the University of Minnesota, with actable translations of playwrights like Hjalmar Bergman, Stig Dagerman, Kaj Munk; or an advanced institute for Polish drama, say, at Wayne State, yielding superior translations and productions of Witkiewicz, Rózewicz, Gombrowicz. Or what about a German and Austrian drama center, where Schnitzler and Wedekind, Kaiser and Hofmannsthal, among others, would be worthily translated and performed? This is the far-ranging, cinematic vision our theater could acquire: outstanding modern and classical plays from abroad, equals of the Fellinis and Antonionis, Bergmans and Truffauts.

Granted there won't be mass migrations to the plays of, say, Ghelderode or Audiberti, Zuckmayer or Ramón del Valle-Inclán. But the more successful productions could be toured around, and civilized minorities everywhere would be drawn to them. This means generous subsidies; it might also mean the enactment of high-level cultural agencies as yet undreamed of. But the important thing is to start thinking of theater as a high, perhaps even aristocratic and unpopular art, and to stop wasting foundation moneys on little theaters in Oklahoma and Texas, which, though they start with *Macbeth* and *Candida,* soon find that William Inge, Neil Simon and replicas of Broadway musicals are more profitable. Meanwhile, we move outward to the conquest of space with our Apollos, movies and TV, but that inner space that is the domain of the dramatist remains unexplored as long as our theater is *Promises, Promises* and *Play It Again, Sam.*

A BRIEF FOR BREVITY

(1970)

If WE HAVE NO theatrical bread, let us eat rolls. If there are no good new three-act plays to be had, what about good old one-acters? Almost all great playwrights, at least since Chekhov and Strindberg, have written them, and they are less performed even than the longer works of the masters. Until recently, in fact, the one-act play has been done mostly in community theaters or high-school auditoriums: either in little halls or by little people, and generally to little avail. Although off- and off-off-Broadway have taken up its cause with relish, Broadway has been churlishly inhospitable, making a few exceptions only for new one-acters by established playwrights.

In recent years, there have been two double bills by Peter Shaffer: one good (*The Private Ear* and *The Public Eye*), one not so good (*White Lies* and *Black Comedy*); the four paltry, pretentious and passé one-acters by Robert Anderson, *You Know I Can't Hear You* etc., which succeeded largely thanks to Walter Kerr's proselytizing; three musical one-acters of meager merit, *The Apple Tree;* and, latterly, two efforts by Neil Simon: *Plaza Suite* and, disguised as a three-acter, *The Last of the Red Hot Lovers*—both of them hits. But the public is presumed not to like one-acters, which may be why Simon resorted to a masquerade as convincing as those horses made up of two clowns joined face to bum.

Why this putative and, to some extent, real hostility to the one-acter? For the same reason that short stories sell less well than novels, and that poems sell far less well than prose. In the solid capitalist bourgeois, or in his interior decorator, some-

thing there is that does not like a wall, and one of the cheapest
ways to hide a wall is with books. The bigger the book, the
more it covers, and your fat Uris or Michener out-tapestries
a modest collection of stories or slender volume of poems. Beyond that, a novel gives you more pages per dollar, and is
easier to read. Easier because its main dimension is longitude,
and its meaning and impact are, or seem to be, evolved gradually and painlessly. A story or poem, unable to bask in length,
must operate in depth, height and thickness. It must set up
inner relationships, echoes, implications, suggestions; utilize
the space between the lines; curl up on itself to achieve preg-
nancy.

This means that you have to go diving into a poem or story;
there is no leisurely novelistic stream for you to drift along
daydreaming in your canoe. The same, to an extent, applies to
the one-act play. Everything here is speeded up and, if the
play works, fraught with greater significance per line, per word,
than in the usual full-length play, where you can afford to miss
lines because of the immoderate guffaws of a self-indulgent
audience, your neighbors' animated conversation, poor delivery
from the stage, or your own inattention. A good one-acter
needs more intensive concentration and greater than ordinary
rapidity of perception in the theatergoer. Empathy has to come
much faster—a burden primarily on the playwright, but second-
arily, and not inconsiderably, on the audience as well.

Yet think of the gain in variety. Suppose a Broadway producer were to offer a first-rate mounting of three one-acters
by, say, Pirandello, Wedekind and Ghelderode. Or by Synge,
Ionesco and Sam Shepard. Or by Molière, Max Frisch and
Tennessee Williams. Or Courteline, Lorca and Brecht. The shift
in time, place, mood, spirit and technique would easily make
up in diversity for the lack of sustained élan; and if the plays
were well matched, for development of plot and characters, we
would get variations on a theme, different answers to a question
or questionings of an answer—a dialogue of playwrights as well
as of characters. Inexpensive scenery or unit sets could reduce
costs, and the same actors would play three very different roles
in one evening. This would widen their scope and, by creating

a kind of repertory situation within a long-run setup, keep them from getting bored and falling off their toes. The audience, in turn, would delight in watching the actors' transfigurations, and get a chance to see the shorter, less known, but not necessarily lesser works of important dramatists in other than impecunious or inexpert productions.

And if the audience does not like the opening Strindberg, there are still the Beckett and O'Neill to come. But if the whole thing is Neil Simon or Robert Anderson, whether in three acts or three one-acters, what hope is there of changing horses in mid-swamp?

All this, to be sure, is predicated on the assumption that people want theater—more specifically, good theater. If they don't, if small gemlike plays by master jewelers do not mean anything to them, then we cannot save the theater. Or people, either.

ADVICE TO THE HATELORN

(1972)

In an average week, I get about two or three fan letters to some nine or ten pieces of hate mail. I enjoy both equally, though naturally I am more grateful for the former. But the latter may prove more useful: several magazine and book publishers have mentioned the possibility of my producing an annotated anthology of these bizarre, uproarious and ideologically often fascinating poison-pen missives. And those sent to my publishers and Xeroxed for me are considerably more numerous and even more provocative—though hardly provoking. Most interesting is the demand that because the letter-writers (often backed up by friends) disagree with me—or because I don't seem to like any play and, therefore, theater much—I be summarily sacked.

Now, there are three points explicit or implicit in this that bear examination. First, the notion that a critic who likes few of the plays or productions he sees must ipso facto dislike theater. This is bad logic and worse mathematics. Literary and dramatic values are always formulated by the supreme court of time, also known as posterity. If works and writers are considered worthy, it is because they have survived the test of time. Now glance at the number of new plays that open in a given season; then look up in the authority of your choice (lexicographic, scholarly or critical) the number of surviving plays from any season ten or more years ago. Finally, decide whether the number conforms more to the seasonal number of raves dished out by me or by—you supply the name.

Which leads to the second question: are my few laudatory

notices given to the right plays? If "right" means from the point of view of time, we—or more likely our successors and descendants—will have to wait and see. But if "right" merely means what the outraged epistolarist considers so, the problem is simpler. It is reducible to who is more likely to be right: the critic or the irate complainer.

Who is the complainer? He or she may be a literate, theater-loving outsider; or more often, a vociferously self-satisfied pretender, whose lack of culture and discrimination is reflected in his or her inability to cope with the English of mere letter-writing, never mind the vastly more complex and subtle language of art. Sometimes the correspondent is a practicing theater person—in which case, there is usually a personal ax to be ground. Let us take him to be an average concerned citizen who likes theatergoing, reads the reviews in the *Times,* and perhaps even an occasional theatrical book. He knows something. But what of the critic who from infancy has loved theater, been involved with it in one way or another, seen it and read about it much more than the most dedicated dilettante, traveled all over in search of it, and cultivated a number of arts related to it (extending from opera and ballet to music and painting)? Indeed, a critic who can endure what is hurled at him almost daily under the abused rubric of theater must be either a strong-stomached and weak-minded ostrich who can placidly swallow anything, or someone who, despite his passionate jeremiads, continues to believe in and love the theater, and exults in its rare but genuine glories.

It is a curious, rampant if not endemic, symptom of an arrogantly, unthinkingly pseudoliberal society, this assumption that everyone's opinion about theater is as good as anyone else's—and if it happens to be that of an indignant correspondent, not merely equal but better. I wonder: do these superiorly enlightened consumers write similarly insolent letters to engineers, physicists, biochemists, twelve-tone composers and structural anthropologists, to name but a few? Of course not, because even they realize that they know little or nothing about engineering, dodecaphony or enzymes. And yet (to take engineering) have they not crossed innumerable bridges? Well, is theater less of an art and skill—less of a discipline with its rules, devices, structures, aesthetics, problems and imponderables—than bridge-building? It is not even that bridges collapse more unequivocally than plays or performances; it is only that they last a little longer than most plays, and that until the collapse, their defects are considerably better concealed.

But the expert can detect both hidden failures and virtues—along with obvious ones, if any, of course. His expertise—in perception, comparative assessment and expression, if he is a drama critic—is not available to the common man, or even to the frequent theatergoer. This fact has to be accepted in the case of the *qualified* drama critic just as in that of any other expert. Not slavishly accepted, to be sure—certainly not to the extent of abrogating cultivation of one's private thought and taste. But it has to be reckoned with at least to this degree: "Damn it, there is a good chance that in the long run *he* may be right!" Then, if one still wants to write a dissenting letter, based on cogently developed arguments or facts that the critic overlooked, very good. But the mere loudness of one's opinions, even backed up by a large number of similar loudminds, is meaningless.

What is especially quaint is the assumption of these gab-gifted amateurs that because of their presumed numerousness or actual vociferousness, the dissenting critic should be fired. If criticism were merely a business (as, alas, it is for some), the customer might be "always right." But serious criticism is an art, a mode of perception and expression, an ability to evaluate based on multiplicity of experience and—less definably—taste. And here mass opinion has historically more often been proved wrong than right. Like any other artist, then, the critic would be suspect if he did not—by not being only of his time—antagonize the multitude.

And then there is that supreme fallacy of letter-writers: that there is such a thing as objective criticism. This is one of those *pseudodoxia epidemica* or "vulgar errors" Sir Thomas Browne liked to compile, and it is common among nonletter-writers too. For people tend not to know what criticism is. In their innocence, they take it for a science, when in fact it is an art. It is the art of cultivating one's taste, of reasoning well in behalf of that taste, and writing so well about it as to make that writing become art. But most people expect the scientifically arrived-at critical absolute somewhere at the turning of a page. No, criticism is the art of persuasion, civilized polemic and—sometimes—inspired debate. It is founded on intelligence, sensitivity, experience and concern. It evolves in the critical consciousness through an endless process of comparing and contrasting, sifting and evaluating. It means having lived with and for an art at the cost of much more money, time and effort than even the most dedicated layman can afford to spend on it.

There is also something else. The true critic is a visionary. He sees somewhere deep inside him an ideal play, a perfect production, a flawless performance. This is almost never achieved, nor should it be. It would be horrible for the critic, just as it would be dreadful for the director, actor or playwright, to have attained perfection beyond which nothing remains to be desired and striven for. It would be artistic and critical suicide. Which of course is not to say that praise and enthusiasm should be denied where they are due, but the tide of inflation should be stemmed, in criticism as in the economy.

Some demolition jobs become critical landmarks. More often it is judicious, illuminating appreciation that assures lasting critical renown. But the mediocrities and worse that a critic praises become the rubble under which his name will lie buried and forgotten.

A STEP IN THE
RIGHT DIRECTION

(1970)

IF THERE IS ANYTHING our theater needs as desperately as subsidies and a National Theater, it is directors. We have some very good actors and actresses, designers, even playwrights (not so many as we would like, but where else are there appreciably more?), and we have no end of edifices. But when Arnold Wesker asked me recently to recommend some American directors, it was like being asked to name the novelists of Greenland. And a theater without directors is a directionless theater, with no one in it to develop performers, draw out playwrights and draw in audiences—all of which great directors have been known to do. For they are geniuses working cosubstantially with the dramatist's genius, for which German has the splendid word *kongenial*, meaning not just congenial, but fellow-genius.

Oh, we do have some few directors who have a useful specialty—who are jugglers with sight gags, solid geometricians of bodies in a drawing room, or who, like Bab-O, can get everything out of a kitchen sink: blood, sweat and platitudes. But we have no all-around directors of stature who can tackle a whole spectrum of plays, and while adding their own shading, not distort any play's individual coloration. Probably the three last theatrical directors of stature in America were—the past tense is deliberate, though all three are alive and in need of kicking—Elia Kazan, William Ball and Mike Nichols.

Kazan was the master of moody realism, of the brooding, pregnant atmosphere that whelps thunder and lightning, of heavily impasted local color. For Williams, Miller and Inge, he was the man, sometimes choking the breath of honesty out of a play, but always increasing its theatricality. I am not sure what drove Kazan out of the theater, but it may well have been his fiasco with *The Changeling*, which he misdirected for the old Lincoln Center theater. Confronted with a play that was not contemporary, not even vaguely naturalistic, and with a poetic diction and psychic intensity beyond those of his usual encounters, Kazan proved utterly impotent and turned the terrible thrills of the play into cheap frills.

William Ball directed at least two absolutely stunning and memorable productions, *Under Milk Wood* and *Six Characters in Search of an Author*, in which his fidgety, overwrought, somewhat precious sensibility came to full expression without squelching the playwright. In the Pirandello, there were certain undesirable exacerbations, but the whole thing pulsated, trembled and shook like a long paroxysm, complete with premonitory tremors and, after the crisis, a few receding spasms. But more recently, with his ACT company in San Francisco, Ball has yielded to a queer blend of exaggeration and attenuation, so that his productions look like bouts of shadowboxing.

As for Mike Nichols, who could make Neil Simon farces look like sophisticated comedies, and whose staging of Ann Jellicoe's *The Knack* was an exemplary fleshing out of a skeletal script, the moment he turned to something else—specifically, the period melodrama of Hellman's *The Little Foxes*—he managed to turn the play, despite all his angling for effects, into a water out of fish. Anyway, he has found a new home in the movies.

Which is one of the main reasons we have no stage directors: almost all of them are in films. There are three main reasons for a director's preferring film: he has greater control over the entire production (for example, by means of editing), his style can show in many more ways (for instance, in the framing of shots), and the film is preserved *in toto* on celluloid, whereas a stage production is remembered only by a few photographs and imperfect accounts on paper. And though I shudder to mention it, there is also the difference in remuneration. But the theater has something else to offer the director:

to work with the great dramatic geniuses of all ages, rather than to be saddled with a mediocre screenplay—often, to be sure, of his own devising. Also there is the further challenge and glory of not hopping on a merrily rattling-along bandwagon, but kissing a great and dormant art into awaking.

What we need immediately is a crash program for the making of directors. It is significant that some of the most heavily subsidized programs in the country are geared to the developing of playwrights and actors, even of drama critics, but only marginally or not at all to the creating and training of directors. What would be more natural than the establishing of a handful of centers—at repertory theaters, universities, professional schools—for the exclusive teaching of directing, perhaps by visiting dignitaries; of course, all aspects of theater would be represented in, and profit from, the finished productions. What would be easier than to provide grants for qualified young people to be sent to observe and study under great directors in several countries successively (there might be a little language requirement here, which wouldn't hurt anybody); however, those chosen should be truly young and flexible persons, not middle-aged, halfway-successful hacks of the sort foundations love.

And something else. Many of the great European directors —Stanislavsky and Okhlopkov in Russia; Lugné-Poë, Copeau, Dullin, Jouvet in France; Gustaf Gründgens and Fritz Kortner in Germany; Ermete Zacconi in Italy; and any number of Englishmen—were also actors, or began as such. In America today there is virtually no such animal as the actor-manager, or actor-director, so I think it is among the actors themselves, and particularly the younger ones, that we should look for and encourage the directors of tomorrow. Otherwise we will stumble along as we do now, with directors who are mostly stage traffic-directors, and with the grim possibility of there being less and less traffic for anyone to direct.

DEFINITIONS

One of the frequent problems with criticism is that it does not define its terms. It is principally in this sense that "definitions" is used here: attempts to make clear to the readers from what bases my criticism proceeds. It may well happen that readers will find some of these very personal definitions agreeable, even if they do not find their specific application to their liking, or the other way around. We are all of us made of theory and practice—sometimes called soul and body—and in grouping these, as it were, theoretical definitions together, I hope that some readers, less comfortable with the body of my criticism, may discover that at least we are soul mates.

WHEN YOU
WRITE THAT, SMILE!

(1968)

Mᴜᴄʜ ʜᴀѕ ʙᴇᴇɴ ᴡʀɪᴛᴛᴇɴ about critical standards, though these are hard, if not impossible, to define. But something more can be said about critical attitudes, which have not received all the attention they deserve. What is, or should be, the critic's attitude to his work? We have known doctors to make it on their "bedside manner"—a term dating from the old days, before the gravely ill patient had to rise and go to the doctor's office. Well, critics still go to the theater, though it has been gravely ill for so long that there can be no cause for alarm, only for exasperation. What sort of "stageside manner," then, is the critic to have?

We critics are always reminded that, first and foremost, we must love the theater. Those who do the reminding, to be sure, are not drama critics, so it's easy for them to talk. And, indeed, we do love it. No one but the most passionate, inveterate lover (or the most raving masochist—but, come to think of it, the two are not mutually exclusive) would return night after night to the theater, the scene of *someone else's* crimes, unless some fatal passion or, what is much the same, compulsion were gnawing away at his bosom. The plays and productions, more often than not, are brutally horrible. These are horrors the Average Theatergoer knows nothing about.

The A.T. goes to see the season's best, most lauded plays, and has, at season's end, one out of two reactions. Either he says to his spouse: "Well, another sorry season is over. Still, we did see a couple of good things." Or he may say: "If they can't give us more than two or three good things a year, why on earth do they bother?" But the A.T. has seen a dozen shows at the utmost—and *he* is griping! Now, the person—critic or other—who has to swallow everything that comes along, every last abominable insult to human intelligence and dignity that is spewed forth, sees an entirely different theater. The difference is a little like that between what the officially guided and surveyed visitor to Red China is allowed to see and what the natives behold from day to day. Only much greater. And despite all that, the critic goes back unto the breach again and again, and feels expectant, excited, agog each time the curtain rises, or the actors pelt him with flowers or roll around over his feet, depending on which kind of play it is.

Love for the theater, certainly. But let us remember: *qui bene amat, bene castigat*—who loves well, chastises well. A girl friend of mine once described the difference between an unfavorable review by Robert Brustein and one by me. The gist of it was that when Brustein rapped, it was more in sorrow than in anger; but that when I did, it was to beat the recipient down so that *that* ugly head would never rise again. There may be a little truth to this, but only when I am at my worst. Scholars are invited to compare, for example, Brustein's negative review of the Old Vic's 1962 visit to New York (*Seasons of Discontent*, pp. 231–34) with mine (*Acid Test*, pp. 160–64).

Or compare these two descriptions of the same actor, Rip Torn. Brustein, reviewing him in *Desire Under the Elms,* writes: "Rip Torn and George C. Scott contribute generously to the general incoherence, both demonstrating that acting has long since left the neurasthenic stage, and entered the pathological. Torn, playing Eben like a refugee from a Texas lunatic asylum, giggles when he is in despair, stares blankly when he is happy, and spits when he is undecided." Reviewing Torn in *Daughter of Silence,* I wrote that the director "must also be allowed his share in Mr. Torn's booby prize: it has to take at least two persons to evolve such an elaborately rotten performance. Gazing yearningly out into the audience à la Olivier (but somehow always managing to forget to pull his gaze back), throwing lines away like Orson Welles at his slatternliest, and doing his best to look like Henry Daniell's death mask, Mr. Torn allows words to revolve wanly in his mouth like a jingling key chain in a bored man's pocket. Marlon Brando, another one whom Mr. Torn emulates, cannot, even during his most narcissistic silences, produce such an illusion of a nonfunctioning sound track as Mr. Torn conjures up throughout most of his speeches."

It may indeed be that my review dwells more lovingly on what seemed to me wrong—more lovingly and more chastisingly. But Brustein, with greater concision, gets his message across just as sharply, just as devastatingly. Neither of us, however, stopped Mr. Torn from developing into a very fine actor (in such plays as *The Deer Park*), and into a perhaps even finer director (e.g., *The Beard*). And of course, stopping anyone is not the intent as a rule—only stopping someone, if possible, from proceeding in *that* direction. Sore losers, however, will always be sore; when Edward Albee, on TV, named the critics who should be shot, the sorrowing Brustein and the sardonic Simon were felled with equal deadliness by Albee's imaginary bullets.

Now, it is true that newspaper reviewers tend to be overrespectful of personalities on, or behind, the stage—this is true even of the best of them, Walter Kerr, when he writes about Broadway (off-Broadway he is apt to be less reverent). But you can't clean the Augean stables with polite disapproval. You probably can't clean them by any other means either, but it's worth trying. And no wonder that serious critics become sardonic wits in self-defense: to contemplate and describe what a critic must, and not relieve oneself and the reader with a joke, even with a cutting one, would result in serious repressions and madness. But what one writes with is not *Schadenfreude;* it is more like a version of what Yeats called tragic joy. At least some unfunny comedy or humorless performance will, in the critic's pages, die laughing.

IS THIS THE
RIGHT WAY TO REBEL?

(1968)

I N FRANCE IN 1891 symbolism with its subsidiaries ruled the literary roost. Jules Huret was conducting an inquiry into "literary evolution," when a telegram arrived from the novelist Paul Alexis: "Naturalism not dead. Letter follows." Naturalism, or more exactly, realism, of which naturalism was an offshoot, is always declared dead or dying, yet there is also always word arriving by telegram or letter that it is alive and well somewhere or other. The numerous indignant letters that protested Albert Bermel's recent and rather mild attack on Arthur Miller in the *Times* may be still another set of missives implicitly affirming the aliveness of realism.

WHILE PARTISANS and enemies of realism argue its timeliness or datedness, its demise or indestructibility, few people stop to ask themselves what "realism" really means. Edward Albee says that *Who's Afraid of Virginia Woolf?* is a realistic play, while Eugene Ionesco makes the same claim for his very different sort of plays. I remember going along happily with my college textbooks' definition of "realism" until I discovered in a work by the distinguished scholar Mario Praz that realism was just a form of romanticism. In painting, there is even something called "magic realism," which is an instant contradiction, like Nescafé. On the whole, "realism" has become either a term describing certain French writers like Balzac, Stendahl, Flaubert, or the English novelists that preceded them, or else a term of praise or derision meaninglessly brandished about.

Yet almost every modern playwright (indeed, almost every artist), when pressed, would call himself some kind of a "realist." This, I am sure, goes as much for Beckett and Genet as for Williams and Miller, as it must have gone also for the great forerunners of current modernism; thus even Artaud speaks of an "objective unforeseen" that is an image "suddenly and *realistically* materialized." And the Surrealists, as the name indicates, considered themselves more real than the realists. Frequently we hear such strategic equivocations as "poetic" or "heightened" realism. No artist, even if he is a painter producing hard-edged or soft-edged daubs, or a film maker scratching directly on a loop, wants to be accused of lacking reality, of not being in touch with the world and telling it "like it is." This would be like being caught with one's artistic pants down—or, times being what they are, up.

Here a definition suggests itself. To a given artist, "realism" means the conveying of what he understands by reality. This is why *Virginia Woolf* and *The Chairs* both seem "realistic" to their authors, who, each in his way, tried to reproduce a personal vision of reality. The situation has its ironies. A play like Ionesco's *The Lesson* may be highly unrealistic in its technique (the circular form, the stylized and symbolic action, the nonsense words), yet convey what most people would call a sizable chunk of reality: it is *this* absurd concept of education that led to the student revolutions at the Sorbonne, Columbia and elsewhere. On the other hand, plays like *Incident at Vichy, Cat on a Hot Tin Roof, Bus Stop* and *I Never Sang for My Father* may make a great show of "telling it like it is" and use straightforward techniques, yet strike most discriminating viewers as bundles of attitudes: mere posturings conforming to the current expectations of middlebrow theatergoers.

The difference between "realism" and "reality" in the drama, as I see it, is that the former tries to live up to the decent, solid citizen's view of what is true and real, usually by means that will not puzzle or offend him; whereas the latter tries to satisfy an individual author's vision of a reality behind the everyday reality, generally by means that emphasize the private, idiosyncratic inner language of the playwright. From this it should not be inferred that the theater of realism is necessarily inferior to that of reality. "Realism" has genuine value when it thoughtfully explores some area that has not yet been subjected to scrutiny; the theater of "reality" is valuable when the dramatist's inner-directed vision strikes at a hidden truth that in due time imposes itself on the audience.

Thus *The Boys in the Band* is, by and large, a realistic play: it views the homosexual ambience as any tolerant and understanding, but otherwise quite ordinary citizen would view it. There are no profundities, no flights of fancy, no arcane or innovative techniques employed—merely honest (well, reasonably honest), generally able and dedicated workmanship. But by exploring an area that the theater has not yet explored, the play's realism fulfills a needed and commendable function. For this is the first serious play that places the homosexual in the context not of the heterosexual world from which today he is largely able to withdraw, but of the homosexual subworld in which he is progressively more able to ensconce himself, and which has characteristics and problems interesting to homosexuals and heterosexuals alike, though not necessarily for the same reasons.

Conversely, the amoral world of a play like *Loot* is not realistic and does not correspond to any milieu we may know. But the playwright's bitter vision of greed and stupidity and perversion making the world go round may strike us as a fairly accurate though symbolic representation of certain worlds: big business, politics, Hollywood. However, productions of the Theater of the Ridiculous, like *Gorilla Queen* or *The Conquest of the Universe*, are not at all realistic in their approach, but express, I think, what their authors conceive of as reality: a world ruled by a camp sensibility, in which moral and aesthetic outrage is the desirable basic unit of experience. This seems to me a "truth" of so sterile a sort, of such limited applicability, as to represent not heightened but lowered reality.

From this we can postulate that the realistic theater is essentially journalistic, sociological or historic: exploring a society, a period, current psychological or even biological states. As such, this theater is likely to be time-bound and more perishable than the theater of reality. Yet this is not always the case. A play like *The Iceman Cometh, Hedda Gabler* or *Uncle Vanya* is essentially realistic: though it may in some inconspicuous ways depart from the normative views of the period (and these departures may prove, ultimately, most significant), it does not challenge those views, nor does it resort to intensely innovative techniques. Yet such a play penetrates beyond realism via something else: its language. It has found an intensity of expression—individual yet universal, fresh, accurate, but also charged with dark resonance—which propels it into poetry. Poetry, of course, is the very element of the other theater, the theater of reality; but this poetry is more personal, elusive, oblique—in short, more difficult.

The realistic theater thrives when there are new realms of life to be explored. These may be political or sexual, social or psychological. Whenever a new taboo is broken—as, for example, when sexual intimacies or deviations become permissible on the stage—or whenever the political or social order changes in some significant and ostensibly new way, the realistic theater has its legitimate chance. If religious beliefs or family ties atrophy, if heart transplants and freezing of human beings become the order of the day, if space travel arrives and new worlds open up, the realistic theater can, simply and forthrightly, make its contribution. But when, as in *The Price*, it addresses itself to social problems of the Depression thirty or forty years too late, and in a language that (as usual with Miller) is either trying too hard to be poetry or finding it too easy to be prose, there is no reason for preferring this copy to the originals: Ibsen or O'Neill, Odets or even earlier Miller. Conversely, even such slight musicals as *Your Own Thing* and *Hair* (especially in the vastly superior off-Broadway version) *do* address themselves to some part of contemporary reality, and make the grade as realistic theater if not as theater of reality.

THE THEATER OF REALITY, however, is never out of season, except when, as all too frequently happens, the playwright's view of the real is not worth much—is not a view of life that nourishes the intellect and emotions, that extends our range of feeling and thought, if only by finding new and telling formulations. Thus our present theater of reality is in trouble for the most basic of reasons: its distrust and rejection of language, which is, along with gesture, the first reality of the theater.

Let me explain. There are ways of using language that are radical and revolutionary, yet still real and valid. You can make language into a kind of desperate, maniacal game, to prove that you are still alive, as in Beckett. You can make language into a buzzing swarm of hallucinations or platitudes that symbolize the world, as in Ionesco. You can turn language into a magic ritual that is supposed to transmute the world, as in Genet. You can mold language into a mask under which the unspoken is the truth, as in the rare privileged moments of Pinter. You can let language become a mere comic incantation, with pitch and volume changes conveying moods and madnesses, as in Ann Jellicoe or Edward Bond (though this, I must say, is stretching language pretty thin). But in all those cases language is still at work. When it becomes unemployed, as in Happenings, our brains and hearts are out of work, too, and the theater becomes a new kind of escape—work-shirkers' compensation. Thus when a dramatic text by, say, Paul Foster or Rochelle Owens, though it is still a jump ahead of or behind Happenings, becomes little more than an excuse for directors and actors to improvise fancy stage effects, we have not gone forward into reality but backward into the unreal: toward D'Avenant's *Siege of Rhodes* or the extravaganzas of Colley Cibber.

Forthwith, in the name of reality, meaningful gesture is also expelled from the theater. So in the theater of mixed mediums—or, more simply, Happenings—as opposed to the "literary drama," there is no more "plot, development, climax, characterization, and dramatic explicitness." Instead, in this nonliterary drama, "the theatrical situation reverts to its barest essentials, time and space; and the creator's primary problem becomes animating the space and time he allots for himself." I am quoting from Richard Kostelanetz's *The Theater of Mixed Means*, the most literate book on the nonliterary, or illiterate, theater—though in such books literacy is at best only relative.

The gestures in the new theater aim at filling time and space

—and what a pitiful view of reality this is! It is based on the notion, as stated by Allan Kaprow and quoted by Kostelanetz, that life, chaotic life, is the model for chaotic theatrical events. But of course the function of the artist is to strive to understand the chaos, and, by understanding, lessen it—or at least fortify us for our encounters with it. Those who merely transpose it on the stage (or into any other medium) are not friends of art or man, only friends of chaos. And sure enough, we find Mr. Kostelanetz classifying as works of art Times Square, Wall Street (not the architecture, the bustle) and a space shot. These, to be sure, are realities, but not the realities of an artist. It is now to the theater itself that the famous stage direction from *Titus Andronicus* applies: Enter the drama, its hands cut off, its tongue cut out, and ravished.

This profound new theatrical reality is, in fact, at best an attempt to stimulate hopelessly coarse artistic taste buds; at worst, an extension of know-nothing hooliganism. When a Jerzy Grotowski stages *Doctor Faustus* so that, in the name of greater reality and audience involvement, actors and spectators all sit at the same banqueting table, what is achieved—besides seriously limiting the possible number of spectators? If Marlowe's reality can be conveyed only by jolting the audience by such gimmicks, that audience is *ab ovo* beyond—or below—Marlowe's reach. For if, to respond, you need supposed demons elbowing you and jumping up on your plate, the subtler stimulation of Faustus' poetry will be lost on you—assuming that it can be heard at all in such pandemonium. If, on the other hand, you can respond to the "reality" of a fine actor movingly speaking Faustus' lines, you will prefer to sit in your dark, secluded seat and concentrate on the isolated highlighted stage.

But there is worse: the "real" theater as a place of orgies and violence. Consider something like Richard Schechner's *Dionysus in 69*. Do we really need to see the unimpressive breasts of those actresses, the hairy anuses of those actors; must we have the performers jumping and tumbling all over us, when not actually luring us to frug with them or submit to their undressing and groping us? In *The Bacchae* of Euripides, King Pentheus was an intolerant despot who would outlaw sensual and sexual freedoms. In this version of Schechner's, it is the god Dionysus who is a fascist, forcing sexuality and violence on all, advocating a freedom that includes "burning down slums and listening to the screams," and together with the other performers, inflicting malodorous attentions on the audience. Needless to say, along with the baby, bath water has also been thrown out by the new theater.

WHAT HAS brought about this shabby view of reality, and with it the depoetization of the theater of reality? An alliance of intellectual malcontents and anti-intellectual hoodlums. On the one hand, there are the gifted and bright people who are so incensed by the indifference and crassness of the majority, and its materialism and politics; on the other, there are the various dropouts from school and society who are cashing in on what often is no more than incompetence and ignorance by calling it idealism and protest. And it is the fault of our society to have become so callous as to make all protest, no matter how crude and self-indulgent, at least nominally a shining alternative.

There have always been coalitions between the dissenters at the top and the rowdy malcontents at the bottom—think of the figurative union between Nietzsche and the Blond Beast. But by massively relaxing its discipline while stupidly refusing to engage the imagination; by being permissive of absurd excesses without setting worthier examples; by allowing itself to become (in a rapidly changing world) even more outdated than it usually is, the Establishment seems to have become grosser and weaker than ever, while the weapons for combating it have become more readily available.

To the extent that the current theater of reality is an attack on the existing order, it is good and no different from all rebellious drama: Ibsen's and Strindberg's, Brecht's and Genet's. Indeed, some of the rage with which certain Eastern Europeans like Grotowski and Jan Kott have modernized (and butchered) the classics out of all recognizable shape may have been an impotent fury against the oppressive political establishment taken out on defenseless masterpieces. Similarly, the favorable eye with which our own brilliant Robert Brustein has viewed some dubious dramatic experimentation, from unactable Prometheuses to unstomachable Hamlets, may stem simply from his uncontrolled disgust with the political, social and theatrical establishments.

But there can be found in today's theater, though not easily, a language and reality beyond realism and superior to mere window-smashing or opting out. We have seen it, earlier, in such plays as *The Zoo Story*, *Gallows Humor*, *The Connection* and *The Brig*. There are playwrights around today who have a highly specialized yet potentially universally significant view of reality. Thus in recently performed plays by Sam Shepard, John Guare, Israel Horovitz, and perhaps also in works by Leonard Melfi, Rosalyn Drexler, Ronald Ribman, Lanford Wilson, and, a little more remotely as yet, in productions of the new black theaters, something seems to be stirring. May it be a new dramatic reality—or, failing that, a new, honest and timely realism.

WHAT IS TASTE?

(1970)

Pᴿᴼᴮᴬᴮᴸʏ the most terrible thing you can say about a critic is that he has no taste. The most terrible and the most vague. For what is taste, really? *De gustibus non est disputandum,* the scholastic proverb proclaimed: there is no quarreling about tastes. And ever since, almost all critical quarrels have been about matters of taste, which is not surprising when you consider that taste cannot be defined—at least not in a way that would be to everyone's taste. But what is surprising is that so few people should even have tried to define it, or attempted to come to grips with the problem, except in specialized journals of aesthetics, written by professors of philosophy for one another. In what follows, I shall make some suggestions about what taste might be in the field of dramatic criticism; if some of my remarks should bear on the question of taste in general, so much the better.

Aꜱ I ʜᴀᴠᴇ ᴏꜰᴛᴇɴ ᴏʙꜱᴇʀᴠᴇᴅ, a critic must be an artist, a teacher and a philosopher. But, especially if he is a front-line critic, one who addresses himself to new plays as they come up, he must also have taste. In writing about the drama of the past, or of the firmly established dramatic reputations of the present, most of the work—perhaps all—can be done by scholarship, dedication, persuasiveness, a good style and a humane world view. If, however, one is up against something brand new, about which one has to make an unaided, partly intuitive and completely personal pronouncement, one's taste is what one has largely to rely on. Now, there have been scholars, connoisseurs and art collectors who were renowned as men and women of taste: Vernon Lee, Bernard Berenson, Harold Acton. But these have almost always been specialists in the fine arts whose expertise and exquisite tastes bore upon the art of the past, not on what was being created around them.

Oddly enough, as far as I know, no critic was ever considered a man of unusually refined taste—the possible exception being Oscar Wilde, who was indeed a remarkable critic, but whose taste was of a rather special, precious kind. The critics' failure to show in this category may mean simply that to be a so-called man of taste, and surround oneself with objets d'art, one must have more money than a critic can expect to make in this life. Or, perhaps, the man of taste must be an amateur who does not commit his opinions and choices to the printed page, where his errors of judgment persist in shaming him in a way that an occasional lapse in furniture or furnishings does not pursue its perpetrator.

There is, I believe, one critical absolute: the verdict of posterity, the test of time. This in effect is the taste of the ages, and to have held it in one's lifetime argues a critic a man of taste. To have preferred Shakespeare to Kyd and Chapman, to have picked Shaw over Pinero and Jones, to have recognized the superiority of O'Neill to Odets and Maxwell Anderson (I am choosing rather obvious examples) would argue someone, decades or centuries later, to have been a critic of taste.

But what sort of standards of taste can be posited, or at least sketched in, for the present—before it has turned into the historic past? It is a tricky business, when you consider that even such great critics as Sainte-Beuve and Matthew Arnold were proved the less right the nearer to their own time the writers they were judging. And even an artistic and critical genius like Goethe could turn down, in his capacity of theatrical director, Kleist's *Penthesilea,* a masterpiece, but of a type that was to the taste of the future rather than of its own day.

Taste varies considerably from era to era, but the true works of art transcend this sort of period taste; nevertheless, the best collective taste of certain periods can be fairly reliable for all but those masterworks which, almost by definition, are the future made manifest in the present, and are therefore premature. Yet just what that "best taste" might be is immediately apparent only in certain kinds of periods. These are usually eras in which society is structured along strictly pyramidal, hierarchic lines, with the court and the aristocracy at the apex. One thinks of France under the Sun King or of Restoration England, when the sovereign and the court, however dissolute, were functioning as the arbiters of elegance, manners and good taste in the arts. The only trouble with such ruling-class taste is that it tends to be consciously or unconsciously preservative of the interests of the ruling class, and to spurn revolutionary talent as being, precisely, in bad taste.

But what, if anything, does the very word "taste" tell us? It is interesting to note that it comes from the Vulgar Latin *tastare*, derived from a frequentative form of *tangere*, to touch. Then, by way of Old and Middle French *taster*, meaning both "feel" and "taste," we get our English "taste." But in the course of this evolution, the sense, in both senses, changed: what was done with the hand, the sense of touch, now switched to the tongue and the taste buds: the sense of taste. And in all modern languages I know of, the word for "taste" in the sense of discrimination in matters of behavior, art, and so forth, is identical with the word for what we experience when we eat something. Thus, for instance, the French *goût* and the German *Geschmack*. Why did this second, higher meaning of "taste" not evolve until the primary meaning migrated from fingertips to the root of the tongue? I suppose because, however dimly, the wisdom of languages realized that taste in the figurative sense is something less tangible and more internalized, more to be savored than seized—something to be realized gradually, like the deliciousness of an apple, rather than immediately, like the hardness or sharpness of a stone.

We may perhaps further deduce from this that taste is something both very general and very private, for although every kind of honey tastes sweet to everyone, two people are very apt to disagree about which kind tastes sweetest. There is much more room for disagreement here than about which surface is rougher or smoother. But taste tends to be a matter for disagreement only until certain criteria are historically established: once honey from Hymettus, or Ming china, or plays by Molière have been hallowed by time, it is easy to make the proper choices, provided one can afford to indulge one's "tastes." But how does one know about a drama critic who picks play A above play B, both of which have just opened, whether he has taste?

Well, if we assume that taste, like the act of savoring a new food, only more so, is a slow, experimental process, then the tasteful critic is likely to be the one who spends the most time developing his taste. This means, to begin with, exposure. The critic who has trained his taste harder, by reading and seeing plays, by studying drama both through the words of great teachers and through the work of great directors and actors, by keeping abreast of scholarly and critical thought at home and abroad, stands a fair chance of being more discriminating than the reviewer who stumbled onto or was shoved into his particular slot because of some quirk of newspaper or magazine publishing. But of course there seem to be people with inveterate bad taste (whatever that means) whom no amount of exposure manages to refine.

The next thing, then, to look for in a critic is pervasive sensitivity, which usually is an indication of taste. But how does one spot such sensitivity? By a critic's awareness of details, of a variety of fine points that tend to escape the lay theatergoer. Thus the critic who is alert to the greatest number of diverse phenomena may be presumed to have the most highly developed taste. I remember how shocked I was when one of our more influential drama critics asked me whether I paid much attention to such things as sets, which, he said, were not the sort of thing he usually noticed. A person not sensitive to sets—or costumes, or lighting, or background music, or make-up, or whatever else—is not likely to be all that sensitive and tasteful about theater in the larger sense.

IF I MAY SWITCH to films for another example, there is a movie reviewer so color-blind that someone has to write the color of his ties on their backs. Yet this same reviewer will invariably write that a film was in "lovely," "beautiful," "handsome" or "gorgeous" color—four stock epithets that someone must have written on the backs of the respective films for him. And there is your clue: anyone who writes so perfunctorily about color most likely does not have an understanding of it. So, too, the critic with taste will be recognizable by the subtle shading and variety he brings to his descriptions of even such phenomena as recur, with small variations, in every show he has to review.

Again, in the discrimination with which a critic uses language, a reasonably accurate image of his general taste will be reflected. Of course, there have been some writers of criticism with good styles and nothing much to say, but there have been almost none with wretched styles yet the most exquisite perceptions. Study, therefore, whether a reviewer has a sense of prose rhythm (the fact that he may work on a short deadline is almost irrelevant here). Are there well-modulated cadences in his prose? Do his paragraphs have an aural shape? Are his images suggestive, his words soigné? Such characteristics are a good index of taste. One of our younger reviewers and his wife make a point of looking as porcinely disreputable as possible when they come to the theater; they are also given to loud gum-chewing and heaven help the persons sitting in front of them. This crassness, this tastelessness, you may be sure, shows up in the reviewer's work. It is all right for an artist to be a slob in his general aspect and manners; in a critic, where the emphasis is not on creation but on discrimination, such boorishness augurs ill.

But let us get back to less speculative ground. If we agree that the test of time determines what is art, as it also determines which reviewer had the good taste to be, as it were, a previewer of the judgment of the future, certain deductions can be made from the past history of the drama. It is clear that plays of various types survive: comic and tragic, realistic and surreal, naturalistic and poetic. If a reviewer seems to favor one or two kinds at the expense of the others, chances are that he does not have a catholic enough taste. What is even clearer, however, is that only a very small percentage of what is written and produced survives. Therefore, the critic with taste is not likely to become enthusiastic about many things he reviews: a reviewer you see quoted in the advertisements of every other show is not, you may be assured, a critic with taste.

HERE A DIGRESSION imposes itself. Can a critic praise only the truly good plays, those with a future, or must he also praise those with some sort of present—lest the entire theater become a thing of the past? This is not a simple question to answer, but I would say that if there is a real need for theater in the world (and I hope there is—I, for one, would not care to live in a theaterless world), it is by upholding the highest standards possible that the cause of the stage is best served. We need the kind of criticism which, to the extent that it is feasible, forces today's prevalent commercialism to surpass itself.

If a show supplies pure entertainment of an expert sort, provided only that it is not untruthful about human nature, it deserves a pat on the head—enough so that mere fun-seekers should not be deterred from seeing it. But there is no reason to encourage bad entertainment, grossly mendacious escapism or titillating sensationalism under any circumstances. What is at stake in such cases is the survival not of theater but of vulgar and tasteless commercial managements—the survival of something unscrupulous and outmoded that may make it hard for the new and better theater to come into being. The phoenix is reborn from its ashes, not from a few pitiful embers kept alive by a bunch of reviewers breathing unearned superlatives on them. Some kinds of respiration are just too artificial.

To return to the matter of taste, however, and specifically to what I referred to earlier as ruling-class taste. Since we have no aristocracy today, only a plutocracy functioning as an aristocracy, it follows that the taste of the period (a much lesser kind of taste than that of the ages, yet a taste that matters for the moment) is dictated by money. In the fine arts this is causing the worst kind of havoc, with rich but uneducated and uncultivated collectors patronizing and enshrining garbage; in the theater, the situation is somewhat different. There exists an inexpensive theater—call it avant-garde, revolutionary, experimental—where money does not call the tune. Yet it would be unwise to assume that this theater is automatically on the side of the ángels—I mean the kind with wings, not with checkbooks. But it stands a better chance of being so than an expensive theater, like Broadway, which is largely dominated by what the moneyed classes want. And if the money is not in the hands of a civilized group but of more or less newly rich parvenus, Neil Simon becomes God and the reviewer who blows the loudest horn for him, his archangel.

But whatever the theatergoing reader may assume critical taste to be—I submit these notes tentatively and chiefly in the hope of starting much-needed speculation and discussion—let him beware of committing that most vulgar error of assuming that good taste is that which agrees with his. Somebody recently wrote one of my editors to the effect that I had no sense whatever of the tastes of my readers or the public at large. He was, unintentionally, paying me a great tribute which I can only hope I deserve. For it is extremely hard not to be influenced by the tastes of one's milieu; yet resisting them is precisely the critic's duty. It is only in being uncompromisingly himself that a critic performs a true service, and as a man of taste (not infallible taste, for there can be no such thing), goes down in history, or as a man of no taste, goes down the drain.

CRITICAL PROGNOSIS:
NEW CHAPS AND OLD BOYS

(1971)

IT'S TIME AGAIN for theatrical forecasts, and it seems appropriate to predict what drama criticism will be like in the coming season. Such forecasting is desirable because we have drifted far from that happy moment, some fifty years ago, when C. E. Montague of the *Manchester Guardian* could write: "All first-rate critics are, in some measure, banded in one army, fighting in the same everlasting war, and substantially agreed in distinguishing the uniforms of trash, the immemorial enemy, and of sound work, the friend." Either trash has become so clever that it changes uniforms with a hand quicker than the critic's eye, or first-rate critics are too few now to band into an army; moreover, their ranks have been swelled with all sorts of irregulars, sans-culottes, Hessian mercenaries and soldiers of misfortune.

In the coming season, as usual, there will be two chief kinds of drama reviewers in our leading newspapers and magazines: the chaps who are for the New against the Old, and the boys who are for the Old against the New. For the New Chaps, the history of theater begins with Brecht, a venerable though somewhat hoary ancestor, to whom one must pay periodic lip service as proof that one is up on one's ancient history. After Brecht there is virtually nothing till Beckett and the absurdists; after that, except for Pinter, there are no more playwrights, only directors who rewrite plays, the greatest among them being Brook and Grotowski. For the Old Boys, on the other hand, whatever the New Chaps like is ipso facto anathema. Instead, they praise the well-made play, the boulevard farce, the musical (preferably nostalgic), the revival of anything from the twenties or thirties, and an occasional production of a Classic, provided it is routine.

If you look to *The New York Times* for critical assistance, you'll get it—from both sides. The scrupulousness of that publication knows no bounds: you're given two reviewers, a New Chap and an Old Boy. But they are both clever fellows and, being aware of the weight of their opinions, know how to hedge their bets. The resident New Chap will warble in ecstasy over the latest daring experiment at LaMama: two hours' worth of the vowel "A," pronounced with various intonations by nine naked men interestingly entwined with three clothed women (who afterward take off their clothes and are revealed to be men or, worse yet, Julie Bovasso). Nevertheless, he will add several witty caveats about his dirty mind, rather special tastes, and concede that while the whole thing may be considered stultifying, it is surely stultification of genius. When reviewing the new-old musicals of the current past masters, our reviewer will permit himself some generally unfavorable remarks, but will find just the breezily qualifying statement to take the edge off his carping—say, about his being only one grouch among an audience of grovelers, and what avails his jaundiced eye among all those gleaming reflections in the golden eye of the majority? Most of the time, however, our man will manage paragraphs, even sentences, that will start with a raised thumb and end with a lowered one, or vice versa, like those Spanish sentences that are framed by two exclamation points, one aimed at the dust and one reaching heavenward. If self-contradiction were an art, this critic's brow would deserve to be covered with enough bay wreaths to make it outshine a Corinthian capital.

But the *Times* also has its Old Boy, whose methods are even subtler. Though his soul thrills to the old, he knows when to capitulate gracefully and has never been the last by whom the new is tried. When almost everybody accepted Anouilh or Beckett or Pinter, our critic managed to discover that the time was *now* ripe for A. or B. or P.; or that with *this* play, A. or B. or P. at last proved himself worthy. Brecht gets the back of his hand to this day (which may, of course, be for reasons of politics or religion, but we don't mention such words in a family paper); and Ibsen, also a modernist, is shown not to handle exposition half so well as the author of *Butterflies Are Free*. But let anyone revive some collaborative farce by Kaufman and Hart, or Hecht and MacArthur; or let Richard Rodgers cough up another musical and let there be in it some Grand Old Star (preferably female) who turns every stick of scenery into a betel nut—and our critic will be singing benedicites to the show and printing love letters to the star such as she might well carry about inside her bodice forever. The reviewer's masterstroke, however, is to find a playwright who under a veneer of pseudo-newness will provide a jovially doddering boulevard farce; thus the next Murray Schisgal item will again be hailed as the prototype of the *truly* innovative, and our critic will prove conclusively that he is no old fogy.

Meanwhile the *Post*, the *News*, the—but stop! Nobody gets those papers for their drama reviews. The *Village Voice* will run no fewer than three totally divergent reviews of a play that no one, even assuming he wanted to see it, could locate in time. *Newsweek* will forage in the caves of the new deeper than the underground press, and emerge at the antipodes; conversely, *Time* will stick to the old, except if there should be something new from Oliver Hailey, even a return of Hailey's comet. *The New Yorker*, though favoring the old, will continue to pronounce *King Lear* unactable, and extol anything of Hibernian authorship. One denominator, though, most critics will have in common: the earnest desire to keep show-biz alive, in some form or other, lest they lose their livelihoods. Before long, therefore, they'll discover a few unquestionable gems that will put the theater on its feet, their quotes on display, and your teeth on edge. As for your critic, he will continue to police his fellow watchdogs—alas, to no avail.

MUST THE REST
BE SILENCE?

(1970)

Wɪᴛ ᴀɪʟs our theater? The economists declare that
the theater has priced itself out of competition with movies
and television. The youth-oriented hold that the theater does
not offer young people the "relevance" they find elsewhere—
say, in pop music. And the avant-gardists claim that the theater
lags behind other art forms, and must stop being tradition-
bound. To these theoreticians, subsidies, an injection of rock
into the lyric vein, a groat's worth of Grotowski could solve
the problem.

There may be some truth in all this—though less than
meets the anastigmatic eye—but I do think that what the
theater is most afflicted with is the agony of the word. The
word, which was in the beginning, threatens to drop out at
midpoint, or wherever it is that we are. And theater has always
been sustained by the word. Certainly, as its very name, derived
from the Greek *theasthai* (to view, to watch) indicates, theater is, first of all, a visual medium. Yet as a person may begin
by winning us over visually but must, to hold our attention,
back this up with a mind that manifests itself in words, so the
theater must have some idea behind its comeliness and al-
luring movements. And so *theasthai* is related to *theorein*
(to look at), whence the word "theorem"—an object of study.

The stage today has fallen victim to the general mistrust,
dislike and recession of the word—the word which in all
theaters but the most recent was equal in importance with
movement or action. Let us remember that the two are by

no means polar opposites: the most primitive form of language is precisely pantomime; conversely, language often functions as gesture. Put most simply: words caress, wound, stir us to action. Or, as R. P. Blackmur wrote in *Language as Gesture*, with reference to poetry, "We feel almost everything that deeply stirs us as if it were a gesture, the gesture of our uncreated selves."

When you come to think of it, the Greek theater was almost all words, except in the choric passages, where, however, the action was dance. I suspect that the classic "decorum," which consisted of keeping things like violence and sex off the stage and relegating them to narration, i.e., words, had less to do with ethical or even aesthetic considerations than with the mere fact of novelty; that word, the onstage word, was new and infinitely fascinating. To hear a messenger tell of Jocasta's death or of Oedipus' blinding himself (to be sure, in the language of Sophocles) was every bit as remarkable, thrilling and new as seeing such things acted out was to be for later, more jaded audiences. When the word—at least as socked and buskined to us—lost its novelty, visual excitement came to be more in demand. And significantly, as technology, which is the opposite of poetry, grew more accomplished, the mechanics of the stage became more dazzling and the words began to go into eclipse. Of course, the dramatic poet— or, more exactly, the undramatic one—was also to blame: the stage had to freeze while the wordmonger savored the sound of his vice [sic].

Nonetheless, as late as in the days of Shaw, dialogue was still an eminently stageworthy craft, and a play like *Heartbreak House* could get along on token action and compellingly gesturing language. But that was half a century ago, and verbal gesture has dwindled to gesticulation or less. I suppose the choking clutter of print, radio talk programs, demagogic speechifying and proliferation of propaganda must have contributed to giving the word a bad odor. And again, infatuation with technology and gadgetry, which could so easily be applied to music, the plastic arts, the movies, but had more or less exhausted its scenic potential, and never had much to offer other writers (I doubt that even an audience of computers would enjoy computer poetry), may have lured budding playwrights into nonverbal realms.

Though nonverbalness first affects the general public, its indirect effect on the theater is still a mighty blow to the windpipe. Characters in Albee's plays sometimes apologize for speaking in paragraphs, which is as if a sober person excused himself for walking a straight line. But truly young people astonish me with their inability to speak even in sentences, never mind paragraphs. Although the last great wave of theatrical inspiration we have witnessed, the Absurdist, still made use of words, it played them off against the stage action: each tripped up the other until both collapsed. Words were mocked, browbeaten, used to wipe up the stage with. Finally Beckett, like Prospero, renounced his magic in an *Act Without Words,* and in rushed every kind of inarticulateness from Happenings to Grotowski. Explorers searched out every nook and cranny between deathly silence and deafening pandemonium, by-passing only the word.

Have words failed us, or have we failed the word? Until recently, the chief topic of the theater, as of general conversation, was Lack of Communication: husbands and wives, parents and children, X's and Y's who simply could not, would not, did not speak to one another. No doubt this is largely a social sickness, but I wonder whether it is not almost equally a verbal one. Have we not allowed television, traffic noises, rock, war and other germ-carriers to infect our craniums and tongues with a roof-and-mouth disease rendering us unable to think and speak words in meaningful, beautiful, moving ways that engender confidence, love and action? This is what causes failure of communication in our lives, and those dreary platitudes about it onstage.

Let our youthful rebels beware: social and political commitment without commitment to articulateness and poetry will do little for the world beyond transforming it into a monstrous discothèque, free and equally brutalizing to all. The necessary revivification of the word might well start in the theater. Just by ceasing to shout, by talking softly to people, it might oblige them to listen.

FULMINATIONS

*The number of pieces in this section is the greatest, and
the facile conclusion would be that they therefore represent
the true nature of the author. But it is just as possible that
they represent the true nature of our theater—or if you prefer,
the theatrum mundi, the great stage of fools on which we all
perform.*

*Schopenhauer observed that the man who goes up in a
balloon does not see himself as bigger—he only sees the rest
of the world as smaller. The critic, to gain his overview, must
have a balloon that takes him up high enough to afford a
panorama; but this does not mean that history does not have
a balloon that ascends higher and longer than any critic's,
and that from the vantage point of this superballoon the
critic's view may yet come to look as earthbound as that of
any troglodyte.*

*Nevertheless, I can say of these fulminations that they
were begotten by genuine anger, however facetiously phrased.
And, unlike the Church, I do not see wrath—at least the kind
that can be called intellectual indignation—as a vice. I see
it as a passion which, if history should bear it out, becomes
sanctified. If not, it remains a profane passion, but even that
appears to me better than the kind of mundane tolerance that
is indistinguishable from indifference—the only true, and
truly contemptible, critical vice.*

MUGGING THE BARD
IN CENTRAL PARK

(1965)

Sнакеspeare has had a hard time of it in America. Not only is there no Shakespearean acting tradition and adequate schooling available, but also what theatrical method has prevailed here is the exact opposite of the style, or stylization, that Shakespeare requires. Thus the Bard has fallen into the hands of either academicians and their student productions, or culture-mongering socialites banding together with the backwash of Broadway to Theatre-Guild the lily. Typically, the American Shakespeare Festival at Stratford, Connecticut, wallows in both errors: a representative production there is a *Measure for Measure* done as a Strauss operetta in Old Vienna, with a company full of Broadway has-beens or mincing eunuchs, and directed either by a cast-off director of the Old Vic with his wonderfully Edwardian ideas, or by an ex-college professor with no stageworthy idea whatever.

But my concern here is with the New York Shakespeare Festival, to be had in Central Park every summer, and singled out for every kind of praise by every kind of reviewer. Night after night it sells out—not its seats, which are gratis, but its artistic standards, which, if any, are gratuitous.

Two points should be made right away about Joseph Papp, the man who conceived and produces the Festival. He is passionately dedicated, and he was able to get the project going over all manner of opposition and, what is worse, indifference. He raised the money, and, God knows, it's easier to find sermons in stones than to squeeze blood or money out of them.

107

But though Papp is a gifted money-raiser, this does not yet make him a theatrical producer of quality—and certainly not a valid artistic, let alone stage, director. He has undeniable talents for getting things started, and no idea where to stop.

As I look back on many summers of Central Park theater-going, I see few things to recall with genuine pleasure. Perhaps no more than three: Philip Bosco's Angelo, Penny Fuller's Celia, and John Morris' music for *Love's Labour's Lost* (or, as the Pappians in their non-U way spelled it, *Love's Labor's Lost*). Even there I cannot be quite sure about how much additional dignity Bosco gained by the cloddishness of Marianne Hartley's Isabella, how much Penny Fuller's stature was raised by the total collapse of Paula Prentiss' Rosalind, and how much Morris' unpretentious melodiousness profited by contrast with the customary claptrap of David Amram. In any case, what are these few bright spots as against that army of Rorschachian blots spreading across Mr. Papp's scutcheon?

What, for example, of Frank Silvera's Lear, a vapidly self-pitying whiner from beginning to end; of Nan Martin's Beatrice, all leaden cutenesses; of Colleen Dewhurst's and Michael Higgins' turning *Antony and Cleopatra* into the humdrum affair of an Irish washerwoman with an Irish cop, complete with brogues? What of Julie Harris' baby-talking Ophelia; of Papp's staging of *The Merchant of Venice* so that Shylock emerges the undisputed hero; of Gerald Freedman's directing *The Tempest* as a series of vaudeville acts bristling with sight gags and stage tricks further obscuring the already mumbled and uneasily rattled-off poetry? And what of the repeated casting of performers like Betty Henritze, who has only to appear on-stage for the aesthetic eye to boggle; or Jane White, who has only to open her mouth for the civilized ear to revolt? Or take the current directorial trio, Gladys Vaughan, Gerald Freedman and Papp himself; individually, I dare say, they could be matched, but I defy anyone to adduce a threesome as monumentally untalented.

Consider the most recent Park production I have seen, Mrs. Vaughan's *Coriolanus*. Here were crowd and battle scenes of which a third-rate discothèque would have been ashamed;

swordmanship that looked like a bunch of tourists in Chinatown insistent upon using chopsticks; blocking that had, for example, Coriolanus bidding farewell to his beloved wife from clear across the stage; low comedy involving the Volscian servants lingered over with much more gusto (though no more taste) than any of the tragedy surrounding the protagonist; a Valeria interpreted not as a noble Roman matron but as an Eve Arden-style comic-relief *Hausfrau;* and an entire cast mispronouncing the Volsces as "the Volskis"—shades of the Russkis, perhaps?

The individual performances, with the exception of Robert Burr's manly and personable, though hardly great and tragic, Coriolanus, were foul to middling; of these the most hauntingly horrible were the tribunes of Alan Ansara and James Earl Jones, the Virgilia of Kate Sullivan, and—hysterically cheered by reviewers and audiences alike—the Volumnia of Jane White. Jones sounded like a one-stringed double bass with a faintly Calypso accent, and rolled about like a huge barrel set in motion by a homunculus within. As for Miss White, her every look, gesture and move is that of a fishwife suffering in equal measure from neurasthenia and megalomania. But the supreme giveaway is her voice, inflating every sound, blowing up every syllable into an egomaniacal balloon, until her entire hypertrophic ego is wafted heavenward on bloated, unnatural vocables.

Both Miss White and Mr. Jones are blacks, which brings me to yet another trouble with Papp's productions. Out of a laudable integrationist zeal, Mr. Papp has seen fit to populate his Shakespeare with a high percentage of black performers. But the sad fact is that, through no fault of their own, black actors often lack even the rudiments of Standard American speech—itself well behind British English in musicality and appropriateness to Shakespearean verse; moreover, they have been unjustly deprived of sufficient training and experience in even the standard American repertoire, such as it is. As a result, desegregation will take even longer on the poetical than on the political plane.

But it is not only aurally that Negro actors present a problem; they do not look right in parts that historically demand white performers. As the painter Larry Rivers—neither a high-brow nor a square, but possessed of an acute visual sense—remarked during a recent symposium, "I don't think putting Negro actors in white parts is possible—I don't see how you can keep life out of the stage." Thus a black Henry V runs counter to the lifelikeness of the play—all the more so when, as frequently happens, his brother is played by a white actor. With Mrs. Vaughan's Roman citizenry about four-fifths Negro, Rome clearly became the capital of Abyssinia, the few whites presumably accountable for as missionaries. The trouble with this sort of thing is that it cannot help setting off wrong responses, so that it is scarcely surprising to find the innocent who passes for *Cue* magazine's drama critic commenting that "the bitter clashes are sometimes startlingly suggestive of Bogalusa or Selma." Fine, except that unfortunately this is not remotely what the play is about.

The critical evaluations of Papp's enterprise have been consistently and thoroughly misleading—whether because of the assumption that something free of charge and for the people must be evaluated along democratic, not dramatic lines, or simply because of the popular reviewers' abysmal lack of discrimination, it would be difficult to say. What, for instance, is one to conclude from Judith Crist's review of *Coriolanus* in the *Herald Tribune,* which reads in part: "Whenever the play bogs down in talk or scene change—and this play does—director Gladys Vaughan has set a citizen to scrambling about, a flag to waving and a lackey to pratfalling. None of this is excessive, all of it is part of the excitement generated by this handsomely dressed, fast-flowing production." The conclusion, I suppose, is either that Shakespeare at the height of his creative powers was a bungler happily rescued by Mrs. Gladys Vaughan, or that Mrs. Crist, at the height of her critical powers, is beyond rescue.

What justification is there for feeding audiences not Shakespeare but pap—whether with one or two p's? Some twenty-five years ago, arguing for the movies as they then were, the playwright Gerhart Hauptmann wrote: "One does not drag down *Peer Gynt* when one makes a film of it; but one may, perhaps, raise an audience consisting of decent chambermaids, hansom cab-drivers, or even of all kinds of uncontrollable elements, up to its level." Rather than the Germany of 1920, this is the democratic America of 1965 with hardly any chambermaids or hansom cabbies left (though a few of the latter survive, precisely along the perimeter of Central Park), but Papp's Shakespeare today is very much what a 1920 silent-film version of *Peer Gynt* might have been. No doubt there are those—drama reviewers included—who enjoy, of a sticky New York evening, going into the summery Park for an uplifting sermon against Governor Wallace, but those whose concern is with Shakespeare, theater and art will find little or nothing of value in it.

Mr. Papp is not really interested in art, let alone poetry, about which he manifestly knows nothing. To him, Shakespeare is the friend of the common man, the spokesman for the underdog, the social, or socialist, Messiah. But Shakespeare was no such thing, and in the attempt to wrench him into that, his true magnificence is irretrievably lost.

The New York Shakespeare Festival had best be considered as an act of charity for underprivileged New Yorkers, and should, as such, be reviewed by those reporters whom the papers regularly send out to cover charity balls and bazaars. Or is that whom they have been sending all along?

LOVABLE LITTLE PEOPLE

(1967)

IF THERE IS a character so ubiquitous and universally beloved of Broadwayites that he may safely be considered
immortal, it is the Lovable Little Man, who in some cases
appears as the Lovable Little Woman. There are many impure
manifestations of the LLM, but let me try to describe here his
provenance and main features in the pure state. The character
was not to be found in the plays of O'Neill, George Kelly and
the early S. N. Behrman. It is the sentimental Marxism of the
WPA playwrights that begot him upon the democratic opti-
mism of the American public, and it was not till the thirties
that the figure emerged full-fledged. But it was the postwar
culture boom, bringing an ever more pseudocultural and self-
deluded audience into the theater, that gave him the supreme
accolade.

What are the characteristics of the Lovable Little Man? He
must, first of all, have a heart of gold. This is a *sine qua non*.
He may have almost any failing you like—though quirks are
preferable—as long as he has his heart of gold. This solid-gold
ticker may not be fully revealed until the closing scene; in
fact, it is best not to unveil it completely till then, and keep
the audience in genuine 24-karat suspense about it. But not
quite in suspense, either. Underneath the suspense they should
really have no doubt about this buried, beating treasure. While
the LLM (or LLW) is raising, for example, fiendishly insuper-
able obstacles to Daughter's marrying that nice young man—
just because he isn't a catch, or a college graduate, or Jewish—

it must be secretly clear to the audience that in the end, the hurdles will prove superable.

Or, if the LLM suffers from a ridiculous shyness (downright unmanly but, mind you, nothing effeminate!) about proposing to the charming widow next door, merely because she is so dazzling, witty and popular with men (though, I need hardly remind you, she doesn't sleep with any of them), you must fear that he'll never do it. But at the same time you know that in the end, after the matter has been dragged out for three acts, he will clumsily, by accident—but what a cute accident!— pop the question all the same, just as you guessed he would. And, as you likewise guessed, be accepted. That's the LLM for you. And that's entertainment.

Heart of gold, entertainment and recognizable foibles. It is good if these little shortcomings of the LLM or LLW can be identified as one's neighbors' or best friends'. Or better yet, one's wife's or husband's. It is not fatal even if they turn out to be one's own, since the creature is so lovable, after all, that everything will be forgiven. Nevertheless, it is preferable for these peccadilloes or comic idiosyncrasies not to be one's own—except, perhaps, in a caricatured and thus harmless form. It is nice to be able to feel superior to the LLM. That is what makes him so lovable.

But enough of this theorizing, and on to actual practice. Where on Broadway today do we find the LLM or LLW? Why, just about everywhere. Well, not in *The Homecoming* or *The Killing of Sister George* or *Marat/Sade* or *At the Drop of Another Hat;* those are foreign shows, about foreigners, where- as the LLM is, among other excellent things, American. Abroad they have plays that do not particularly go in for the LLM, and this may be what is called art, and of course one should go to see it, too—one should, in fact, definitely make the effort of seeing it, because though entertainment is better for seeing, art is better for being seen at. But it can't hold a candle to shows about the LLM and LLW, like *The Odd Couple* or *Hello, Dolly!* or *The Impossible Years.*

Down to specifics, then. Take *The Apple Tree.* Did you think Adam and Eve were great heroic, epic or tragical mythical figures? Well, perhaps mythical, because that the LLM and LLW certainly are. But great, heroic, epic, tragic? No! Little and lovable. Wasn't the book even based on something by Mark Twain, or Hal Holbrook, who is the LLM turned philosopher? Or take *Don't Drink the Water*. There is no denying it, its caterer hero has a mean streak. Yes, but his meanness proves quite ineffectual in the end, and he does keep writing doting letters to his boy back home, and he is sweet to his wife when she really gets shaken up, and finally he does let his daughter marry the wrong, i.e., the right guy. Who, naturally, turns out to be the LLM junior size.

But with *Cabaret* all is truly well again. It might be objected that this show has something to do with stories by Christopher Isherwood, who is, or was, English. Not at all; by the time the librettist, Joe Masteroff, and the lyricist, Fred Ebb, and whoever all the other unwicked cooks were, got through with this broth, it became a veritable breeding ground, or bacterial culture, of LLM's and LLW's. The purest and most nearly archetypal of them all is a Herr Schultz, who did not exist in Isherwood, and who, despite his ultra-Teuton name, is, in fact, a Jew. This, though not a prerequisite, is always a nice thing for the LLM to be. Schultz has a song in which he comically—or so the authors think—informs us that being a "meeskite," which is Yiddish for someone ugly, is not a bad thing at all. And the whole character—all bumbling, fumbling, mumbling good will—is meant to be an illustration of how wonderful a homely nonentity really is. Aristotle and Brecht, our two most important dramatic theorists, though they disagree about virtually everything else, would be in perfect accord on rejecting this sentimental "meeskite" as the fraudulent trash he is. But the spectators know better: if they themselves are "meeskites," they feel vindicated and ennobled; if they are not (or think they are not), they can bask in feeling superior and nobler yet.

Or consider *I Do! I Do!* The wife in the show is a perfect LLW and is portrayed by the greatest interpreter of LLW's, Mary Martin. Not only does she get a chance to utter every platitude that we associated with LLW-hood, but also, the

way things are fixed, we can take the clichés at face value
and laugh *with* them, or we can feel above them, and laugh
at them. You see, the important thing in writing about the
LLM and LLW is *not* to have a point of view. If you are manifestly for them, the audience or even the critics may accuse
you of being naïve or trivial or old-fashioned, which will not
hurt you at the box office, but might hurt your ego. If you are
against them, the critics are quite likely to hail you as a
master (even if your play is as phony as *The Homecoming*),
but the audience will resent you, and this might hurt the
B.O. The safe thing, then, is to poke gentle, likable fun at
your LLM and LLW, and allow for any interpretation; this
means that your play will be mindless and spineless, but definitely not audienceless. To illustrate: the wife in the show has
an extramarital dalliance, but it is only a) subsequent to the
husband's unfaithfulness, and b) platonic. By the double standard still dear to our audiences, it is all right for the LLM
to be a wee bit unfaithful (and is it ever wee here!), but the
Mother of the Children—perish the thought! Still, in the name
of women's rights, she must assert herself. Hence the obvious solution: she shall be platonically unfaithful!

Yes, the fallibility of the LLW or LLM must be strictly
controlled. Take *The Star Spangled Girl* by Neil Simon, who,
if there were such a thing as LLM and LLW Enterprises,
Inc. (and I am not absolutely sure there isn't), would be
chairman of the board. Here we have a girl who is the young
LLW personified; the only trouble with her is that she is
a Southern reactionary and as stupidly prejudiced as they
come. Moreover, she falls in love with a man because of the
way he smells, but that, we are to understand, is not idiotic
but cute. Well, this model Birchite might be overstepping the
boundaries of permissible paltriness; so, come the last scene,
she must be converted to the extreme opposite: maniacally
uncritical, eternal-opposition liberalism. Clearly two such antithetical follies nicely cancel each other out, and our LLW
is to be viewed as a wholesome bit of Americana, not as a
double moron.

Again, take *Sweet Charity*. This, too, you might remonstrate, has something foreign in its origin, but, never fear, it has become Americanized, homogenized, lobotomized to the point where the LLW is no longer a prostitute, but a dance-hall girl, which allows the authors to imply out of one corner of their mouths that she is really a sweet, innocent thing, as the movies have taught us taxi-dancers are; but also enables the audience to grin along with the other corner of the author's mouths, full of innuendos to the contrary. And of course, whereas the ending of Fellini's *Nights of Cabiria* was bitter-sweet, in this "adaptation" it is merely sweet and sour: an LLW must never come to excessive grief, or we might lose our faith in things as they are.

And what about the hero of *Walking Happy*, as played with insufferable servility by Norman Wisdom, who, as the ads inform us, "is irresistible" according to "Walter Kerr and everybody else"? To be sure, this, too, is based on a foreign, in this case English, play; but by the time its authors are finished with it, it is about as English as a Shakespeare History performed at Stratford, Conn. This LLM is so arch-pure that he ceases to be a man at all, and becomes a worm. But as we all know, a worm will turn, and, by the last scene, Mr. Wisdom is well on his way toward masterful self-assertion in his career, marriage and entire personality. Now, whereas the LLM or LLW must never be a prostitute, it is more than all right for the performer enacting the part to be an arrant whore. Mr. Wisdom, though English, does what most successful American stars have done: every look, every gesture, every intonation of his shrieks (or, perhaps, reeks): "Love me! Love me! Love me! Look how little, how defenseless, how lovable I am!" With this kind of shameless pandering to the public, small wonder that our LLM ends up irresistible to the two forces that count: Walter Kerr and everybody else.

The relentless LLM and LLW industry grinds out its platitudinous and false fabrications without surcease. We have not yet had a musical of *Macbeth*, but we did have something that looked like the book for a musical of *Hamlet* called *Those That Play the Clowns*. It was written by the librettist of *Bye, Bye, Birdie* and *Hello, Dolly!* and if it had only not forgotten to get a catchy title like that and a few songs, it might be with us yet. What we do have with us—and apparently will have forever—is a musical-comedy version of *Don Quixote* called *Man of La Mancha,* the ads for which try to make us feel guilty if we have seen it fewer times than twice, whereas we should feel slightly ashamed if we sat through it once.

Don Quixote, who was a tragicomic champion of noble but obsolete values, has become in *Man of La Mancha* an exemplary LLM. He is no longer larger-than-life-size, no longer superbly and preposterously trying to turn the clock back. Now he is a lovable little fellow who persists in being "idealistic" in spite of adverse circumstances. This Don spouts vermiculate commonplaces about dreaming the impossible dream and righting the unrightable wrong, and is just a sweet little fellow on the side of the angels but, alas, impractical. Call him a dreamer, or, better yet, a lovable little man. Cervantes may whirl around in his grave as if his quietus had been choreographed by Jack Cole, but an audience full of LLM's and LLW's, real or imaginary, nightly weep for and cheer this great figure's reduction *from* the absurd to sheer banality.

LET ME make it plain: I am not for a return to Greek tragedy or medieval miracle plays. I do not demand that my drama be about great heroes or saints, about spectacular figures, whether heroic or villainous. I am perfectly happy with plays about ordinary people as long as these people don't stink with cuteness, improbable lovableness, disingenuousness, smugness ("How much more wonderful to be little, ordinary, average!")—in short, with dishonesty. Brecht, that great—but by no means, as for certain fanatics, only—master, has given us a whole gallery of little people who do not exude lovableness from every pore. Instead, they exude sweat. Also cupidity, stupidity, cowardice, and at other times, common sense, shrewdness and decency. And sometimes even lovableness. Nor is Brecht the only example. Examples abound in the modern theater: from Ibsen, Chekhov, Pirandello down to Beckett,

Ionesco, Genet, to name only those most familiar—though, apparently, not familiar enough.

Visualize a Peer Gynt, for instance, or a Mother Courage. They go through countless misadventures, comic or shattering, brought about by their obtuseness and greed. They learn nothing, and have no core of goodness. But they plod on, they persist; their scurviness is human. We end up caring for them in spite of them, in spite of ourselves. Such plays reveal us in our nakedness, and, catering to no false contentment, urge us to understand and, if learning to be better is beyond us, at least learn to forgive.

But, of course, the LLM's and LLW's will go on forever. Oscar Wilde has warned us about the rage of Caliban at seeing, as well as at not seeing, his face reflected in the mirror. The solution is to present lies with a little truth in them, or truths with a lot of lie. The LLM answers Broadway's crying need to have things both ways. He is less than life and less than art, but what matter: if you multiply two minuses, don't you get a plus? Quite so. But what happens when you are merely adding up minuses?

NEW, NEWER, NEWEST

(1969)

"Speed kills!" is the drug-traffic signal displayed on many walls with which Kilroy tries to head us away from Methedrine. But an even more dangerous killer is our living speed itself: the speed with which we embrace and drop fashions, tastes, beliefs; the tempo of our race through aesthetic and spiritual environments for the sake of being contemporary, mod, now—with it, ahead of the game, out of sight. But there is just as little sense in outrunning the Joneses as in keeping up with them; in either case, we are living our lives to impress others, instead of to express ourselves.

Most of us would resent being called cultists, yet we are sectarians and victims of the Cult of the New. We want the latest models of cars and clothes, this year's hit songs and school of painting. In automobiles and other technological commodities the new model may indeed introduce significant improvements, though more often than not it is just a new line here, an additional gadget there. The master car, the Rolls-Royce, changes minimally, if at all, from year to year. Clothes, particularly women's, change radically but pointlessly every year. Just when we get used to the miniskirt, we must learn to love the maxi, both of which may coexist while anathemas are hurled at the midi. (Which, of course, will be next year's fashion.) At least these changes are insignificant and seldom irreversible; indeed, reversibility is what they depend on.

But when we come to art—and I don't mean pseudo-art, like pop music—this greed for the new becomes disastrous. Yet it cannot all be blamed on the producers and middlemen; a large part of the guilt is the consumers'. For in the arts, as elsewhere, the obsolescence is built not so much into the product as into the consumer's mind. It is there that, thanks to various overt and covert forms of advertising, the "new" has been implanted as an end in itself. And a very convenient criterion it is for minds that neither know nor care much about the arts; for whereas it is extremely hard to determine what is good and what is bad, anyone can distinguish the new from the old. The Theater of Cruelty succeeds the Theater of the Absurd, and is itself closely followed by the theater of improvisation whose heels are trampled by the theater of mixed mediums, which is jostled by the theater of total participation and theater in the streets, which is tailed by theater in the nude. In art, merely to enumerate all the movements that have cropped up since the still-surviving abstract expressionism would easily use up the rest of this column.

There are three main causes of this unappeasable itch for novelty. First, there is the snob value of the new, the one-upmanship in having already bought, read, seen, heard, smelled (there was a short-lived cinematic gimmick—smellies!) the latest thing. There is even something vaguely endearing about this: next to being creative and innovative, being a pioneer in recognizing and promoting significant innovations is held to be best. But there, alas, is the catch: the innovation has to be significant.

Secondly, there is the misunderstanding of the nature of art. Some people confuse art with technology (this group, by the way, includes a good many so-called artists). Thus the new painting, which uses a shaped canvas, is seen as an improvement; the new sculpture is better because it moves—as if sculptures were supposed to race one another (someday, no doubt, this too will come); the new stage production is better because it uses mixed mediums—you get several genres for the price of one. This derives from equating an art form with a contraption —say, a television set, which may indeed be more useful for incorporating ultra high frequency; it is also the ultimate offshoot of that debased and debasing doctrine, "the medium is the message."

Art is also mistaken for news. In our news-oriented culture

(which at all levels tends to confuse information with gossip), it seems only natural that Clive Barnes should be a more important critic than Walter Kerr because you read Barnes the next morning, Kerr only next Sunday. By the same token, television reviewers are becoming more important yet: you can have them the same night as the dramatic event. Least noteworthy is the serious, speculative critic, whom you might have to wait for as long as a month or more. What good is he, when the movie or play he discusses opened weeks earlier?

The third, most crucial and disturbing, reason for the Cult of the New is boredom. The same boredom that lies behind far more distressing social ills: divorce, suicide, certain types of crime. One is tired of looking at the same kind of paintings, listening to the same kind of music, going to the same sort of shows. This, regrettably, is tantamount to being tired of the same partner in love, tired of the same *modus vivendi* within the law, tired of life itself. It is ultimately a failure of understanding and love—in our case, understanding and love of the arts.

In a recent interview in *Book World*, the novelist Doris Lessing remarked, "I tend to like slow-moving books, books that take their time and contemplate all the way through." Of course, such books also take the reader's time, but the choice is painfully simple: either we create time, or our lack of time destroys us, turning us into automata or addicts, time-servers or good-time chasers. The test of a true work of art is that it does not tarnish: an opera like *Wozzeck* is good for any number of hearings; a painting by Rauschenberg or a sculpture by Oldenburg *should* bore us from the moment after we've looked at it, for it is a façade over a void. If within a short time we get bored with a work of art, either it is not a work of art or we are not art lovers. It is understandable that one of the creators of the most boring pseudo-art, Andy Warhol, should have praised the dullness of Albee's *Tiny Alice* in order to elevate boredom to a positive artistic value.

ONE OF the big problems here is overabundance of money in hands short on culture and taste. This is particularly noticeable in the fine arts, where collectors like Robert and Ethel

Scull have been leaping (to adapt a phrase of Harold Rosenberg's) from vanguard to vanguard, without showing the slightest resistance to any new movement. Such people turn art into a vulgar market place. There, as Hans Magnus Enzensberger has written, "the future of the work of art is sold before it has even occurred. What is steadily being offered for sale is, as in other industries, next year's model. But this future has not only always begun; it is also, when tossed out into the market, always already past. Tomorrow's esthetic product offered for sale today proves, the day after tomorrow, a white elephant, and, no longer sellable, wanders into the archives in the hope of the possibility that, 10 years later, it might still be palmed off as the object of a sentimental revival." This is how camp is born—but that is another story and does not concern us here. (Enzensberger's important essay, from which I quote, is entitled "The Aporias of the Avant-Garde," and is reprinted in *Modern Occasions,* edited by Philip Rahv.)

Observing that "the forcing of creation by promoters of novelty is perhaps the most serious issue in art today," Harold Rosenberg goes on to note: "Novelties in painting and sculpture receive notice in the press as new *facts* long before they have qualified as new *art*. . . . To deny the significance of the new product begins to seem futile, since whatever is much seen and talked about is already on its way to becoming a *fait accompli* of taste. By the mere quantity of interest aroused by its novelty, the painting is nudged into art history."

This is the art-as-news fallacy I spoke of before, at work with a vengeance. It is the dishonesty and suspect friendships of art dealers, the vainglorious inanity or sheeplike conformity of museum directors and curators, and the ignorance, gullibility and moneyed mindlessness of the collectors that bring about ultimate chaos. The buyers are not even able to recognize that most of their novelties are really old hat. As Erich Kahler says in his important but little-known book, *The Disintegration of Form in the Arts,* "Dada, this exuberantly inventive movement, uncommitted, flexible, humorous as it was, using all imaginable means of provocation, anticipated everything that today is carried out by pedantic bores." The same absurd, anachronistic state of affairs is noted in poetry by the British critic A. Alvarez, who comments on "the odd phenomenon of the latest avant garde being largely a rewrite of that of 50 years ago." No one, he says, exaggerating only slightly, is "bothered that Pound looms behind Charles Olson's shoulder and William Carlos Williams towers over Robert Creeley's. The stuff is felt to *be* modern simply because it *looks* modern. The avant garde is acceptable because it is essentially reactionary, harmless."

THE LINE of defense against these abuses should be drawn, at the very least, in reviews and critiques. The public is often just as willing *not* to be duped, but untrustful of itself, looks for critical spokesmen to bolster its conservative impulses. The critics, however, tend to fail it. The most insidious reason for this is what has aptly been named the Hanslick Syndrome. Eduard Hanslick (1852–1904) was a powerful Viennese music critic, able in many respects, but now remembered mostly for his attacks on Wagner, which posterity has proved wrong. The majority of our critics—excepting the obvious lowbrows, and not even all of them—are afflicted with the Hanslick Syndrome. Turn to *The New York Times,* and you will see the wildest fatuities of a Ronald Tavel or Julie Bovasso hailed as delightful contributions to our drama.

In 1934, after a visit with the philosopher Henri Bergson, the great poet and critic Paul Valéry jotted down in his notebook: "He too thinks of sensibility as a kind of resistance. I was surprised." This aperçu is even more needed in 1969. We live in a time when critics are only too eager to jump on any avant-garde bandwagon that pulls up before their front doors. They are so afraid of becoming the laughingstocks of the future that they are perfectly willing to reduce the present to a bad joke. Although most reviews are written on wood pulp, they should be as carefully thought out as if they were committed to paper with 100 percent rag content. This will not ensure the critic's rise from rags to riches, but at least the mind he'll save may be his own.

To be sure, this critical "resistance" must not be overdone. It would be just as deleterious to reject all new art out of hand as it would be to throw the old overboard as if it were so much ballast. Back in 1918, one of the idols of today's American youth, Hermann Hesse, pointed out the absurdity of the categorical rejection of either the old or the new. The critic who nowadays wants to be fair to both, Hesse observed, has "a bitterly hard time of it. But why shouldn't critics have a hard time? That's what they are there for." What precepts can one give critics, even assuming that they wanted them? The basic critical method—perhaps the only one—is still, as T. S. Eliot put it, "to be very intelligent." But what about the public? Are there any practical hints for the audience?

Here again, the solution is to think more about art, or not to think about it at all. If one's interests do not truly lie in the arts, there is no point in force-feeding oneself or allowing others to do it to one. But if this is the case, one should abstain from pontificating, vociferating, and trying to dictate tastes. Instead one should content oneself with the old, much-maligned formula of "knowing what one likes," in whose name much less damage has been done than in that of liking what one thinks one *ought* to like. But if one is going to get seriously involved with the arts, even as an appreciator, one simply has to drink more deeply from the Pierian spring, and this inevitably means reading up on the arts, not just consuming them. Nothing is more meaningless than the ever-increasing figures of concert, theater and museum attendance that the foundations are so fond of recording and crowing about. Exposure alone guarantees nothing; it is apt to be just another form of rubbing against, gaping at and reaching out for the new, without absorbing anything.

Probably the most useful thing the layman can do is to find two or three very different critics or writers on the art he is interested in, and, like any jury, decide on the basis of hearing out at least two sides of the argument. The only difficulty here is in finding a decent conservative critic of the art in question. Things have changed in a most remarkable way. The wholesale obsession with the new in the arts—as well as a generally much greater, though often merely neurotic, concern with the arts—

has as its consequence that far-out, avant-garde movements are no longer consigned (as until now, often unjustly, they were) to the lunatic fringes of art; rather, they have become the dead center, the very Establishment. When Thomas Hoving exhibits a huge monstrosity by Rosenquist in the Metropolitan Museum (where even genuine still-living artists have not been accorded such testimonials); when paintings by true masters such as Poussin and David are dragooned from their usual place to spotlight and lend prestige to Rosenquist's mural, a piece of ill-painted poster art, as the most casual inspection of the sloppy application of pigment revealed; when Robert Scull, the owner of the picture, is, again unprecedentedly, invited to fill up the pages of the Met's Bulletin with uncritical praise of the modern masterpiece he owns—a radical change is upon us.

As recently as half a century ago, as large and important a group as the Surrealists still passed for artistic buccaneers and outlaws; now, however, any miniature movement—say, the light-show makers or the minimalists—is exhibited, sold, written about and extolled wherever you turn. The periphery and dark corners—where one is barely noticed, exhibited, subsidized, published or heard from—are reserved today for the conservatives: artists, critics and scholars. I am not arguing that the conservatives in art are better than the radicals. But I am saying that until they too are heard from, the serious danger exists that our arts will become ever more frantic, psychotic, solipsistic and, above all, divorced from any relevance to humanity.

SHOULD SHUBERT ALLEY BE
RENAMED MEMORY LANE?

(1971)

Nostalgia is something that settles, like verdigris, on any public monument, however awful, after it has been standing around for a sufficient length of time. As green as the green pastures of our youth, its greening process is felt especially in the theater, which in the youth of most of us was one of the chief purveyors of illusion, and unlike the movies, does not get desentimentalized on late-night television. Everything past in the theater is fair game for waxing nostalgic about, from old shows to old drama critics.

Only recently (April 11, 1971), Walter Kerr published an encomium of *No, No, Nanette* and the old-time musicals in *The New York Times Magazine.* He voiced his hope for more revivals of the kind of twenties and thirties musical that "just wants to be happy and to make you happy, too, and . . . doesn't give a hang how it swings it." But Kerr himself is the object of some people's nostalgia. In his 1969 book, *The Season,* William Goldman published a lengthy tribute-lament to Kerr, who had switched from daily to weekly reviewing. It began: "Walter Kerr's loss was the theater's loss too. Kerr was the best. He wrote funny and he wrote smart, and he got better as he went along." Mr. Goldman's writing here, as usual, is too good and too ungrammatical for mere prose. It should have been a lyric: "He wrote funny/ And he wrote smart,/ Made you feel sunny/ Or clutch your heart.// And he got better/ As he went along./ Now he's turned quitter/ And done us wrong." Set to music, this may prove the showstopper of a future nostalgia-musical about the good old days of show business and play-reviewing.

The term "nostalgia" comes from two Greek words: *nostos,* a return home, and *algos,* pain. From these derives the New Latin word *nostalgia,* which, like the German *Heimweh,* means a painful yearning to return home from far away. The very etymology indicates that it is not a good thing: a pain, a sickness, whose cure may not exist. As Thomas Wolfe knew: You Can't Go Home Again.

Why can't you? Because the nostalgia involved here is not that of a traveler abroad who can return to his country any day, but that of the aging man who can't return to his youth. To the middle-aged, youth is where they were always happy; whatever might have besmirched those lambent days is conveniently swept under the carpet of oblivion. "One is always at home in one's past," writes Vladimir Nabokov concerning some ancient Swiss governesses' mooning about prerevolutionary Russia, "which partly explains those pathetic ladies' posthumous love for a remote and . . . rather appalling country, which they never had really known and in which none of them had been very content."

Memory is treacherous. Kerr saw *No, No, Nanette,* he tells us, when he was ten, and it was his first show; he was taken to it by two maiden aunts who, I dare say, thrilled to it. For the ten-year-old lacking any standards, whose first visit to that wonderfully grown-up thing called the theater this show was, the experience, even without the mediation of maiden aunts, must have been overwhelming. Now, if in middle life, we encounter our first love, what do we do? We look past the dumpy matron or overcosmeticized career woman before us and see the swan we once knew—the swan that was no swan at all but an ordinary duckling.

There is nothing wrong with our idealizing our past, erecting a mnemonic temple to our youth. Man lives by pipe dreams, as O'Neill so powerfully reminded us, deriving his lesson from Ibsen's *The Wild Duck,* which teaches us that the destroyer of illusions may also destroy life. But there is a vast difference between nursing the pleasurable pain of nostalgia in private, and turning it into something public; between savoring the sweet drug of "How lovely it was then!" within our own addicted bosoms, and hypostatizing a universal artistic principle from our personal, inartistic needs.

No, No, Nanette is trivial, banal, mendacious and stupid beyond the rights of any show, however escapist, to be in this day and age. The main plot, if there is one, concerns a young girl's almost losing her stuffy fiancé (whom it would be a blessing to lose) over a trip to Atlantic City with a bunch of other girls and boys. One subplot concerns a Bible publisher's almost losing his wife over three girls he keeps in different cities, and with whom, it emerges, he has entirely platonic relations. Another subplot deals with the near-collapse of the publisher's lawyer's marriage, when the rather rakish lawyer pretends that these non-doxies of his employer's are really his. The entire show is concerned with dalliances that really aren't, yet cause rifts in relationships that, but for a *deus ex machina* (or three), would upset a whole convoy of marital apple carts.

What is Kerr's special pleading for this colossal foolishness? (He himself speaks of the audience's "conniving with . . . idiocy gleefully.") These musicals, he argues, were not made to make sense. They were meant to accommodate delicious production numbers, songs and clowning. In that case, why not have musical revues, variety shows and circuses, which do not make any pretense of plot? The lies we get from today's musicals, like *Company* or *Follies,* are, to be sure, almost as gross as those of *No, No, Nanette,* but at least they are today's lies and illusions. They are not saddled, for example, with yesteryear's moral censorship, and can at least make gestures in the direction of truth.

But what about the songs, production numbers and clowns of a show like *Nanette,* on which the defense rests its case. Take the most famous song, "Tea for Two." Melodically it is almost as simple-minded as the sound of train wheels nocturnal travelers cannot get out of their insomniac brains: one does not come out humming "Tea for Two"—one runs out pursued, bugged, hummed by it. As for the lyrics, Frank

Fay had a very funny monologue questioning what on earth they mean, and Brendan Gill has since put something similar into print in *The New Yorker*. That the lyrics truly don't mean anything has recently been admitted by their author, Irving Caesar. Or take the second-best-known song, "I Want to Be Happy." It is so platitudinous, sappy and schematic that its lyrics seem to be some sort of found object—say, a grade-school paper that accidentally rhymes, and onto which someone slapped a tune.

Quoting a Larry Hart lyric of the period, Kerr writes, "You don't believe in love songs that behave like that, you just relish the trickery and accept it as mockery . . ." Well, in those Caesar lyrics there is hardly even trickery. But suppose there were pots of it: why should we consider trickery a positive value? And even if we concede trickery to Kerr's example (the rhyme Crusoe-trousseau), why is trickery tantamount to mockery? Trickery is mere cleverness; mockery implies a standard from which something considered inferior to it is derided. It is a long, long way from sleight-of-word to satire.

And production numbers? The grandest one in *Nanette* is called "Peach on the Beach" and has a handful of girls treading large beach balls more or less in unison. Any provincial circus elephant can do it better, but if our own four-year-old can recite a poem badly, that's not butchery, that's wonderful. And that, folks, is nostalgia. It is our own youth, our own childhood, stammering, stumbling, puling up there on the stage, and because it is ours, it is marvelous. "Just as there are wise and foolish virgins—that is the rumor, anyway —can't there be wise and foolish musicals?" asks Kerr in his summation. I can see him subtly smiling as he writes this fine, allusive sentence, and adds the parenthetical remark as a fence in the middle for himself to sit on in case defending the indefensible should become too tiring.

There are, in fact, neither wise nor foolish virgins any more, except perhaps in kindergarten. As for musicals, there may be more and less foolish ones, but it is not, I think, up to the distinguished critic of an important publication to defend the right of the foolish musical to proliferate. There will always be trash, and there will always be people to promote, consume and devise jesuitical sophistries in its behalf. But they should not be serious critics. The Kerr doctrine is a dangerous one: should there also be wise and foolish statesmen, doctors and teachers? And wise and foolish critics? Or is it just that theater does not really matter, and may as well be the receptacle for any kind of silliness?

But I have not yet covered the clowning in *Nanette*. The principal clown is Patsy Kelly, the comic chambermaid who does not go but shuffles about her work, and is continually at war with vacuum cleaners, doorbells and telephones. Is this still funny? Rather less funny nowadays than that there actually were once live, live-in maids in middle-class households. One of the principal people involved in bringing us this revival (I won't name him and cause him future job trouble) ran into me just before the opening and wondered what I'd think of it. "It went over big in previews with the kind of people who hang $100 laminated Coca-Cola signs on their den walls." Comedy—except for the greatest—dates much more quickly than any other genre. We seem to cry at much the same things as we always did—our mortality, say, and the transience of all good things—but we laugh at new, or new-seeming, jokes more than at old ones. Laughter depends on surprise.

What, then, accounts for the success of *No, No, Nanette?* The nostalgia, the homesickness we project on it. And another sickness: camp. In case you have forgotten, camp is the patent, flagrant stressing of the unreality of something: the outrageousness, absurdity, monumental impracticality or anti-life quality of the thing. It tends to appeal especially to the more ostentatious deviates, to whom defiant unreality seems much less threatening and excluding than what, rightly or wrongly, they consider the hostile heterosexual world.

But camp is less important than nostalgia, which can put across—or, more precisely, *over* on us—such things as *Nanette*, or *The Two and Only* (Bob and Ray in an interminable evening of long-terminated jokes), or *Love Story* (today's college kids represented, lyingly but comfortingly, as those of the fifties, when an occasional four-letter word and a little premarital puppy-sex was the worst a doting parent had to fear), or *Follies,* which makes people feel that the good old Ziegfeld Girls, the good old songs and routines, and the good old routine of marriage will somehow totter on forever.

When I first chastised *No, No, Nanette* and the mentality that engenders and supports such revivals in my review of February 15, the editor and I got more hate letters (along with some others full of gratitude) than for any other critical attack I've ever launched. The missives ranged from one-word, anonymous obscenities to elaborate but usually no less hysterical anathemas, impugning everything from my virility to my religion. A woman from Philadelphia's posh Rittenhouse Square wrote, in effect, "Immigrant go home!" A thirteen-year-old from New Jersey, prompted perhaps by a stern paternal voice, called me a faggot. I cite this merely as instructive, though not necessarily conclusive, evidence of the defensive fury with which people try to perpetuate their misconceptions.

For it is legitimate and necessary to understand and accept one's past, and it is also comprehensible that in a swiftly shifting and unusually harsh world one might wish to avoid reality. But the past must be embraced as it really was, not misconceived as footling capers and witless horseplay to be pedestalized behind a proscenium. You may even idealize the memory of your youth, but you should not enshrine a crass oversimplification of it. And you may want to retreat into such misconceptions for the good reason of dreading the present with its political crises and personal promise of old age, sickness and death. Yet to regress into an infantile myth is merely to be dying backward instead of forward, with your bib instead of your boots on. There is a tragic laughter to be extracted from the present that is a bright encouragement to ourselves and others, and is far better than giggling your way back into the womb.

The overarching defense for the Nanettes of this world (though truly, they are neither of this nor of any world) is "light entertainment." As if all great comedy, even the most eternally, universally relevant, were not also light entertainment. But it is light entertainment transcending itself into truth and art, and requiring a modicum of awareness, culture and thought. Can you imagine an advertising slogan like "Nanette gives you less for your money!" or "Nanette's lie-content is a guaranteed 100 percent!"? But business is a serious business; whereas theater is merely show business or monkey business or, at most, box-office business. As for art—what's that?

"WHAT CAN I DO
IN THE WATER?"

(1966)

FEELING, as E. E. Cummings said, is first. And feeling leads to thought about feelings, and this expresses itself in action, of which artistic creation is one form, which in turn elicits feeling, and the circle recommences. There have been ages in which feeling was suspect, and they produced a classicizing, rationalistic art. There have been ages when reason was in bad odor and they instigated a romanticizing, antirational art. Alas, we have come to an age in which both reason and feelings are suspect—or simply lacking—and that gives rise to anarchy, anti-art, non-art. Or if you prefer, Events, Activities, Happenings.

By their names you shall know them. Who wants theater —a word that comes from *theasthai*, "to view," "to see"? He who would see, respond in every way to what he sees, and acquire insights and opinions—who wants to feel and think. But who needs Events, Activities, Happenings? He in whose life nothing is, or seems to be, happening; who must contrive artificial events, synthetic activity to fill up the void. Theater, which is an art, i.e., a "joining together," attempts to create schemata, views of life; Happenings, which are a jumbling together, are an attempt to create a substitute for life, a rival life (or non-life), which is either the evasion or the total misunderstanding of art. It is worse than barking up the wrong tree; it is trying to bark a nonexistent tree into being. Richard Schechner quite ingenuously diagnoses the New

Theater. One gets rid, as he says, of plot "which Aristotle . . . calls the 'soul' of drama"; one minimizes the text, which is "the heart of traditional theater"; "the performer is treated inanimately . . . as material"; the whole thing is called, in Michael Kirby's phrase, "nonmatrixed," i.e., emerging from no womb. Quite so: total dehumanization. The supposed analogy with such arts as painting and music is, at the very least, specious: colors, shapes and sounds are not inextricably part of the human being, and can (not necessarily to best advantage) be treated as independent from recognizably human situations. But a theater that uses human bodies, words and actions cannot ignore, transmute or travesty them without becoming something else—without ceasing to be theater.

What is behind the New Theater? Fear, hatred or stupid absence of such feeling and thought as are embodied in the old theater, which, from Aeschylus to *Everyman* from Shakespeare to *Godot,* has been able to express and even foreknow changing perceptions, aspirations and sensibilities without having to deny and destroy its essence. The exponents of the New Theater are, at best, painters, dancers, musicians *manqués,* who may suspect deep down that making large, limp, plastic telephones and other soft machines, or turning thirteen television sets on and off, does not a sculpture or a composition make. At worst, they are people incapable of genuine differentiation and evaluation of experiences, and who therefore manufacture an experience-surrogate on which, as Mr. Schechner proudly affirms, no comment is necessary or possible. At best, ineptitude in an existing art; at worst, moral abulia, intellectual aphasia and an emotional St. Vitus' dance.

But it is not only a question of trying to combat emptiness in the easiest (and least rewarding) way possible. It is also, and above all, a way of shirking responsibility. It is clear from Mr. Schechner's article—as from Happenings themselves—that the twin Muses of this New Theater are Chance and the Machine. That one follows a rudimentary "scenario" and will "let what happens happen" is the wooing of Chance; that many Happenings are "programmed in much the same way as one would feed alternatives to a computer" is the reliance on the

Machine. Now, the Machine and Chance might strike us as mutually contradictory Muses—and so they are, which is why, conjointly, they can produce such beautiful chaos. Clearly, Chance and the Machine can be absorbed and subsumed by art; no less clearly, they have their greater uses at the gambling table or in the laboratory and factory; but they cannot be the begetters of theater—not until a royal flush or a smashed atom constitutes a work of art.

But such a concept of art does avoid responsibility while bringing prestige. As Mr. Schechner tells us, it "resists . . . analysis," is free of "traditional obligations" and basks in a lack of "human intentionality." When things happen chiefly by free association, accident or mechanism, obviously no one can be held responsible for the anything or nothing that results. If, moreover, the Event is perishable by definition, and cannot be fully recorded or repeated, it is exempt from the tests of critical interpretation and endurance in time to come. If, furthermore, as Mr. Schechner and Company would have it, "one cannot ask 'Why do that?' but only, 'How well have you done what you set out to do?' " we are back with that ancient and dishonorable piece of sophistry that has always been invoked to justify hack writing as *intending* only to amuse, pass the time, etc., and having to succeed only at that—by which standard *Tobacco Road* is the equal, indeed the superior, of *King Lear*, as to most Happeningists it undoubtedly is.

Happenings, I suspect, are less a branch of theater than an attempt to induce hallucination, and as such should be discussed under the heading of Drugs rather than Drama. (There is, however, a vast difference between the artist who uses drugs to induce artistic creation and the fellow who uses what he thinks to be art to induce hallucinations.) Mr. Schechner tries to gild Happenings by association. When he finds their "audience in those who support the Freedom, Peace, and Student movements," he is merely reminding us that the young, with their mixture of energy, enthusiasm, inexperience and injudiciousness have as often taken up a good cause as been taken in by a bad one. Opposition to the New Theater, however, comes, we are told, "from humanists who feel offended."

The implication is: from outraged old fogies. This is laboring under the delusion that humanism has outlived itself, when in fact the only trouble with it is that it has not yet caught on.

I am not saying that all this bluster and bustle cannot cough up an occasional device the real theater can use. I am not even excluding the disastrous possibility that this New Theater may conquer the old. Only that would be something like the conquest of Rome by the Goths; what would survive to inspire and enliven the future would be the civilization of the conquered Romans, not that of the conquering Goths, Huns and Vandals. For even at its worst—well, second-worst—the old theater addresses itself to questions like "What is good, happiness, life?" and not, like a typical Happening, to "What can I do in the water?" But there is more splash and, ultimately, money in putting on Happenings than in teaching water polo. It is also easier.

Personally I was most enlightened by Mr. Schechner's conclusion that the New Theater "directly explores the inanimate human being." This should make it of great interest to any audience consisting of inanimate human beings; and since "the place of the performance is whatever it happens to be: a loft, Grand Central Station, a health club pool," I would suggest as especially apposite the inside of a mass grave. The vague surface animation that the outside participants would bring to the proceedings would not—in the certifiable absence of heart, soul and intentionality—differentiate them enough from the inmates to cause them any serious discomfiture.

HOW MANY OSTRICHES
CAN DANCE ON A PINHEAD?

(1974)

Robert Wilson's *The Life and Times of Joseph Stalin* takes twelve hours to perform, from 7 P.M. to 7 A.M. It ran for four nights only at the Brooklyn Academy of Music, but Wilson is considered such a unique prodigy that no money or effort was spared even for such a noncommercial venture. There have been similarly extravagant Wilson premières from Paris to Persepolis, sponsored by no lesser potentates than Pierre Cardin and the Shah of Iran. These are always Happenings, in which diverse, tenuously connected events litter the stage and surrounding area; *Stalin* is made up of seven unconnected acts, yet so loath is Wilson to let go of his audience that scenes are offered in front of the curtain during the intermissions. The show cost some $200,000, largely foundation money, and it costs the viewer twelve hours of his short waking life—though some people, like the *Time* drama critic, sensibly converted several of these into sleeping hours. Or perhaps not so sensibly, because they would have slept better in bed.

The work has been described as an opera, although there is no singing, and the musical background, when there is one, is apt to be either diluted neoromantic claptrap or the same two scratchily recorded bars of music repeated to near-infinitum. It has also been called a play, although it contains only a few, often reiterated verbal fragments here and there—a further de-naturation of the already very watery Gertrude Stein—and long, droning readings of Marxist texts to which amateurish dancers unfocusedly sashay about. It has been called pantomime, too, although mime distills scattered human busy-ness, whereas Wilson's stage animals (some of them real) and people (none of them real) mosey around in a somnolent phantasmagoria with no discernible relation to reality.

Still others have dubbed this choreography, although ballet, at its most rarefied, remains an orderly translation of music into visual terms (without in any way diminishing the music), and modern dance, at its most tellurian, is still a celebration of the human body's mobility and nobility. In *Stalin*, movement consists of phenomena like a bathing-suited jogger trotting to and fro across the stage at irregular intervals (a marathon running gag); a bunch of women in a Victorian dormitory jumping in and out of bed as an incoherently muttering Father Time inches his way forward and backward; people in animal suits lolling about in a barred-off cave while, outside, gamboling seminudes are superseded by Goyaesque figures in a stately processional (something about lost animal innocence here); a pair of legs doing a fake high-wire act just beneath the proscenium arch; a man periodically coming through the audience with a long pole, to set large metal rings on a wire strung over the spectators' heads jangling and humming (a marathon humming gag); a huge but effete black man parading onstage from time to time in ever more outrageous get-ups, and with genitals ever more outrageously thrust out; and so on and on and on. What dance there is is repetitious, aimless, barely coordinated slithering or circling about, mostly watered-down Merce Cunningham, of which even the original is deliquescent and amorphous enough.

The most plausible defense of Wilson's work is based on its pictorialness, the creation of "a flowing gallery of pictures," in Stanley Kauffmann's words, "with theatrical means." Yet there is, for me, a basic fallacy in this argument: a modern painting (classical painting is hardly relevant here) works because of its immutability and equilibrium, through which it reorganizes or reinterprets form and space, evoking an alternative world that clarifies or criticizes this one. By constantly reshuffling images, you get not a work of art but a deck of cards. Painting utilizes permanence: its power is in capturing something, not in dissipating it. As for using the stage for purely painterly purposes, it means depriving theater of two of its essential modes of making a lasting impact: words and meaningful actions. And subtracting from a medium, diminishing it, is as mindless and arrogant as expecting an audience to stare for twelve hours into a giant kaleidoscope.

Many have tried to justify Wilson's work on the basis of its resemblance to dreams. Well, dreams have been exploited in works of art since time immemorial: from the Bible, which is full of them, to *Finnegans Wake*, which is all a dream. But a dream is made artistically relevant when its individuality is rendered universal: as, for example, when Joyce's dream subsumes history and myth; or when René Magritte's paradoxically interpenetrating indoors and outdoors, day and night, foot and shoe, become objectifications of the eternal yearning to have things both ways. But when Wilson gives us, in slower-than-slow motion, a black woman murdering her children, before and after which she mopes around for hours with a stuffed crow attached to her wrist, the meaning is purely private—an incident from the life of a dumb boy that struck Wilson, a former stutterer who worked with dumb children, and who still seems to be gesturing in public for an audience he takes to be made up of dumb children. There is no resonance here, still less integration of details into a meaningful whole.

Wilson's opus has been compared also—approvingly—to drug fantasies, and twelve hours of it, I dare say, constitutes drug addiction. Yet the drug experience is not art. Countless artists have used drugs to stimulate their creativity; nonetheless the finished works, carefully articulated, always strive to enhance and sharpen their audience's perceptions and understanding. Wilson, in trying to hypnotize his spectators with the sheer length and soporific pace of his spectacle, wants to blur, blunt, break down our faculties. He is as much an artist as is Timothy Leary.

Most curiously, some have called Wilson a genius; so, for instance, Martin Gottfried, the *Women's Wear Daily* critic, who went on to define the quality of genius as "creating something unlike anything created before." This is a poor definition:

Bartók, Stravinsky and Webern, let's say, are not simply unlike
Strauss, Debussy and Mahler, any more than Balanchine and
Cranko are simply unlike Petipa and Ivanov. Genius is the wedding of the traditional and the new—arduous, as many marriages are—into an individual vision that is as like as it is unlike
what has been. For something truly unique, you must go outside art—say, to Hitler's extermination camps or to America's
nonimpeachment of Nixon.

Except for his elephantine elaboration and misuse of his
mediums, Wilson is, in fact, all too like some of his predeces-
sors. His visions, if such they be, were anticipated in poetry by
Rimbaud and Lautréamont and their followers; in visual art,
by certain primitives, and by the Dadaists and Surrealists; in
the theater, by Alfred Jarry and his successors, from Apollinaire to Artaud. Wilson is anywhere from fifty to a hundred
years too late. Frequently, though, his borrowings are more
immediate: the mumbling heads sticking out of holes were
managed far more purposefully by Beckett; the chorus line of
ostriches pranced about more hilariously in Disney's *Fantasia*.
If what mind Wilson possesses does not strike me as particularly
original, however, this has not prevented it from being, in turn,
an influence on things like his great admirer Jerome Robbins'
dismal ballet *Watermill*, or some of Peter Brook's most recent
pseudotheatrical Happenings.

Wilson's main device is accumulation—repetition in ever larger quantities at ever greater duration. *Stalin*, which has virtually nothing to do with Stalin (whose name Wilson, during one
of his several onstage appearances, manages to mispronounce),
incorporates shorter, revised versions of all of Wilson's previous
works, e.g., *The Life and Times of Sigmund Freud*, which
dragged in Freud quite gratuitously and brazenly; *The King of
Spain*, which did the same for Philip II; and so forth. Quantity
is set not just above quality, but indeed above meaning itself:
if one Negro mammy appears, soon there are 4, 8, 16 and still
more; later, one cavorting ostrich similarly proliferates into 19
—not 16, as a bleary-eyed Clive Barnes reckoned it around six
in the morning. Accretion, agglomeration, reiteration, extension
—the devices that come easiest, and can most readily be re-

duced to triviality and banality—are Wilson's mainstays. In Iran, one of his works spread over a whole week (the way Persian culture has been going lately, the Andersen tale may have to be rewritten as "The Shah's New Clothes"). How long will Wilson's next work, incorporating *Stalin,* stretch our endurance?

Of course, there are people who are fascinated by watching, for example, a man in a huge frog mask sit at a banquet table for two hours, be served food and drink by a lackey, and mumble "Thank you!" once—the *Women's Wear Daily* critic laughed blissfully at this. But what is it really? Camp. The sheer, absurd excess of Warhol letting one shot of the Empire State Building turn into an eight-hour movie; of Robert Rauschenberg nailing a stuffed, green goat to an oversize canvas, or hanging a stuffed eagle from it; of this *Stalin* that drags on for twelve hours and drags in some 140 or 150 performers, some of them in drag, and including Wilson's own aged grandmother, who should have been in bed long before. Basically, camp represents the homosexual sensibility defying a heterosexual world by flinging enormous exaggeration into the faces of the smug straights: if they swallow it and proclaim it genius, the joke is on them; if they end up outraged, with mudpies on their mugs, the laugh is still on them.

In small doses, as a spice, camp can be effective—see some of Al Carmines', or the current, cleverly campy *Candide.* But whereas steak *au poivre* is tasty, who would dine on pepper on pepper? In twelve hours of your short life you can see the three late masterpieces of Eugene O'Neill; or the best ballets of Balanchine, Cranko and Robbins; or *The Rake's Progress, Ariadne auf Naxos, Wozzeck* and *Bluebeard's Castle;* or all the best current films, from *The New Land* to *American Graffiti;* or you can even live a little. In twelve hours of Wilson's farrago, you merely age and die a little. It is an artistic and human scandal that falls somewhere between *Watermill* and Watergate. It is for escapees from thought, feeling and confrontations with reality, however transfigured by art—food for Philistines.

Oddly enough, a work of Emile Durkheim that I chanced upon offers what strikes me as a perfect critique of Wilson's "art." In *Moral Education,* the French sociologist writes: "Social man necessarily presupposes a society which he expresses and serves. If this dissolves, if we no longer feel it in existence and action about and above us, whatever is social in us is deprived of all objective foundation. *All that remains is an artificial combination of illusory images, a phantasmagoria vanishing at the least reflection; that is, nothing which can be a goal for our action.* Yet this social man is the essence of civilized man." If you consider the sentence I have italicized, you have a discerning diagnosis of Wilson. Art is, loosely but not flaccidly interpreted, something that points toward a goal for spiritual action. It is a way of making us feel and understand, think and exist; not by foisting restrictive models on us, but by eliciting self-discoveries we can variously apply.

Now, Wilson's *Stalin* tosses out images that are artificially rather than artistically combined, that vanish from the consciousness not only on the least reflection, but also on the slightest passage of time, and that cannot tell us anything we need to know. Even when Wilson comes closest to significant imagery, as in the cave where people become cut off from beasts, slowly but definitively, by bar after thuddingly dropping bar, the image has no resonance. It does not make clear its intent: that the four-footed cave-dwellers are purer or more genuine than the two-footed paraders outside the cave's mouth. In fact, when an honest-to-goodness dog and sheep are thrust among the animal puppets or performers in beasts' clothing, the real animals very quickly and sensibly leave. For Wilson's beasts express little or nothing about animal being, or about being per se: they loaf around, or move about aimlessly, or perform a clumsy little dance fragment. If there is no more than that to being an animal, we might as well remain human.

Wilson's creatures are all pretty much the same, and that is precisely the trouble—the interchangeability of all that goes on onstage. If everything were reversed in time, place or meaning, it would make exactly as much—or as little—sense. Wilson's agglomerations are, despite the elaborate *mise en scène,* an invitation to indiscriminateness, to a kind of passivity that, along with its opposite, hysteria, is the favorite mode of American audience participation. Yet all art consists of actively making choices—not necessarily what we would consider the right ones, but choices susceptible of evaluation. Even such an extreme case as Mallarmé's pursuit of the perfection of the blank page —nothingness conquered by the poem—is a rational choice: the attempt to re-create the self-sufficiency of inanimate, uncaring matter and space within the friendly (because man-made and human) poem. There is no such choice in Wilson, where pure or impure arbitrariness is merely given a grandiosely wasteful orchestration.

I see nothing more in *The Life and Times of Joseph Stalin* than its tune-in-turn-on-and-drop-out value. And for that, marijuana is both easier to come by and less expensive to produce. Pot, moreover, is unpretentious. In using Stalin, Freud and the rest as nominal excuses for his nonsense, Wilson becomes guilty of pretentiousness to the point of indecency. Stalin appears briefly as a photograph in the beginning, is cursorily mentioned a few times, provides the justification for a character labeled Stalin's Wife (though unrecognizable as such without, and even with, the program), becomes the pretext for the protracted background readings from Marxist texts, and finally gives rise to some simulated broadcasts denying the sickness or death of the dictator. All this is sheer rodomontade, invocation of a big name on which to sell one's paltry wares.

The fact that the particular big name is a heinous one does not lessen the distastefulness of its being used for self-indulgent and self-promotional purposes. Auschwitz and Hiroshima are surely as ghastly as Stalin, yet nothing is more unappetizing than their being dragged in as the moral excuse for the excesses of countless underground movies and two-bit theatrical experiments, by way of a facile hortatory climax. Or take that pretentious and untalented painter Robert Motherwell, who had the arrogance to palm off his vacuous daubs as "Elegies for the Spanish Republic," another great historic catastrophe, although they could more appropriately be called "Laments for the State of Painting," testimonials to a different kind of disaster.

The point is that the doodlings and diddlings of a Robert

Wilson, however brontosaurian their dimensions, belong in a much more modest niche of infamy than that reserved for the gigantic tyrant in whose posthumous memory the Solzhenitsyns and Sakharovs, the Rostropoviches and Panovs, as well as countless others of our day, continue to be harassed and victimized.

THEATRICAL
DISORDER OF THE DAY

(1969)

J AN KOTT's previous book, *Shakespeare Our Contemporary*, has become a cult object, and Kott a kind of McLuhan of the theater. The basic ideas of this Polish critic—that Shakespeare was a Beckett *avant la lettre* and that *Lear* is really the *Ur-Endgame*—were espoused by men of the theater like Peter Brook and Peter Hall, and reinterpretations of Shakespeare and the Greek dramatists became the disorder of the day. Kott may have owed some of his success to the fact that his was mistaken for a liberal voice out of Communist Poland—though the fact that he had to read Shakespeare in Polish translations might as easily have given pause as delight. At a recent symposium, Kott announced in apparent seriousness (and manifestly broken English) that he would have the Ghost in *Hamlet* played by a mole, because Hamlet refers to him as "old mole." One would like to think that this was meant as a joke, but when the joke becomes a full-length book, it is no laughing matter.

In the new volume, *Theatre Notebook, 1947–1967*, the rabid innovator and woolly theoretician mostly yields to a Kott of a different color: a theater buff and women's-club lecturer. The book consists of short pieces, some of which may have been reviews or magazine articles, and is divided into halves; the first deals with Polish plays, playwrights and performers; the second has Kott covering theater from Spoleto to Edinburgh, from Tunis to China. As journalism, the book is not half bad, for Kott is much better at describing landscapes and performances than at analyzing plays and productions. He is a born enthusiast; if memory serves (and it is a serviceable memory indeed that can recall much about this book two minutes later), there is only one adverse opinion expressed in these 268 pages. This would not be a drawback if the various encomia and adulations were in any way novel or penetrating. But at this late date we scarcely need to be told that Sophocles and Molière are full of contemporary relevance, or that Kafka's world is that of dream and nightmare.

When he is dealing with Polish subjects, Kott is mildly interesting, but this is due only to our scantier knowledge of these matters. No clear idea of the work of, say, Gombrowicz and Witkiewicz, Rózewicz and Mrozek can be gained from these spotty, lopsided tributes; still, we may be grateful even for haphazard crumbs that mitigate our ignorance. But when he describes Polish performers—or, in fact, any performers—Kott becomes evocative, sometimes even eloquent; such pieces as the one on Gustaw Holoubek are among the best in the book. For Kott is first of all a buff, a literary stage-door Johnny; he gushes about a dressing room and the actress in it, about making a date with her and the "perverse fascination of meeting Lady Macbeth in a café." The rest of Kott is a dreamer-up of absurd theories and a mangler of facts. On the first page of the book we are told that "Ubu's every other word is merde," whereas Ubu never says *merde*, only *merdre*, and this only a few times in the course of the play. Or we are informed that Shakespeare "knew well who murdered Marlowe and why," a secret that Shakespeare evidently passed on only to Kott.

Let us examine the Kottian method at work. "In Racine's *Phèdre* the story is only a pretext. Phèdre examines her conscience in a world that is morally unacceptable; in which love exists, but every love is a sin; in which the need for happiness exists, but happiness is impossible; in which God exists, but God is blind, deaf and vindictive. It is not Phèdre who is tragic, but Racine's world." This looks impressive, even magisterial, to the cursory glance; on closer examination, it crumbles to dust. In every great play the story is only a pretext; every tragic author is concerned with a morally unacceptable, i.e., tragic world—look at *Prometheus Bound,* or *Lear,* or *Life Is a Dream.* Every love in *Phèdre* is not a sin; in the full sense, only the heroine's is. Happiness may be impossible, but then, that is the premise on which all tragedy is based. As for God's vindictiveness, this is Kott's anachronistic fantasy: Venus is not God. And obviously it is not Phèdre who is tragic but Racine's world, for there is no Phèdre outside of Racine's world: she is his creation, his illustration of the world. As usual, Kott has slapped together inaccuracies and platitudes, and coated them with a declamatory grandness.

Kott's style is undistinguished, except when he tries for fancy effects like the repetition of a phrase, at which times it is distinguished by its awfulness. However, it must be admitted that his translator, Boleslaw Taborski, also needs translating into English. We read, for example, of a grenade being thrown *"to* the chief of *the* police." There are even whole sentences that are gibberish, for which it is hard to say who is responsible: "Slowacki combined within the elements of *Macbeth* and *A Midsummer Night's Dream,* a seemingly impossible achievement, he wrote an astonishing tragicomedy that is both fairy tale about the beginnings of Poland and a stinging contemporary satire." Perhaps the most sensible thing is to blame the publisher.

There are in *Theatre Notebook* a few anecdotes, bits of information and aperçus that are not without interest. But they hardly justify a book; still less do they justify the author's international reputation. Yet the reputation is perfectly comprehensible: "I like all impurities," Kott declares at one point. There are few heights in today's arts and letters that cannot be scaled by piling impurities on impurities.

GROTOWSKI'S
GROTESQUERIES

(1970)

THERE IS A NAME in the theater of our time that is more
prestigious than any other. It is perhaps more of an incantation
than a name, and even more than an incantation, a magic formula. It is the words "Jerzy Grotowski," the name of the
founder and director of the Polish Laboratory Theatre of
Wroclaw. I remember when, as judge at the Yale Dramat's
Festival of College Drama (or whatever the thing is called),
I was accosted by a lanky youth from a Midwestern university. He wore dungarees and paratrooper's boots, and spoke
in a manner unburdened by literacy. Where, he wanted to
know, could he read about Jerzy Grotowski? When I mentioned
the *Tulane Drama Review,* he said, somewhat impatiently,
that he had read all that, of course; where could he get more?
I suggested a trip to Poland, and he earnestly replied that, if
he could only afford it, he'd go. I realized then that the theater had acquired its own guru, its *magister ludi,* on a par with
Marcuse and McLuhan, and one who, unlike Strasberg, tran-
scended national boundaries.

Last fall, there appeared in the Sunday *Times* an ad, no
more than a quarter page in size, heralding the coming of
Jerzy Grotowski to the Brooklyn Academy of Music. I am told
that people who sent in checks no later than the following
Monday were informed that their requests could not be met;
those who did get their tickets apparently sent for them that
very Sunday, or even the night before, when the paper hit
the stands. No one but the Mage of Wroclaw could have pro-

duced such an effect. Of course, the number of spectators for
Grotowski's productions is very small: sometimes no greater
than forty; never over a hundred. The opening night was in-
stinct with confusion. Grotowski had found the facilities in
Brooklyn unsuited to his stagings, and at the eleventh hour
shifted his activities to a Greenwich Village church with re-
movable pews. Many people were unaware of the change of
location; moreover, the starting time was announced one way
on the tickets (which, incidentally, looked more like illustra-
tions for some ancient book on magic than tickets, and also
conveniently listed the telephone number of the Laboratory
Theatre in Wroclaw, in case one wished to make inquiries)
and another way in the *Times*. So the chosen few waited ex-
pectantly and long for the stragglers from Brooklyn to arrive. It
was found, however, that the Brooklyn Academy had oversold
tickets, and the excess ticketholders, who were rigorously ex-
cluded, proceeded to bang away vengefully on the church
door, as if they were nailing on it at least ninety-five theses.
These people were later accommodated at additional performances, which, alas, made Grotowski cancel his Los Angeles
engagement, leaving deprived West Coasters without even a
church door on which to take out their frustrations.

The opening bill was Grotowski's adaptation of Juliusz
Slowacki's (the nineteenth-century Polish romantic poet's) adaptation of Calderón's *The Constant Prince*. For it, the audience
is seated on two tiers along three sides of an oblong playing
area: one tier may be six feet above the arena; the other, ten.
Ushers led the long-waiting folk to seats on one of the two
levels of planks, and fitted each arriving behind into a little
space of board by peremptorily directing other behinds to
huddle closer together. Everyone was in his seat, which on
opening night legitimately, and later on the black market, cost
up to a hundred dollars, a trifle high for an enterprise that
calls itself "the Poor Theatre." A few executives of the sponsor-
ing Brooklyn Academy were standing inconspicuously at the
back of the upper tier, but were promptly driven from the
temple at Grotowski's behest. The Master was present, as at all
performances, watching and occasionally making some small

adjustment, such as shifting one of the two spotlights a little. He is a piece of walking chiaroscuro: a pudgy expanse of very pale face punctuated by blackish glasses (for an eye ailment, we are told); below this, a sizable stretch of black suit separated from the equally black tie by a white shirt. This is the *ne varietur* uniform, and suggests a cross between a secular priest and a hieratic IBM executive.

Ellen Stewart, the eponymous director of the LaMama Theatre and a co-sponsor of Grotowski's visit, toured the bleachers and walked around the arena, whether to survey or for display, I cannot tell. The off-Broadway reviewer of *The New Yorker* dropped her notebook into the acting pit with a moderate thud. A dread hush fell on the already cowed audience. Was this the signal for the beginning? Or some act of *lèse majesté* for which the offender would be promptly punished? Finally the play began, and lasted, like all these Grotowski productions, a therapeutic fifty-five-minute hour; Calderón's version must take at least three times as long, but may well seem shorter.

The five men and one woman in the cast cavort, contort, skip, wallow, prance and dance about. They shrill or rattle off words, unintelligibly even for Poles; they sound like human hurdy-gurdies, whining, shrieking, chanting, howling. The only piece of scenery is a slant-topped slab of wood on which a prisoner is stripped, castrated, and admitted to the group; then another prisoner, the Prince, is brought in. All in white, he is stripped to a white loincloth and tortured by the others, who wear absurd black costumes—a mixture of styles and periods including togas, berets, a cardboard crown, an umbrella, a red cloak that at one point becomes a bullfighter's mantle in a mock corrida. The umbrella, like all Grotowskian props, also undergoes metamorphoses, and the whole affair is suggestive of kids discovering a trunk full of old clothes and horsing around in them. The gentle and Christ-like Prince does not give in to his tormentors, who, by their grotesque millings, hoppings and mumblings around him, supposedly convey that they are as impressed and reverent of him as they are envy- and hate-ridden.

The performers split into little groups and bound and gesticulate about in amorphous imitations of modern dance. They strut, leap and yell in various distorted voices. Much of the shouting is done into the plywood walls or, prone, into the floorboards. There is no attempt at maintaining character: just after the Prince has been tortured, he turns into a living wind machine and provides wind sounds by which the others can be buffeted about. The Prince is finally killed, but his spirit (or in this windy context, more accurately perhaps, his breath) conquers his slayers. I cannot give a more detailed account because a) hanging over the railing and sandwiched in between bodies, I was in no position to take notes; and b) I was so dumfounded by the infantilism and coarseness of the proceedings that sheer amazement kept me from even trying.

The next production was *Akropolis,* based on a 1904 play by Stanislaw Wyspianski. In the original, the action takes place at Cracow Cathedral and the Royal Castle, which together form a kind of Polish Acropolis. On the eve of the Day of the Resurrection, figures from the Bible and Greek mythology out of the Cathedral tapestries and Castle statuary come to life; their appearance here makes the place into "the Necropolis of the Tribes." In the end, Christ-Apollo is resurrected and leads a triumphal procession that spells the redemption of both Poland and Europe. Grotowski has transposed the action to another necropolis—the Auschwitz death camp. It is now the inmates who act out various Biblical and mythological scenes by way of a temporary reprieve from the horror of the camp. Finally they all disappear under a scrapheap they themselves have built up on the stage—the crematorium—and a matter-of-fact voice is heard saying: "They are gone, and the smoke rises in spirals."

For this production, the audience was scattered in small handfuls fitted in among the platforms of the irregularly shaped playing area; slightly larger groups were around the fringes of it; the rest were up in the balcony, but on only two of the balcony's three sides—for no other reason, presumably, than so as not to exceed the mystic figure for attendance that Grotowski has prescribed. On the center platform there was a goodly stack of sections of stovepipe; above the platforms, a network of ropes. A beat-up iron bathtub and a battered wheelbarrow could also be discerned. The actors appear in costumes made of sacks with holes in them, the holes lined with material suggesting torn flesh. On the feet, ungainly wooden shoes that make a fearful clatter; on the heads, berets. Between periods of slave labor, the prisoners perform their Biblical and Homeric scenes involving the stories of Laban, Jacob, Esau and Rachel (including Jacob's combat with the Angel), the love of Paris and Helen, and the prophecy of Cassandra. It is all in grotesque distortion: from time to time, a prisoner plays cacophonous versions of popular songs on a creaky violin, and the scenes are acted out in a similarly grotesque, ear-assaulting fashion. The death of Laban is the murder of one prisoner by another; the marriage of Jacob and Rachel is a procession following a prisoner clutching a piece of pipe bedizened with a rag for a wedding veil; the love duet of Helen and Paris is performed by two male prisoners cooing at each other while the rest jeer at them; the combat with the Angel has one prisoner, Jacob, kneeling and holding up with his back the wheelbarrow in which another prisoner, the Angel, lies with his head hanging toward the floor. The Angel bangs the floor with his head and tries unsuccessfully to kick Jacob's head with his boots; Jacob cannot shake the wheelbarrow off his shoulders. We are to understand that they are two prisoners nailed to the same instrument of torture.

A little reflection will show that all this, apart from its obvious ugliness, is nonsense. For if the prisoners were enacting visions that are supposed to fill them with hope and a sense of the transcendent, they would not portray them as ghastly travesties. If, on the other hand, the prisoners are jeering at their cultural and spiritual heritage, their actions become a grim charade so nihilistic that no one would bother enacting it in the shadow of death. Grotowski has confused—inadvertently or deliberately—the horrible experiences of prisoners with their hopeful fantasies; the result is not harrowing enough to convey the death-camp experience, and sheds no new light on it; even less is it able to express the persistence of human dignity and imagination, for which task it lacks poetry. But, someone is sure to say, why this insistence on historic or psychological *verismo,* or even verbal poetry? Why shouldn't Grotowski amalgamate the agonies and aspirations of the inmates into an image that subsumes both? Has not Grotowski written of an "element in our productions variously called 'collision with the roots,' 'the dialectics of mockery and apotheosis,' or even 'religion expressed through blasphemy; love speaking out through hate' "? The answer to this is, as always when facile symbol-mongering is at work, that you have to make your scenic event credible on some basic level before you can expect it to function on a higher plane; neglecting the base of the pyramid for the sake of the apex is bound to produce castles in the air. For me, *Akropolis* produced only one effect—of studied repulsiveness, which made the incineration of these creatures come none too soon.

I reproduce some notes scribbled on my program during the performance. "Prisoner bangs floor five times with head. Hissing sounds from cast. A prisoner bangs various pipes with a stick and declaims through them. Cast brays. Soft singsong by woman prisoner at one end of acting area; antiphonal choir from others at far end. Love talk of two men, regularly interrupted by gales of sneering laughter. Two men recite in low, croaking voices; woman interrupts with little pigeon cooings. Woman does weird push-ups, dances around, tears at clothes, is bent double from time to time and ululates pathetically. [The Cassandra scene.] They stand, back to back, in a double file of three, one man on their shoulders, chanting and gesticulating. This turns into a howl. They enact what looks like the turning on of the gas: they face in different directions, some sitting, some bending over and clutching their outfits at the neck; all are shrieking or praying or keening. They stumble up the platform in a wavering line, lift a dummy off the ropes, stagger around with arms uplifted, chanting and howling. This is interrupted by one of them doing a coy little *sotto voce* recitation. General screaming. All disappear through trap door, whence more chanting and a few words."

This, I submit, is how it strikes a viewer if he doesn't speak Polish (as most of Grotowski's admirers don't), but Poles I know have assured me that they too find it hard, if not impossible, to make out the words. When the prisoners go about nailing down pieces of pipe to the floor, or hanging up other pieces from the ropes above, or when they suspend themselves or one another from these ropes, brutality does come through clearly enough—a brutality, however, that I never found moving. As Robert Brustein sees it, "Grotowski operates on the anti-pleasure principle. His work is profoundly sadomasochistic, in the manner of the imitation of the Passion of Christ—flagellating and painful both for actors and audiences."

In the third bill, *Apocalypsis cum Figuris,* the two spotlights are side by side on the floor, the stage is the entire floor space of the church, the actors are dressed in bizarre, mostly white, parodistic outfits, and their shadows are projected all over he walls. The audience of forty sit along two walls on narrow benches. The piece is a retelling of the Christ story, with the Christ figure enacted by the Simpleton (shades of Kazantzakis), and the other actors assuming the roles of Peter, Judas, John (author of the *Apocalypse*), Mary Magdalene and Lazarus. Grotowski and his actors—again the five men and the one woman—first rehearsed the action without words or with improvised ones. When the action was set, words were found to match the various parts of it—from the Bible and *The Brothers Karamazov,* from T. S. Eliot and Simone Weil—"sources which could be regarded," as the program puts it, "as the work not of one writer but of the whole of mankind." I think the whole of mankind would arrive at these texts about as soon as a thousand monkeys would type out *Hamlet,* but let that pass.

"The cast," as I wrote in *New York* magazine, "go about their standard business of beating, raping and crucifying one another." There are homosexual as well as heterosexual rapes, there is our old friend castration once again, and here is a great deal of that cruel, infernal laughter these productions abound in. There is, further, the administering of a footbath acted out in veristic detail (perhaps so that the water can be bottled and sold to the faithful), there is a delightful scene in which the entire cast takes turns vampirizing a wound in the Simpleton's side and falling over backward like replete leeches. There is much copulating with a loaf of bread, and there is one bit where an actor transfers some snot from his nose into that of another's. Bits of liturgy are chanted, and the final sequences are acted out by the light of candles, which the last departing actor snuffs out.

Let me quote from the program the text of one of the ensemble scenes. "These invocations from the Song of Solomon follow straight after the love-making scene between the Simpleton and Mary Magdalene. Now Judas and Lazarus take up the roles of bride and groom. *Judas:* How fair is thy love, my sister, my spouse, thy necks is as doves [*sic*]. *Lazarus:* How fair is my love. *Judas:* Make haste, my beloved, and be thou like to a roe or to a young hart on the mountains of spices." What, we may well ask, is that supposed to mean? To be sure, I rather like "thy necks is as doves," in which I recognize the voice of the whole of mankind, but other than that? Why should Christ and the Magdalene be making love? Why should Judas and Lazarus then ape that love-making? And why, above all, should Judas and Lazarus make love to the text of the Song of Songs? For shock value, I suppose, but whom, besides a few pious Polish Catholics, who most likely stay away from the Laboratory Theatre, can this be expected to shock? Grotowski's answer would presumably have it that this is to be:

> *confrontation* with myth rather than identification . . . while retaining our private experiences, we can attempt to incarnate myth, putting on its ill-fitting skin to perceive the relativity of our problems, their connection to the "roots," and the relativity of the "roots" in the light of today's experience. If the situation is brutal, if we strip ourselves and touch an extraordinarily intimate layer, exposing it, the life-mask cracks and falls away.*

This is the typically hieratic, arcane, incense-clouded and humorless diction of Grotowski. First we are supposed to

---

* Jerzy Grotowski, *Towards a Poor Theatre* (Simon and Schuster, 1970). All quotations from Grotowski, when not otherwise indicated, are from this book.

clothe ourselves in the ill-fitting skin of myth, then strip to
an extraordinarily intimate layer—some kind of metaphysical
quick-change act—but presently things get hairier yet:

> Even with the loss of a "common sky" of belief and the loss
> of impregnable boundaries, the perceptivity of the human
> organism remains. Only myth—incarnate in the fact of the
> actor, in his living organism—can function as a taboo. The
> violation of the living organism, the exposure carried to out-
> rageous excess, return us to a concrete mythical situation, an
> experience of common human truth.

Why must theater be mythical? I wonder. What is a "concrete
mythical situation"? Are there abstract ones? And are we to
understand that "common human truth" can be experienced
only in terms of violations of taboos? And must the "viola-
tion of the living organism" be "exposure carried to outrageous
excess"? Well, outrageous excess Grotowski's theater certainly
does provide, but even this outrage, as we shall see, is ambiguous in effect and limited in efficacy.

Let me quote again from my earlier account: "Before
Apocalypsis [the spectators] are loudly commanded to read
the program carefully; as they enter, they must divest themselves of everything they carry, including these programs,
which they are permitted to pick up as they leave. At that
time they are also handed a kind of icon, a woodcut emble-
matic of the play, along with a lengthy statement from the
Master explaining with hierophantic modesty and in absurd
detail how these productions are group efforts in the truest
sense. Sold also are expensive, mystagogic and totally un-
readable books in which the Master sets forth his teachings.
And the program notes, by Grotowski and his literary adviser,
Ludwik Flaszen, consist of the most portentous lucubrations
this side of scientology." Next to a needle's eye, the door to
Apocalypsis was the hardest thing for us ordinary camels to
pass through.

But few critics are ordinary camels. "At present the theater's
only hope of life-giving heresy seems to rest in the hands of
Jerzy Grotowski," begins Richard Gilman's tribute to him

in *New American Review* 9. Thanks to Grotowski, Gilman
continues, the theater "has felt itself in the presence of something very like a redemption." In the *New Republic*, Stanley
Kauffmann wrote enthusiastically: "These three plays—together, more than as separate entities—were a major theatrical
experience in my life . . ." But at least that "together, not as
separate entities" strikes me as right, for the Grotowskian
theater cannot present plays—it presents only Grotowski. Everything is reduced to a common Grotowskian denominator.
Significantly, in a decade Grotowski has come up with only
nine productions; each one of them will be rehearsed some
four hundred times before it is ready for viewing, and Grotowski sits there watching every performance of each production—
which would be enough to drive mad anyone not mad already.
If we read in *Towards a Poor Theatre* what Grotowski has
done with *Doctor Faustus*, a play about which we know and
care more than a Grotowskified Slowackization of Calderón
or some wispy piece of symbolism of Wyspianski's, we see
that the result has little bearing on Marlowe's play and is the
very sort of outrage Jan Kott will perform on Shakespeare.

I cannot seriously be expected to argue logically against
the type of thing one finds on any page of *Towards a Poor
Theatre*. We read, for instance, about "resonators." The average actor, we are told, knows only about the head resonator,
i.e., using the head to amplify the voice. But an actor who
makes a study of it discovers that "he can exploit not only his
head and chest, but also the back of his head (occiput), his
nose, his teeth, his larynx, his belly, his spine, as well as a
total resonator which actually comprises the whole body and
many others, some of which are still unknown to us." I fail
to see to what use, beyond encouraging speculation about
what the urethral resonator might sound like, this kind of
thing can be put. Nor do I see what can be done with this
description of acting in terms of "ideograms": "the analysis
of a hand's reflex during a psychic process can be expressed
through a sign, an ideogram . . ." Now, if the psychic process
is, let us say, the decision to change jobs, I do not see why
this should be followed through all limbs and extremities;

even less do I see why the physiological reflexes, once apprehended, need further translation into signs. But what I see
least of all is how these reflexes can be produced "so quickly
that thought—which would remove all spontaneity—has no
time to intervene." How can anyone who rehearses a production for over a year and watches each performance like a
blinkered hawk speak of spontaneity? Not even *kabuki* and
kathakali, by which all this is influenced, would presume to
do so.

After the three Grotowskian presentations here, the chorus
of praise, sometimes with minor reservations, was virtually
unanimous and included such diverse choristers as Clive Barnes,
Walter Kerr, Eric Bentley, Stanley Kauffmann, Harold Clur-
man, Richard Schechner, Elizabeth Hardwick. In fact, the
only reviewer who shared what would otherwise have been
my solitary indignation was Ross Wetzsteon in the *Village
Voice*, whose two articles on the subject I heartily recommend.
One can understand readily enough what Grotowski means
for Poland. On the one hand, he is the natural outgrowth of
the political violence and religious persecution that have brutal-
ized Polish history; on the other, he may seem a great moral
hero to those Poles who do not want to knuckle under to socialist realism. To disaffected audiences everywhere, the sado-
masochism and homosexuality of this theater (only one woman,
and she quite homely; the handsome Ryszard Cieslak, Grotowski's special friend, always being stripped and displayed),
and its very Artaudian cruelty, may offer corroboration and
sustenance. But it is by examining more closely what Grotowski means to an avant-garde American critic that we can
best get at his essential, dubious appeal.

In reviewing *Towards a Poor Theatre* for *The New York
Times Book Review*, Richard Gilman wrote of Grotowski:
"He has fought to obtain the painful and not yet known truth
beneath appearances and to develop clear signs for their mani-
festation." (I take that "their" to be an error for "its"; clearly
what Grotowski, or Gilman, wants manifested is the truth, not
the appearances.) But how does one find clear signs for a
not-yet-known truth? And by whom is this truth not yet

known? If by audiences, then what is so special about Grotowski? Any halfway clever theatrical event provides something unknown and surprising for the audience. If, however,
the truth is unknown to Grotowski himself, he must be humbly
groping for it and trying to express it by whatever tentative
means; to develop "clear signs" for something you yourself
are in the dark about strikes me as an act of arrogance and
folly.

In his *New American Review* piece, Gilman claims, like
Grotowski, that "life in the present is inauthentic"—as if it
had ever been any more or less authentic than now. By the
very fact of being, life acquires all the authenticity it needs,
though Grotowski apparently demands some kind of myth or
religion to authenticate it, a process that all the alembics of
his laboratory will prove insufficient to activate. But, according
to Gilman, Grotowski is "struggling with a language inade-
quate to the new actuality of what he has been doing." This
"actuality" must then logically be prior to the theatrical language that is to express it, and one wonders just what Grotowski's work in its pretheatrical phase might be. "Artistic
creation," Gilman informs us, "is an order opposed to the order
of the world"; Grotowski and his actors "place us in the presence
of emotion and consciousness themselves . . . of a creation and
not an image of one." And Gilman goes on to speak of "the
only justification art provides: its testimony to the *fact* of
the imagination as life-giver in the teeth of life itself. The wish
to have a work finally 'say' something emerges from a blindness to what it is actually doing—putting us in the presence
of a life our own lives are powerless otherwise to unearth."
But what good is our being put in the presence of some other,
perhaps richer, kind of life if that life does not say anything to
us? How does it benefit us to contemplate the complexities,
subtleties and originalities of Grotowski's art if this art does
not speak to us? And why should artistic creation be an order
opposed to the order of the world? Certainly a poem is written
differently from the way an income tax form is filled out;
love-making is different from the representation of it in an
opera or ballet. But from this to an "opposition" is a long way.

The artist's imagination may express a quarrel with the world or a dream of utopia. But even such creation must avail itself of methods of juxtaposition, assemblage and composition that have their equivalents in biological, chemical, mathematical processes at work both in nature and in the laboratory. And even if the artist's subject matter may seem totally revolutionary, it is never very far ahead of science or history, which, often regrettably, proceed in analogous directions toward identical goals. In any case, the images of *Akropolis, Apocalypsis* and *The Constant Prince* are definitely trying to say someting to us; it is simply that under the delusion of saying it highly originally, they say it primitively and crudely.

But Gilman has not invented his own Grotowski; he quotes directly from the Master: "In art, it is not life itself that makes the context—it is the objects of art. That means to do a great work one must not observe life. That effort is artificial. We observe life as we live it." So far this is no more than the good old doctrine of aestheticism, *l'art pour l'art* restated rather more clumsily than by some of its nineteenth-century practitioners, only to be saluted by critics like Gilman and overwhelmed audiences as some wonderful new truth opposite to life. But Grotowski continues (again quoted by Gilman): "To say that in order to create I must observe society is wrong. Society is always there in our experiences." What seems to remain unperceived by Gilman and the rest is the considerable jump from "life" to "society," treated as if it were no jump at all. What Grotowski seems to oppose is merely socialist realism—which is indeed the depiction of life as officially prescribed by a society, or at any rate by the government of that society. Of this, quite understandably, Grotowski wants no part. But to leap from opposition to a Communist, capitalist, bourgeois or any other society's official view of life to the opposition of life itself—a feat of hyper-Pascalian gymnastics—is humanly and artistically self-destructive. And it does not matter whether it is done knowingly or not, as part of a politically necessary, self-protective stratagem, or out of some insane need to be different at any cost.

What does it mean when Gilman interprets Grotowski's

work as placing us in the presence of emotion and consciousness themselves, of a creation and not an image of one? (Kauffmann, more cautiously, but not cautiously enough, spoke of
"bone-deep truth.") How does Gilman imagine a pure emotion or consciousness being deposited on a stage, or anywhere
else—except, of course, as an image, a representation? But Gilman believes in some kind of pure "creation," which strikes
me as mere word-mongering. A creation of what? If of something unrelated to anything, how can another human being
recognize its meaning? And can anyone honestly believe that
new feelings or emotions can be introduced into our affective
repertoire at this late date? Clearly, there are new ways of
expressing them, but even a *Finnegans Wake* says something
identifiable, and says it with relation to something and someone: words, however boldly combined; and a reader, however
ideal.

But perhaps the best example of Gilman's method, which I
take to be representative of that of many true apostles, is con-
tained in this sentence: "Almost every movement and sound
is what can only be described as 'pure,' without precedent
and predictability, yet wholly inevitable, accurate, created,
true." Here the Master's and the disciple's ravings are in perfect
harmony. If something is wholly unprecedented and unpre-
dictable, to what can it then be true? And in what sense can
it be called accurate? If there is no such concept as "time,"
or if a watch is making up its own time, in what sense can we
call the watch accurate? "Created," yes; but why "inevitable"?
Why is it inevitable that a tortured Prince should provide
funny wind noises for the rest of the cast? What makes such
sounds, or the disfigured recitation of words through spinal
resonators (whatever they may be), "pure"? Pure what? And
all this from a critic who does not even speak Polish, a language of which Grotowski occasionally does make some sort
of use.

There, however, is the crux of it. Grotowski and Gilman are
both against language. They are part of the anti-language
movement that has gained control of all the arts, even those that
make little or no use of words. In a sense, all of Grotowski's

elaborate researches into a *via negativa* (attempts to remove
whatever might block an actor), ideograms, confrontations
with myth, elimination of almost everything but the actor-
audience relationship, are efforts to get past communication
through language. This reminds me of the periodic efforts of
avant-garde film makers to eliminate dialogue and return in
one way or another to silent films as being more pure, more
visual. But the fact remains that the word, even if it is not
indispensable to the stage or screen event, is a great help to
it. It is possible for a human being not to speak, by being a
baby or a Trappist monk, but in theatrical or cinematic communication, at least in a work of some length, a good deal
more gets conveyed if the author and actors are not Trappist
monks or babies. We created the word (or, if you prefer, God
created it) because we need it and find that it serves us well—
even in such highly unnaturalistic constructs as the poems
of Mallarmé, the plays of Beckett, and so on. Anyone wishing
to jettison the word proceeds, I firmly believe, either out of
a jaded *ennui*—boredom with something he chooses to consider
too profuse and ubiquitous—or out of some sense of impo-
tence: that everything has been said already and that there
is nothing further to achieve. But this should stimulate the
creative mind to even greater efforts toward making words
create and perform, rather than give up something so fundamental as *not* to distinguish us from the beasts, which clearly
have it too—in some cases more clearly than our own young
people.

There is also another significant aspect of Grotowski's
work, one that James Roose-Evans has summarized adequately
in his book, *Experimental Theatre:*

> Grotowski is concerned with the spectator who has genuine
> spiritual needs and who really wishes, through the confron-
> tation with the performance, to analyse himself. The very
> physical proximity of the actors and audience is intended to
> assist the collective self-analysis to take place. Does this
> imply a theatre for an élite? The answer is a positive, yes.
> Grotowski insists that this be made clear from the very begin-

ning: "We are not concerned with any audience but a special one."

This worthy aim also elicits serious doubt. What is so special about a theater of collective self-analysis? All art, if we are receptive, makes us examine its values against our own and vice versa, in a dialogue of self-analysis, collective or not. But for the analysis to be effective, the audience must be given something that, on one level at least, it can identify. But when things are so vague that the devoted Roose-Evans, who has seen the show and read Flaszen's explanation that the spectators at *Akropolis* are the living, the living watching the dead in whose deaths they are implicated, can nevertheless write, "The audience, however, is not involved. They represent the Dead," we are in trouble. A Rorschach test by itself—without controlled conditions, guidance and supervision—is not going to be a helpful tool for self-analysis.

But even assuming that Grotowski's "theater of encounter" offers, more than any other, this collective self-analysis, and that such analysis is what is needed; is anything gained by a theater that admits such small numbers of spectators and considers them an élite? Yes, there is that proximity to the actor (Grotowski wants us to "feel his breathing and smell the perspiration"; I don't), but surely this distracts attention from the play. And I believe that people who come to the theater specifically to be psychoanalyzed are not an élite, but a plurality of neurotics and psychotics in need of help—help that they can get much better elsewhere. The sparse admissions, moreover, can be construed in Poland as an act of defiance of the régime, with its programmed, mass-oriented art; in the world at large, they smack of snobbery that may deprive the very people who are supposed to be benefited. At the very least, Grotowski might demand from the forty to ninety people he admits to a performance affidavits to the effect that they are more demented than the hundreds he turns away. It is a terrible waste to inflict his theater on the sane.

APPRAISALS

The pieces in this section are book reviews—i.e., reviews of theater or theatrical matters in book form. The supposed distinction between theater and drama, claiming that the former is enacted on a stage by people and thus living and good, whereas the latter is printed in a book and thus mere dead "literature," has always struck me as absurd. For one thing, the only people to whom "literature" and "literary" are dirty words are illiterates, and to them I have nothing to say. For another, to claim, as so many people in the theater do, that a play as read in an armchair does not exist, shows only how provincial and chauvinistic theater people are. Of course, a play is meant to be performed and seen, but if we had to wait for performances of many a masterpiece, we might have to tarry quite a while, and in waiting for a wholly worthy performance of most of them, we might easily die of old age.

So, I say, better a good reading than no performance or a poor one. An intelligent, imaginative reader can often supply what a run-of-the-mill production cannot, and an unintelligent, unimaginative reader is not likely to see the light by the mere purchase of a ticket and plunking of his backside in the designated seat. True, repeated exposure to good productions will educate a person; but so too will the assiduous reading of good plays. If the pieces that follow make clearer and firmer the connection between theater and printed drama, and even between theater and dramatic criticism or nondramatic reflections by a playwright, it is all to the ultimate good of the theater.

THE DEPUTY AND
ITS METAMORPHOSES

(1964)

WHEN THE GIFTED German novelist and playwright Martin Walser hailed *The Deputy* as "a legitimate offspring of the long overdue marriage of Sartre and Brecht," he was only half right. Though *The Deputy* owes much to Sartre's skill in casting political and philosophical polemics in highly stageworthy molds, it has nothing of Brecht's alienation and epic theater or even didactic satire. Erwin Piscator, who gave the play its first production (in Berlin), was nearer the mark when he called it "a historic drama in the Schillerian sense."

It is certainly true that Hochhuth has all the moral fervor of Schiller, the disciple of Kant, and that the ethical criterion of the play is a categorical imperative that will have no truck with relativist notions of comparative good or comparative evil. However, Schiller's use of the historic in drama is not Hochhuth's. Most patently in *The Maid of Orléans*, but also elsewhere, Schiller was willing to alter historical facts radically to suit his purposes, whereas Hochhuth is at great pains to include all possible historical data and limit his invention to the interstices—sometimes to the detriment of his play.

Actually, among Hochhuth's artistic forebears, two other great German historical dramatists figure more prominently: Kleist and Hebbel. It is Kleist's Romantic passion that largely informs *The Deputy;* its idealistic young Jesuit hero owes something to the Prince of Homburg and even to Michael Kohlhaas, figures whose noble passion makes them politically or socially culpable, but who are more troubled and complex than, say,

167

the hero of Schiller's *The Robbers*. And it is Hebbel's notion of historical drama, based on Hegel rather than Kant, in which protagonists become symbols of their society, their age and the workings of history, that importantly affects Hochhuth's dramaturgy.

This inevitably leads to the question of the role of historicity in historical drama. Does *Richard III* fail as a play because it is unfair to Richard? Does the fact that Anouilh makes his Norman hero into a collaborating Saxon invalidate *Becket*? Does Shaw's cramming *Saint Joan* full of twentieth-century hindsight and Shavian philosophy disqualify it is a historical play? Clearly historic drama can emphasize either half of its name: it can make history subserve the ideas and effects of drama, or it can use the drama as a vehicle for momentous historical truths. Though either approach is valid, the former is more likely to produce a work of art, the latter a tract in dramatic form. But the importance of the literate tract in the theater should not be too readily dismissed, whether it is called *The Cradle Will Rock* or *The Exception and the Rule*.

It is equally clear that a major stumbling block is the question of contemporaneity. It is all right to be fiercely critical or freely inventive, or both, where a figure of the distant past is concerned—where our own world and memories are not incriminated and the plea of insufficient evidence can be advanced. Thus *Becket* may grossly caricature a twelfth-century pope and elicit no more than the arching of an isolated eyebrow, whereas *The Deputy* may make a twentieth-century pope less unsympathetic than its author personally considers him and yet provoke outcries of "Caricature!" from critics all over, regardless of race, creed or competence.

Let us consider the main artistic charges (as opposed to political ones) that have been leveled against Hochhuth's Pius XII. We are told that this Pius is not a worthy antagonist for the idealistic hero—in other words, the "caricature" argument in more sophisticated form; and that *The Deputy*, asserting as it does its historical authenticity, has no business imputing motives of a damaging yet unprovable sort to the Pope. Now, if you believe in a categorical imperative to do right, as

Hochhuth does, Pius can no longer be an equally convincing
defender of an antithetical position, as Kleist's Elector or Antony in *Julius Caesar* can be. Absolute morality compels a pope
to speak up in behalf of six million human beings, dead, dying
or yet to die—even if the consequences, to himself and all Catholics, were more manifestly dangerous than they may have
appeared to be. By keeping the Pope as close to absolute silence
as dramatically feasible, Hochhuth is actually lending the greatest possible dignity to a position he considers untenable. What
makes Shakespeare's Iago a greater figure than Verdi and
Boito's is that, despite minor and inconclusive clues, he remains
silent on his ultimate motivation.

Now for that motivation. Hochhuth has indeed put forward
all conceivable reasons for the Pope's silence: the safety of
Catholics, business and financial considerations, ecclesiastical
politics (danger of schism), European politics (Hitler as bul-
wark against Stalin and Communism), a kind of aristocratic
hauteur and lack of human warmth, failure of nerve. Hochhuth
does not insist on the equal relevance of all—indeed, he allows
directors, actors, audiences and readers to consider some of
them irrelevant. If, however, it is objected that the particular
juxtapositions are misleading, I reply that the need for com-
pression makes them inevitable. And if it is maintained that
there is still too much invention involved, I answer with the
words of Lessing from the *Hamburgische Dramaturgie:* "Whoever reasons correctly also invents, and whoever would invent
must also be able to reason. Only those believe in the separabil-
ity of one from the other who are by disposition incapable of
either."

Here we come to the crux of the matter. If Hochhuth had
written a play about Pius XII and only about him, it is entirely
probable that the play would have been, by accepted standards,
more dense although not necessarily more substantial: much
polemical material that is relegated to the "Historical Side-
lights" of the play's appendix could have been set forth in
greater detail in the play itself. Hochhuth, however—and here
lies what is both the glory and the foredoom of his undertaking—is after something bigger: a historical fresco of the entire

complex of events that begat and tolerated Auschwitz. No matter how important the Pope may be to the play, other elements are of equal importance: the Germans, the Nazi Party, big business and science gone mad, the Catholic Church, other churches, individuals everywhere, and the metaphysics of evil as embodied in the play's one predominantly mythical character, the Doctor. What ultimately drags the play down to some extent is the very opposite of insufficient historical data: the excess of usable, and used, documentation.

We should note, then, that the Catholic Church, for example, is seen in the play not only as the Pope, but also as the Apostolic Nuncio to Berlin (who is a historic figure), the Cardinal (who, I suspect, also has a historic basis), the Abbot, three quite different monks, an important lay adviser to the Holy See, and above all, as the young Jesuit, Riccardo Fontana, who stands for not only the two priests to whom the play is dedicated, but also, in Hochhuth's words, "for those priests, mostly nameless, who instantly set love for their neighbor above all utilitarian considerations—ultimately at the price of their lives." It is thus that the entire spectrum of clerical reaction to the plight of the Jews is represented.

So the deputy—or vicar, or representative—of the title is not the Pope, who shirks his duty, but Riccardo, who takes on the Pope's burden and dies for it. Riccardo is a profoundly religious figure, and it is largely because of him that the play can justly call itself "a Christian tragedy." Indeed, it is the only major religious play written since the last war that I know of, and it is perhaps a fitting piece of worldly irony which would brand this one, of all plays, as irreligious. What makes Riccardo into a Christian tragic hero is not only the fact that he assumes the guilt of his Church and unsolicitedly becomes the vicar's vicar. It is also the fact that Riccardo's magnanimous desperation forces him toward two of the gravest sins a priest can commit: insubordination to his spiritual superiors, climaxing in the contemplated political assassination of the Pope; and an attempt to murder the villainous Doctor of Auschwitz. But something prevents him from committing either of these—perhaps salutary —sins: is it Providence in its wisdom, or just the weakness of the spiritual arm of this world? In his final despair, Riccardo is forced into something graver yet: doubting the very decency of God. (None of this, by the way, remains in the preposterous Broadway version, to list all of whose omissions would require another historical appendix.)

Riccardo's counterpart is Gerstein, who represents the secular hero and the lay sacrifice: the man of moral action who must, in a time of assassins, besmirch himself by ostensibly joining with evil in order to undermine it, and who presumably dies a death which is as anonymous as, but less expiatory than, the priest's. As opposed to these two, there are the two poles of culpability: the scientist whose evil knows no bounds, and the Pontiff whose goodness, unfortunately, does; or to put it more abstractly, the sado-satanist doctor whom metaphysical silence drives to unconscionable crimes, and the high-minded trimmer whom unconscionable crimes leave physically silent.

Alfred Kazin has criticized Hochhuth's characterization of the Doctor for not having the horribly vulgar reality of Josef Mengele, the bestial doctor of Auschwitz. And this is precisely Hochhuth's problem. There is so much fact in his play that whenever he transcends it into fiction, into art, he seems fated to be immediately pounced upon by one group of partisans or another. Thus Kazin ignores the fact that there are several other characters in the play who quite sufficiently body forth the "sadistic clown and frivolous maniac" one might miss in the Doctor.

But if *The Deputy* is too multifariously ambitious to be a complete success, it does not flinch from attempting to pursue a theme into most of its terrible ramifications. In fact, the construction of the play is by no means unskillful in the way it manipulates characters through various scenes—dropping them and picking them up again—toward a final, perhaps somewhat disappointing showdown. The suspense leading up to the Pope scene is ably handled, and there is also an effective contrapuntal construction: scenes involving individuals alternate with scenes involving larger groups or their typical representatives. (Nothing of this, either, on Broadway.)

Where the play really fails—aside from a certain weakness

in some of the characters, partly a consequence of their numerousness—is in its language. Though it is written in free verse,
and not at all in blank verse as Susan Sontag asserted in *Book
Week*, this free verse makes very little sense in its line breaks,
and its rhythms are far from compelling. In truth, it might as
well be written out as prose, though even as prose it would
be no more than adequate. The one exception is the trio of
monologues by representative victims in a freight car on the
way to Auschwitz, where the style becomes more unabashedly
poetic—not, however, with unqualified success.

What is much less successful, though, is the English translation of the complete text by Richard and Clara Winston. That
they were unable to cope with the profusion of juicy dialects
enlivening the language and making it ecumenical is understandable and forgivable, although their haphazard attempts at
dealing with it are less pardonable. Thus they will Americanize
a Nazi doctor who now experiments on "critters," or Eichmann,
who now recalls the first "date" he ever undressed, and will
turn an ironic reference to the Gestapo from "your friend in
need" to "mother's little helper." They can likewise be unidio-
matic or overliterate, as when a bowler is told "Take your
stance!" or when an importunate visitor is urged by a Bavarian
monk "Now please, take yourself off," or when "stir-craziness"
emerges as "cabin-fever" and "easier said than done" as "easy
to say, but hard to do."

The unfortunate truth is that the translation abounds in
errors of taste and judgment, and every once in a while, even
misunderstands the text. Here are a few examples taken from
one passage alone. The Winstons, in their prolixity, will turn
Gerstein's simple statement "The souls of the bystanders are
also at stake" into a wordy bit of Sunday Christianity: "Those
who keep silent are accessories to murder/ and they imperil
their immortal souls" (p. 80). They will miss a piece of *humour
noir* (p. 79), "people cremated on the family plan," by translating it as "whole families pushed into the ovens." They reveal
ignorance when they refer to "St. Loyola" (p. 76), which is
rather like saying "Sir Churchill." When Riccardo (p. 84) uses
the conjunctional *now*, "now, don't you go giving up God as

well," the Winstons translate it as adverbial: "you don't want/ to give up God as well, not now," as if the young priest might condone giving up God later. More serious is the mistranslation of Gerstein's pregnant words (p. 90) "Both of us will not survive this war" (i.e., either Nazi Germany or Western civilization must perish) as "Neither of us/ is going to survive this war."

Some of the worst excesses of the Winstons occur when, for no good reason, they persist in veering toward blank verse: "If you insist on it, you'll die here/ like a snail crushed under an *auto* tire—/ die as the heroes of today *do* die, *namelessly*,/ snuffed out by powers they have never known,/ let alone can fight. In other words, *meaninglessly*." (Italics mine.) But they are fully capable of still more mysterious lapses. Thus when the Pope makes the important statement that he leaves protest against the Nazis to the *Oberhirten* ("chief shepherds," i.e., the episcopate of the respective countries), the Winstons translate: "We leave it to the local parish priest." Again, when the Doctor jeers at a young Jewess who has managed to survive "our recent Feast of Tabernacles, the great autumn wine pressing" (i.e., bloodletting), we read "the Feast of Tabernacles, our harvest-home," which is meaningless. And when Riccardo exclaims, in abhorrence of the Doctor, "What sort of . . . of a devil are you?" we get "What a devil you are!"—straight out of Edwardian farce.

But at least the Winstons try, however clubfootedly, to keep up with the text and respect its integrity. No such thing can be said for the Herman Shumlin-Jerome Rothenberg adaptation we are treated to on Broadway. These two men have cut out, completely or in large part, any scenes of or references to utter horror, Jewish collaboration, Protestant indifference or Catholic inadequacy other than the Pope's. Thus no mention of Himmler's modeling the SS on the Society of Jesus; Cardinal Spellman and Catholic power in the United States; the Holy See acting as bankers for the Italian royal house while also doing business with Mussolini; the Pope's concern with liquidating the Church's Hungarian assets before the Russians march in; the callousness of the German bishops and their active support of the Nazis— and God knows what else. Almost anything beyond a decorous suggestion of Jewish suffering and Papal insufficiency, anything that might really draw blood or tears, is cut. Similarly, finer discussions of philosophy, theology, politics, history, literature— or even just passages where the style is a little more complex and poetic—are all ruthlessly cut.

Inserted, on the other hand, are—besides two scenes that are complete travesties of the original (I, ii; II, i)—the kinds of vulgarity and pretentiousness with which Shumlin and Rothenberg have long been identified (I call special attention to Rothenberg's inept translation of German poetry, to say nothing of his own verse). Thus, for example, the Jew Jacobson, an ordinary middle-class person, a teacher perhaps, is turned here into a violent proletarian type continually complaining about his fleas: "They're killing me, the bastards. Look, my navel is raw from them!" and about "pee stains on my underwear . . . what a mess!" The Doctor is reduced to a *Playboy* magazine fan, "You spread their legs apart and read a textbook: hot confessions in the curls of hair," which does not even make sense. Poor Gerstein is obliged to chant incessant litanies— Rothenberg evidently considers the refrain a highly poetic device—and keeps repeating in two separate scenes, "My name is Gerstein!" and "No matter!"

Here are further examples of Rothenbergian poesy: "By the hair and teeth of God! By the plundered hair and teeth of God!" or "Take the star, priest. The light is in the star. The pain is in the star," chanted antiphonally into Riccardo's ears by Jacobson and Gerstein. This at least might stand as a parody of Christopher Fry; but what of "I supplicate, I beg, I grovel, I beseech, I whimper, I demand!" which can only be taken as a parody of Roget's *Thesaurus*. Again, when a young Italian girl is questioned by a Nazi about her fiancé, the text has her reveal that he died fighting in Africa. Here, however, he is made merely a prisoner of war so that Rothenberg can let the girl scream: "He's blonder than you are! His hair is blond all over his body. It shines in the light."

And so it goes. *The Deputy* on Broadway is like one of those comic-strip versions of a literary classic ("My name is Julien Sorel. I just got here!" framed in a balloon above a head), and as the characters bestride the stage you can virtually see the balloons coming out of their mouths.

What makes *The Deputy,* as Hochhuth has written it, important, however, is not so much the political revelation it may have made. Nor technical devices such as having the same actors enact several contradictory parts, to convey that in our age it is merely a matter of "military conscription . . . whether one stands on the side of the victims or the executioners." Nor the elaborate stage directions which bitterly project certain characters into the future—describing, for example, such and such a Nazi as a solid citizen of postwar Germany. What *is* momentous is that in an age that has progressively convinced itself that its significant dramatic form is dark comedy—that, to quote Dürrenmatt, "our world has led to the Grotesque as to the atom bomb, just as the apocalyptic pictures of Hieronymus Bosch are grotesque, too"—that in this era when "the death of tragedy" has become a literary commonplace, *The Deputy* stands as a valid tragedy: not great, but good, and anything but commonplace.

A ROLLER-COASTER RIDE
WITH KENNETH TYNAN

(1967)

Kᴇɴɴᴇᴛʜ Tʏɴᴀɴ's new book is a roller-coaster ride. The first part of *Tynan Right and Left* is "Plays," and with these play reviews we ascend the heights of contemporary dramatic criticism—judicious (with some exceptions I am coming to), well-informed, well-written, witty and, above all, beautifully structured, having the profile of a work of art, as all true criticism should. Next we hurtle into "Films," and Tynan's film criticism is appalling—modish, irresponsible, insensitive, ill-considered, and for the most part ill-written. The drama pre-empts what is right with Tynan's criticism; film gets what is left.

There follows the section "People," interviews and profiles, and here the roller coaster abandons vertiginous climbs and terrifying falls, and goes in for sportive, lurching little ups and downs. Though Tynan does rather more than justice to lesser lights like Miles Davis and George Cukor, and even to medium lights or light-heavies like Joan Littlewood and Orson Welles, his interview with Sartre is a drop into earnest dullness. The next segment, "Places," starts with a marvelous up, an evocation of Barcelona in all its toothsome topsy-turviness, proceeds downward to routine assessments of San Francisco and the Costa del Sol, and then topples into a piece of perfect fatuity, "The Three-Star Tour," to which I shall return. The concluding item here, on New York City, takes us halfway up again.

But up only to dump us precipitously into a section called inside the book "Comments and Causeries," but on the jacket and title page, rather more demotically, "Events." Most of this is routine literary journalism, except for a few sheer drops into the preposterous, like the ode to female posteriors, though even here Tynan does not touch bottom as he does in a sophomoric pastiche of Arts Festivals, a subject safely beyond—because beneath—parody. The book ends with a sharp ascent into provocative controversy, a quasi-*cause célèbre,* in which Tynan attacked Truman Capote for *In Cold Blood,* with answers from Capote and the main defense counsel, and rebuttals by Tynan.

I have deliberately refrained from referring to the foreword until the very last, because it cannot be fitted into the roller-coaster image, at least not until these contraptions learn to burrow underground. For the foreword is a descent into the pit of Tynan's arrogance, a by-product from which the mines of genius are seldom free, but whose sooty sediments need not be allowed to disfigure the entrance to the mine. Here, among other embarrassing things, Tynan gives us a God's-eye view of himself, direct from the "dossier the Greatest Critic of Them All is compiling for me, Up There," which can be described only as carrying anthropomorphism to the point of having a friend at the highest court.

In his dramatic criticism, Tynan continues the good work of *Curtains,* his previous and excellent collection. I would say that even here he has a fault, but, as faults go, it is a fairly endearing one. At some point in his life—it is idle to try to fix the exact date—Tynan converted to what he thinks is socialism or Marxism, but is in fact Brecht. Having fallen in love with this splendid playwright, he felt, rather touchingly, that in order for the marriage to last, he had to embrace Brecht's religion as well. But Brecht's Marxism was of an unorthodox sort; besides, dogma of any kind is less of a hindrance to the creator than to the critic. Now, it is true that Tynan's leftism, too, is rather peculiar—not excluding snobbery, social-climbing, celebrity hunting, and just plain sybaritism—but it does slant his criticism, to some extent, in a rather predictable way.

So it seems mildly unsettling that Tynan should overpraise a piece of obvious claptrap like Robert Ardrey's *Shadow of Heroes* and undervalue the works of Beckett, but once we understand that he is a political meliorist, not a metaphysical pessimist, we can make allowances for his bias—particularly because his theatrical taste wins out in the end. Thus, his final words on Ardrey are, after all, fairly negative, and his concluding remark about *Happy Days,* for example, suitably laudatory.

But these are minor cavils compared to the delight most of these reviews unstintingly provide. Tynan's basic position as a critic is defined for him by Brecht, from whom he approvingly quotes: "The modern theater must be judged not by its success in satisfying the audience's habits but by its success in transforming them . . . not by whether it interests the spectator in buying a ticket but by whether it interests him in the world." This criterion, though it can easily take on political coloration, is nevertheless first of all a plea for uncompromised standards and for the recognition of the high—though not necessarily unsmiling—seriousness of theater. It is in his capacity of believer in theater rather than in sideshows that Tynan can cuttingly derogate to "the kind of [folksy] fun . . . that ruined the Abbey Theatre"; warn that "too many of our younger playwrights have forgotten, in their passion for novelty of content, the ancient disciplines of style"; or, with regard to certain French dramatists, wittily deplore the ability "to exploit the full capacity of the French language for exquisite, lapidary emptiness."

Thus, Tynan has nothing but justifiable contempt for "the middle-class, postprandial Broadway audience" and a theater wherein "it is permissible for a playwright to condemn the bourgeois as a man but not as a bourgeois." Yet this attitude does not force Tynan into the corresponding pitfall: endorsement of scandal and nonsense as devices *pour épater* or provoke *les bourgeois.* He cogently dismisses Happenings and related phenomena with the axiom "If all the world's a stage, we might as well burn down the theaters."

Of the three talents that probably contribute most to Tynan's excellence and readability, let me mention first the lightning phrase, which in a flash illuminates an artist or performance. Thus we have Vanessa Redgrave "looking as vulnerable as a baby giraffe," or Edith Piaf "walking off the stage . . . like an exalted concierge." There is the instant evaluation of Shaw, "the exuberant, infertile figure of G.B.S." or this unfair but not wholly unjustified sally, "When you have seen all of Ionesco's plays . . . you've seen one of them."

Second, Tynan is extraordinary in his ability to evoke a performance or production with a few coruscating sentences. Read his rousing encapsulation of Maria Casarès' Phèdre, for instance, or of Noel Willman's Claudius: "At his first entrance, Mr. Willman strikes a note of decent banality from which he never afterwards departs. To establish that he is a crafty fellow, he keeps his eyes roving from side to side, like air pockets in a pair of spirit-levels; and he clinches the case against Claudius by eating grapes. It is a rule of Shakespearean production that men who eat grapes are definitely voluptuaries and probably murderers."

Tynan's third supreme aptitude is for parody and persiflage, as when he eviscerates Marlowe's mighty line by rewriting a passage from *Tamburlaine* in terms of "a horde of pills and wonder drugs bent on decimating one another," and he can put his finger on Synge's fatal weakness with a mere one-sentence imitation. But beyond all this there is the review that in the shortest space captures the essential sights and sounds of a production, evaluates the play with the fewest and farthest-reaching words, and gives you the very feel and smell of the event.

Not so when it comes to movies, which, as Tynan made clear in *Curtains,* he values less than the drama. Here we get all the tony Chelsea sophistries (domiciled wherever the *Cahiers* mentality is in vogue) that place Ozu above Bergman, Blake Edwards at least on a par with Antonioni, the Beatles and Jerry Lewis in a special pantheon, and Godard at the right hand of God. In this world, movies are essentially pop, and whereas one sees nothing in the magnificent *Woman in the Dunes,* one is "intermittently unexpectedly touched" by *The Sound of Music.* The worst of it is that Tynan is not even consistent here: he bemoans with unending wrong-headedness the "cult of the director," films in which one individual's signature is on every detail, while out of the other corner of his mouth he is singing the praises of Godard, in whom directorial autonomy rampages like galloping consumption.

As an interviewer and miscellaneous literary journalist, Ty-

nan acquits himself honorably, except for certain lapses noted
above. Most distressing of these is "The Three-Star Tour," in
which Tynan and a wealthy American friend roll from one end
of France to the other in a chauffeur-driven limousine and
pleasant alcoholic haze to sample most of the establishments on
which the *Guide Michelin* has rained a shower of three stars,
its supreme accolade. At one of these Lucullan hostelries, Tynan
is torn between joy over a "gargantuan truffle . . . *en feuilleté*
with sauce périgourdine" and dejection over "a flabby steak
Dumas." His companion "snidely wonders" how Tynan "can
embark on a tour like this and still call [himself] a Socialist."
He is put in his place: "I reply, curtly but sincerely, that good
food should be available to everyone; Socialism which denies
the pleasures of the gullet is Socialism disfigured by the English
puritan tradition." I suggest that Tynan might try plying his
trade in any of the Socialist republics from Russia to Rumania
and see how far he would get indulging his three-star-sprinkled
gullet and chauffeur-driven behind.

This, however, is the one small problem with much that is
best in the book: brilliant dramatic criticism that has to be read
against the parlor-leftist grain. Especially in the theatrical section, *Tynan Right and Left* is superb, except when it is a case
of Tynan left and wrong.

STRANGE DEVICES
ON THE BANNER

(1966)

THERE IS ALWAYS joy in certain quarters when a poet starts
writing for the theater. In the glorious ages of the drama, from
Aeschylus to Goethe and Schiller, drama and poetry lived in
wedlock. The nineteenth century broke up that happy union.
But sentimentalists like to see marriages last, however unviable
they have become, and there seems to be less rejoicing in
heaven over a repentant sinner than on earth over reconciled
spouses. So when Robert Lowell's *The Old Glory* was produced
off-Broadway, when, in other words, a major American poet
was appearing on the stage with verse drama, it was to some—
notably to most of the highbrow critics—as if the world had
suddenly become a better place.

The Old Glory consists of three one-acters: two shorter
ones, *Endecott and the Red Cross* and *My Kinsman, Major
Molineux,* based on short stories by Hawthorne, and one longer
one, *Benito Cereno,* from Melville's novella. In *Endecott,* a
well-meaning Puritan governor of Salem in the 1630's discovers,
as he quashes mixed Indian-and-white maypole dancing, that,
much as he is against King Charles and the Church of England
and their various worldly and opportunistic representatives in
the New World, he is not really for the more fanatical aspects
of his own Puritans. Yet he is forced into severity against the
revelers because "a statesman can either work with merciless
efficiency, and leave a desert,/ or he can work in a hit and miss
fashion/ and leave a cess-pool." Endecott opts for the desert,
but allows for a little bit of cesspool by way of an oasis.

In *Molineux*, a youth from Deerfield arrives in Boston with
his little brother just before Tea Party time. He hopes for a
career through his powerful kinsman who commands the red-
coats in Boston. During a hallucinatory night in which the Bos-
tonians treat the boys with a mixture of hostility and mockery,
the Major is always mysteriously alluded to and strangely un-
seeable—until the boys have to watch him being killed by the
anti-English mob, and are even hypnotically drawn into that
mob.

The plot of *Benito Cereno* needs no summary, but it should
be noted that Lowell has made considerable changes here (as
elsewhere), mostly in the direction of showing the contradictions in the American attitude toward Negroes: "In a civilized
country," says Lowell's Captain Delano, "everyone disbelieves
in slavery and wants slaves." And the play proceeds to show
the rights and wrongs of both blacks and whites.

Clearly, Lowell is trying to capture the ironies, cruelties
and inconclusiveness on which America was built: in *Endecott*,
the ambiguities are chiefly religious; in *Molineux*, political; in
Cereno, racial. Beyond that, though, he is concerned with essential human nature, which he sees as paradoxical, untrust-
worthy, and above all, tenebrose. But, regrettably, there are
three obstacles he cannot quite negotiate: the limitations of
the one-acter, the demands of dramatic form, the problem of
stage poetry.

Endecott, for example, is an interesting figure who manages
to arouse our sympathetic curiosity, but only at the expense of
swallowing up most of the playlet: his psyche exacts much
more attention from us than do the perfunctory characters and
negligible events of the play. In *Cereno*, attempts at writing
some sequences in the manner of Genet, Beckett or Kafka rub
uneasily against patches of realism and even a Hollywood,
shoot-'em-up finale. In *Molineux*, the absurdist mode is fairly
consistent (though not so witty as in Beckett or Ionesco), but
it clashes with stabs at mythologizing—Charon is introduced as
ferryman to Boston, "the City of the Dead"!—and throughout
one feels a certain confusion between symbol and rigmarole.

Again, dramatizing fiction has required such devices as the

confidant, but in *Molineux* the presence of the kid brother is not only illogical, it also dissipates the harrowing isolation of Hawthorne's solitary young protagonist. In *Cereno*, Lowell must supply Captain Delano with a sidekick, the naïve bosun Perkins, whom the poet intended both as butt of Delano's greater insight and wit and as a Prince Hal, who is supposed to end up, as Lowell put it in an interview, "superior to Delano." This superiority is meant to manifest itself, Lowell tells us, in two short and separate speeches, one of which is only six words long, and allegedly hinges on Perkins' ironic use of the one word "sir."

Now, this sort of thing is all very well in lyric poetry, but it just does not register in performed drama. And it is true of all three plays that, though they are aware of the things that make a play a play—not merely action and conflict, as commonly held, but also diversified verbal texture, humor, pathos, variety of tempo, absorbing talk and so on—Lowell is unable either to provide enough of them or to marshal them properly. Thus, action tends to bunch up in one place, humor to sound forced, and the language to become static or inconsistent. Babu, for example, far from remaining a slave fresh out of Africa, turns into a Calypso cut-up and connoisseur of American and European history and conditions.

Yet the final problem is the poetry itself. Though written in free verse, *The Old Glory* attains to poetry only in Captain Delano's speech beginning "I see an ocean undulating in long scoops and swells . . ." But this passage is only a slight reworking of Melville's third paragraph; and where it departs from Melville's prose, it improves on it only in one participle, "swallows sabering flies." Here now is a typical passage:

> *Things aren't really bad,*
> *but the time will come, the time will surely come,*
> *I know the King's mind, or rather the mind of his advisers—*
> *kings can't be said to have minds.*
> *The rulers of England will revoke our charter,*
> *they will send us a royal Governor,*
> *they will quarter soldiers on us,*
> *they will impose their system of bishops.*

What is the point of printing this as verse? Even its most eloquent champion, Robert Brustein, refers to it in the Introduction as a "prose style." True, there is the precedent of Eliot and Fry, but are *The Cocktail Party* and *Venus Observed* worthy of emulation? Verse that is not really verse can add only pretentiousness to a play, confuse the actors and throw dust in the ears of the audience. It may even deflect the playwright's attention from his primary task.

But could one not write truly poetic plays today? The answer, apparently, is no. By far the best twentieth-century poet-playwright, Bertolt Brecht, kept his poetry off the stage. On it, he allowed for song interludes; otherwise, with trifling exceptions, his plays were in prose. Poetry today has, unfortunately, become a minority art, no longer an integral part of the culture, as it was in the heyday of verse drama. Reluctantly we must accept its divorce from the theater, which must at least *seem* to speak the language of the land. The poet, as writer, may still have a place in the theater; poetry, barring a miracle, does not. What history hath put asunder, no man is likely to join together.

GROPE, GRAPPLE, FULMINATE, LAMENT-DON'T JUST SIT THERE!

(1968)

JOURNALS ARE WRITTEN for various, sometimes questionable, purposes; one of the best justifications for them is autotherapy, the need to come to terms with one's own life and, through it, with life itself, and that very unpleasant appendage of life—death. *Fragments of a Journal*, by the French playwright Eugene Ionesco, is the record of an unrelenting struggle with one's mortality: sometimes a witty defiance, more often a dreadful, unequal, yet plucky duel.

If you can imagine Boethius composing his *The Consolation of Philosophy* without any philosophy to believe in, or Thomas à Kempis writing *The Imitation of Christ* without a Christ to imitate, you get some idea of Ionesco's problem. Racked by a sense of the transience and insufficiency of our stay here, and appalled by the absence of an afterlife, his mind gropes, grapples, fulminates and laments. It is one of the most exacerbated cases of *horror vacui* on record: the book lies halfway between a metaphysical journal and something for the medical journals. The theme, to be sure, echoes through poetry—in English, from Dunbar to Dylan Thomas—but it has seldom been voiced so persistently and desperately in essayistic prose.

Actually, the book is not quite so monotonous as that; it leaps with very little organization from childhood reminiscences to political and literary speculations; from angry notes on a Swiss rest home in which Ionesco spent some time to the transcription of numerous often obsessive dreams; from attempted evaluations of the author's career to bits of surreal prose poetry. Some of Ionesco's asides—such as his berating Brecht, Sartre, the *nouveau roman,* psychiatry—are interesting but all too quickly submerged in a sea of private troubles. The book is most useful as a companion piece to Ionesco's later and more earnest (though dramatically less satisfactory) plays, *Exit the King* and *Hunger and Thirst.* Indeed, the *Journal* contains some unused but extremely valuable scraps from the former.

In *Exit the King,* the theme is the pathetic, hideous and ludicrous non-acceptance of death by a decrepit monarch clinging to a meaningless life. The *Journal* contains numerous variations on that theme. In vain does Ionesco tell himself that life is a hoax, thrust upon him only to be snatched away just as he was beginning to accept it; that "love is the air we breathe, our daily bread. But, alas, the air is polluted and the bread poisoned." Even the meanest form of existence remains preferable to non-existence—even though "it would be more 'natural'. . . for nothing to be. For nothing ever to have been." Terrified of death and inept at life, he yet "hopes to win first prize in a lottery without having bought a ticket."

As for *Hunger and Thirst,* it is made up of the very dreams and nightmares that litter this journal. The sinking house, the impenetrable wall, the elusive, unidentifiable beloved are all here. And the theme of the anguished search for the meaning of life. "I have run after life so much . . . I have never been late and never too early, and yet I have never caught up with it: it's as though I had run alongside of it." The situation is Sisyphean. "Presumably there is nothing to understand. But one's got to have a reason, to find a reason. Or else to lose one's reason." The 150 pages of this journal are so labyrinthine that one can easily lose one's way in them, if not one's reason.

Yet the book has its uses, even for a wider audience. In N. F. Simpson's *One Way Pendulum* a character complains that she put a skull on the mantel to remind her of something, but it doesn't work—she can't remember what it was supposed to remind her of. The *memento mori* that Ionesco's *Journal* provides in this section (sequels have already begun appearing in France) is guaranteed for use even by our Pollyanna-ish society—there is no mistaking its message. And the social and political calamities of our day are not enough; we need an Ionesco to confront us with our most metaphysical, and therefore most individual, predicament.

MADNESS AS THEATER

(1966)

THOSE OF US who enthusiastically applauded Peter Brook's production of Peter Weiss's *Marat/Sade* were not exactly acclaiming a set of new clothes without an emperor; it takes something to support and display even the most dazzling wardrobe. We should, therefore, grant the play itself the status of a well-made dummy.

The Persecution and Assassination of Jean-Paul Marat, As Performed by the Inmates of the Asylum of Charenton Under the Direction of the Marquis de Sade by Peter Weiss is a fanciful reconstruction of what might have gone on at the madhouse of Charenton, where the Marquis de Sade wrote plays and staged them with his fellow inmates for the benefit of chic Parisian audiences, who, like any audience, had a taste for a good mad show. In this case, the play-within-a-play is Sade's fantasy of Marat's assassination by Charlotte Corday and the shabby end of revolutions, while the play-around-the-play is the tumult of the actual production: the cast's instability, the asylum director's irritability, and the staff's inability to cope with the impending and eventually exploding chaos.

The play is a cunning conceit that sucks us in deeper and deeper. We, the readers or audience, are we mad to respond with fascination to a crazy grotesquerie in which our own flaws and vices are pilloried, our own sanity certified by madmen as insane? But are those people on the stage mad? They are performing a play that, except for occasional bizarre breakdowns, represents a valid conflict, coherently dramatized. But is it in fact coherent? The author, Sade, may be mad; his actors certainly are—indeed, we can seldom be sure whether Marat, or any of the other characters, is reading a line of the author's or interpolating his private frenzy. Yet surely the events are largely historical, and the rival positions in Sade's and Marat's *agon* time-honored? But the setting here is a madhouse, and does either position really clash with it? Does not Sade's cynical, disenchanted individualism, alive only to dubious sensual pleasures and solipsistic mockery, strike us as derailed? And is not Marat's fanatical, sanguinary zeal for reform—falling, moreover, on deaf ears or swallowed promptly by an upsurge of status quo—more than a little unhinged? And the hypocrisy of the pseudoliberal asylum director who would censor unsavory truths, and the voyeurism of the audience that would revel in unsavory outbursts—do they not, all together, constitute a mad world?

A *Mad World, My Masters* was the title and theme of a Jacobean play by Middleton, and in the asylum scene in *Peer Gynt* it is hard indeed to tell who is madder than whom. By the time of Pirandello's *Henry IV*, the relativity of madness had established itself as a dramatic *topos*, to become equally at home in the theater of the boulevards and the theater of the absurd. But it is to Peter Weiss's credit that by the system of Chinese boxes he has visualized the pursuit of sanity under madness—or of madness under sanity—as an enticing, never-ending endeavor.

Yet holding up a hall of mirrors to nature is, finally, a device; and a suitcase that doubles its bottoms ad infinitum may, in the last analysis, be doing it ad nauseam. I am not pleading against ambiguity in art, and still less for the playwright's duty to take a stand—though Weiss seems to feel the need of this when, after making Sade and entropy triumphant in the play, he publicly declares that his sympathies and hopes are with Marat and socialism. However, I look for two things in any play: progressively increasing impact and individual style. But *Marat/Sade*, like the madmen in some if its scenes, marches in place, while its style parades about from Pirandello to Brecht to Ionesco to Genet, with an honorific "Eyes right!" at Artaud. The argument between Sade and Marat is neither particularly penetrating nor dynamic, and the surrounding hocus-pocus, though spectacular on the stage, remains in the reader's mind a bunch of frenetic epicycles whirling around a vicious circle.

Weiss uses in the play a late medieval German measure, *Knittelvers,* a kind of doggerel with four loosely scattered stresses in its rhyming couplets; but he alternates this with modern free verse and modernistically omits all punctuation, thus stylistically transcending time. Unfortunately, the language is anything but transcendent, so that Adrian Mitchell's verse adaptation of Geoffrey Skelton's English prose version is often superior to the original as verse, even while cavalier about shades of meaning. There are also some peculiar cuts and additions, apparently tailored to Peter Brook's directorial specifications. Such important lines as Sade's "I hate Nature/I want to overcome her/I want to beat her with her own weapons/Catch her in her own traps" are mysteriously omitted, perhaps as being too abstract; some key stage directions are oddly altered, lines are transposed, reassigned or oversimplified, and whole incidents, such as one in which a patient imagines himself a mad animal, are added. (Unless, as may be, the translators worked from some earlier or later version of the text than the one published in Germany.) There are, in any case, some outright howlers: Marat, in Weiss, has visions *(Gesichte),* and not, as translated, faces *(Gesichter);* his teacher calls him an idler *(Tagedieb),* and not a pickpocket *(Taschendieb);* and so on.

But it is not really a matter of faulty translation or adaptation; it is a matter of defective dramaturgy: a striking, static image that neither moves nor moves us. Moreover, Weiss is a confused thinker. Thus Sade, in his first monologue, is for death as a necessary phase in nature, but also against nature for being indifferent to death; he is for spectacular deaths, even by horrible torture, yet describes Damien's terrible execution as an excuse for Casanova to fondle his excited girl and the populace to turn the whole thing into a carnival; he vows his opposition to nature, which permits deaths, either individualistic or mass-produced, but fails to make clear how he will implement the vow, or what the lovingly detailed description of Damien's agonies has to do with fighting nature with her own weapons. On the stage, given a bustling bravura production, inconsistencies disappear and interest is maintained; on the page, it is all rather like a fuzzy blueprint or a limp libretto.

CONVICTIONS

Convictions resemble definitions, but are not the same thing. Here the emphasis is on more idiosyncratic, more unabashedly private points of view, opinions that may seem specially unorthodox and contrary. Obviously, as I argue repeatedly throughout this book, there is no such thing as objective criticism; nevertheless, some views may be more subjective than others. But if criticism is the intensely individualistic activity I take it to be—if in fact, it is a form of art, which is the ultimate of enlightened subjectivism—it may be at its most useful and finally universal precisely when it sets out along untrodden, unpopular paths.

Once upon a time the preeminence of Shakespeare even among mere English dramatists was a highly debatable matter. The asseveration that form, in a very real sense, is content would have consigned an eighteenth-century critic to Bedlam; today it has become a rather tedious commonplace, known (at least in its McLuhanized version, "the medium is the message") to every self-respecting high-school kid. I am not saying, of course, that a minority view or an isolated position will ipso facto be proved right in the long run. But I am saying that it may be as risky to expect a critic to see things "our" way as it is to expect it from a playwright or painter.

THE AESTHETICS OF THE
ACTOR'S APPEARANCE

(1972)

An important but seldom written about aspect of stage aesthetics is the physical appearance of the performer. Many evils have befallen the theater in our time, and I dare say that the decline in actors' and actresses' looks is not the most important among them. Neither, however, is it the least important, for all its being the least discussed. In public, that is; in private, one often hears comments about the unbearable exterior of this or that performer. The problem has become more disturbing of late for two reasons. One is that it ties in alarmingly with a defiant decline in personal aesthetics—the militant slovenliness of today's young. The other is its relationship to the current emphasis on the outlandish and ugly for kicks, as witness a new batch of fashion models in the high-class magazines whose looks range from weird to odious.

There must be beauty in the theater. One of the many suicidal streaks of our stage is the creeping permissiveness that has allowed the faces and bodies of its women to become eyesores. It is just as if the great paintings and sculptures of women in Western art suddenly got the mumps or scurvy, elephantiasis or pernicious anemia, or whatever else disfigures the figure and defaces the face. Let me answer the first objection: why this concern with women's looks and not with men's? I am affected also by the latter, but I am a man, and I get my profoundest experience of Beauty incarnate from women. And I fail to see why this beauty should be abjured by the theater and abandoned to moving pictures or unmoving ads.

195

But even more worrisome, as far as the theater is concerned, is that the unsightliness of its practitioners may contribute to the further cooling of an already tepid interest in theater among its discriminating patrons. For theater once had glamour —some would go so far as to call it a mystique, but I prefer the more secular "glamour"—and a good part of that glamour was its leading ladies: women of marked physical beauty. Let us not speak slightingly of physical beauty just because there is something called spiritual beauty that is generally conceded to be a much finer thing. In any case, spiritual beauty is not all that useful to an actress: it is a slow worker, and in the two hours or so an actress holds the stage it might barely begin to make its presence felt. But physical beauty, as if aware of its transience, wastes no time in casting its spell.

To be sure, acting ability comes first—that nobody can deny. The only trouble is that acting ability may be even more in the eye of the beholder than beauty. Has any account come down to us disputing the beauty of such actresses as Anne Bracegirdle, Anne Oldfield or Peg Woffington? But consider talent, or even genius. Asked who was the greatest actress of modern times, anyone even moderately well read in such matters would unhesitatingly reply, "Duse." Surely "the Duse," as the diva used to be referred to, was an absolute actress if ever there was one. Well, let me take you now on a little tour of investigation of her artistry, and show you how the foremost authorities disagree.

In 1892, the young Hugo von Hofmannsthal gave this exalting account of Duse, noting that the limits of her art lay

not in her appearance, I do not know what she looks like. The words beautiful and ugly have no meaning for her, her body is nothing but the shifting projections of her changing moods. Over her face glide other faces: a coquettish little girl with mocking eyes and lips; a pale woman with the worriedly greedy eyes of passion; a gaunt bacchante with hot, deep-sunk eyes and dry lips around her open mouth, her neck muscles wildly swollen; and a lovely, cold statue with that great peace upon her glowing brow. She has a different walk each time: the springily even one of the great lady, the trippingly balancing one of little Nora, the sensually soft, dragging one of the poor, sentimental cocotte. All her limbs speak a different language every time: the pale, fine fingers of Fédora seem, the next day, changed into the languid, cajoling ones of the lady of the camellias, and, on the next, into the fidgety, frolicsome ones of the woman in the doll house . . .

Hofmannsthal's paean continues along these lines, and is echoed three years later (June 8, 1895) by Bernard Shaw, who also claims for Duse that hallmark of greatness, the ability to transmute herself for each new part:

> Duse's own private charm has not yet been given to the public. She gives you Césarine's charm, Marguerite Gauthier's [*sic*] charm, the charm of La Locandiera, the charm, in short, belonging to the character she impersonates; and you are enthralled by its reality and delighted by the magical skill of the artist without for a moment feeling any complicity either on your part or on hers in the passion represented.

Very good—except for the completely antithetical words of a drama critic of almost equal stature, Max Beerbohm. On March 9, 1907, Max reminisced about the Hedda of Duse, who

> in this, as in every other part that she plays, behaved like a guardian-angel half-asleep at her post over humanity. Her air of listlessness, in this instance, happened to be apt; but otherwise she showed not a shadow of comprehension of her part.

Earlier (May 26, 1900), after seeing Duse in repertory, Max had written:

> From first to last, she is the same in Fédora as in Magda, in Magda as in Paula, in Paula as in the Princesse Georges, and the Princesse Georges as in La Gioconda . . . My prevailing impression is of a great egoistic force; of a woman overriding, with an air of sombre unconcern, plays, mimes, critics and public.

You might with some plausibility argue that Beerbohm is a hostile witness, but here is equally damaging testimony from a sympathetic witness—more damaging, in fact, because it is meant as praise, yet corroborates Max's view of Duse as a "personality," the very opposite of a great actress. Shortly before her death, Duse appeared in New York as Mrs. Alving in *Ghosts,* and Stark Young wrote on November 6, 1923:

> In the course of the writing, a provincialism and drabness of [Ibsen's] mind more than once appears; Mrs. Alving and the dramatist are now and again insistent and parochial and without imagination. Duse has no great opinion of Mrs. Alving, for one reason because, as she said to me, Mrs. Alving is a liar, to herself and to others. But Duse from her very first entrance put distinction into the part. She was a great lady . . . Ibsen's Mrs. Alving now and again falls into platitude, stubborn and prim. Duse turns such passages into what is not obvious platitude but passionate memory. . . .

This is bad business. The prima donna clearly knew that she was "improving" on what Ibsen had written. Because Duse was a great lady, Mrs. Alving too must become one. Even assuming that Ibsen was somehow at fault (a point that Young, perhaps under the influence of Duse, is all too ready to concede), it is not the performer's job to make up for the author's lapses, least of all when the author is a great playwright deliberately portraying a less than admirable woman. The actress who places herself above the part she plays, who makes the part come to her rather than the other way around, is a personality, a star, and something less than an artist in the true sense.

All this by way of demonstrating the relativity of histrionic talent, even the greatest. It would almost appear that beauty, or at least allure, is a less debatable commodity. Consider the assets of Duse's great rival, Sarah Bernhardt, so derided and subordinated to Duse by Shaw (in his column of June 15, 1895), and generally held to be more of a character, personality and inspired ham than a profound and versatile actress. Though her very admirers tended to admit that Sarah was always playing Sarah, even her detractors could not deny her a potently feminine, erotic appeal. Shortly before her death at seventy-eight, Bernhardt was visited by Colette, who was to recall in *Trait pour trait* this vignette of the old actress pouring coffee:

> Her amputated body no longer counted, stuffed into a somber cloth with great folds. But the white face, the little hands, still shone like crumpled flowers. I did not tire of contemplating the blue of her eyes, which changed according to the movements—so lively still—of that imperious and small head. . . . I consign here, with respect, one of the last stances of the near-octogenarian tragedienne: the delicate and faded hand offering the full cup; the floral azure of the eyes, so young in a network of wrinkles; the quizzical and laughing coquetry of the bent head, and that irreducible eagerness to please, please still, please even unto the doors of death.

I have been reading and rereading lately a number of tributes to the grace and loveliness of various performers. The one that moved me most was Gerhart Hauptmann's 1927 necrologue for the celebrated German actress Agnes Sorma (1863–1927), whom even the usually prosaic *Oxford Companion to the Theatre* describes as "a beautiful woman, with dark hair and eyes, and a charming smile." It is this smile that Hofmannsthal recalled as his one indelible memory of Sorma. "Her smile," he wrote, "which shimmered over all of her expressions, could intensify into Circean witchery or become wholly ironic and cool; she smiled as a tragic heroine, until the smile went numb under the horror of fate, but did not vanish entirely—and as Mrs. Alving, this wonderful face let us behold the rarest thing that can be seen: the smile of despair." Yet it was not the neoromantic Hofmannsthal who said the finest thing about Sorma, but the naturalist, or ex-naturalist, Hauptmann:

> This dear and great artist was, so to speak, a queen of comeliness. Whether one saw her in society or on the stage, one felt fortunate: the Graces had kissed her in the cradle. For all that, she was elemental as a performer, but then, again, it remained her greatest appeal to stay confined, even in the strongest outbursts of passion, within the boundaries of sheer womanly loveliness (*selbst bei den stärksten Ausbrüchen der*

Leidenschaft in den Grenzen des schlechthin Weiblich-Schönen gebunden zu sein).

Praising her admirableness as woman, artist and lady, Hauptmann concluded that "the type of this woman has always been a rare and happy accident."

The importance of an actress of such consummate grace is twofold. First for the playwright, who often models his characters on the performers available to him. We know that even Shakespeare shaped some of his characters for specific actors, and when, with the Restoration, women mounted the stage, actresses became paramount influences on the playwright's imagination. Two of the finest parts in Restoration drama, for example, were created directly for actresses who aroused in the authors more than theatrical interest: Elizabeth Barry was the begetter of Otway's Belvidera, and Anne Bracegirdle the prototype for Congreve's Millamant. But let me skip to modern times and quote Giraudoux's comment in *Visitations* (1947):

> The actor is not only an interpreter, he is an inspirer; he is the living mannequin by whose means many authors personify a vision as yet vague; and the great actor: a great inspirer. . . . It is thus that my Alcmène in *Amphitryon 38*, thus that my Judith spared me all hesitation by slipping, from the days of their births, into actresses who immediately gave them complexions, appearances, voices—the former into Valentine Tessier, the latter into Elizabeth [*sic*] Bergner.

But what sort of heroines would your Sandy Dennises or your Sada Thompsons inspire? Yet even when a dramatist does not have a specific actress as the model for a heroine, an attractive interpreter can still serve him well. "I was always of the conviction," wrote Frank Wedekind in *Schauspielkunst* (1910), "that *Erdgeist* played as I conceived it, and without the interpretation of Gertrud Eysoldt, would have aroused ten years ago only displeasure and moral indignation. Frau Eysoldt played precisely that kind of woman and beauty that were, at the time, the prevailing literary-artistic taste in Berlin."

Which brings me to the importance of the lovely actress

to the theatergoing public. Clearly, audiences are impressed and influenced by the beauty of actresses, and model themselves upon them. Today this aspect of suasion has been largely preempted by the film actress, who is seen by many more spectators, and by especially large numbers of the far more influenceable young. There is something else, however, that a stage actress can do more powerfully than her screen competitor; the nature of this comes out charmingly in a contemporary evocation of Anne Bracegirdle by Anthony Aston: *

> She was of a lovely Height, with dark-brown Hair and Eyebrows, black sparkling Eyes, and a fresh blushy Complexion; and, whenever she exerted herself, had an involuntary Flushing in her Breast, Neck and Face, having continually a chearful Aspect, and a fine set of even white Teeth; never making an *Exit*, but that she left the Audience in an Imitation of her pleasant Countenance.

There is a sense in which the "chearful Aspect" of physical beauty and charm is conveyed by the living presence of an actress even to the most moribund of audiences.

I have argued on various occasions for the need in our theater for actresses winning both as performers and as women. But in these women's lib times, when such views are promptly dubbed sexist, I have been consistently misunderstood and excoriated either by feminists or by other readers who, often because of their own unsightliness, bristle at the mention of actors' physiques. Yet it seems perspicuous and ungainsayable to me: the actor or actress performs with everything he or she has, including face and body. If that face and body cannot move us with their comeliness or nobility, the performer is just as much at fault as if he or she were insufficient in *mimesis*, diction, deportment, timing or what have you. When, in *New York* magazine, I attacked Zoë Caldwell as Colette for being too fat and charmless for the part, and when I further questioned the desirability of her baring one vast, pendulous breast (she was nursing at the time), the brouhaha this aroused was

---

* Quoted in J. H. Wilson's delightful *All the King's Ladies* (Chicago, 1958), a book that has much to say about my present subject. See in particular the chapter entitled "The Actress and the Play."

deafening; letters poured in to the editors demanding my dismissal, my head, my eternal damnation. Over and over, the point was made—as it was later even in street-corner discussions—that an actress's looks have nothing to do with her performance, which is all a critic is allowed to review.

This narrow outlook bears out two failures of the popular—and, for that matter, critical—view of theater and theatrical criticism. This view is basically anti-aesthetic, addressing itself only to technical aspects of a performance and perhaps to a few selected attributes of the performer's personality. What remains ignored is the substratum: the man or woman up there on the stage. One might with equal right discuss what a sculptor has hewed and chiseled, but ignore the material he chose to work in. Thus the portrait bust of a fair Scandinavian girl done in darkest basalt would look, to put it mildly, peculiar, however deftly executed. (A related issue here is the insensitivity, innate or cultivated, of audiences to black actors in white roles —the blithe acceptance, for example, of a Negro Joan of Arc or King Lear, as if such casting did not produce unsuitable, disturbing implications.) For historical, psychological or aesthetic reasons, an actor must look the part he is playing: Quasimodo should not have the lineaments of Adonis, and Beatrice-Joanna should not be a harridan.

Obviously, the unprepossessing actress can play character parts; no one in his right mind would demand beauty from the witches in *Macbeth*. But are you a more enlightened, civilized, sensitive spectator if you do not boggle at an aged, fat, dish-faced Juliet, or are you in fact an insensitive clod, oblivious to aesthetic values? Obviously, acting that is so great that it makes you forget all else does exist, but it is comparatively rare; even when Duse, in advanced age, played younger parts without make-up and with her gray locks showing, a good many theatergoers were unable to suspend their disbelief. Others, to be sure, did so. Most performers, however, are not endowed with histrionic gifts able to overshadow all else, and had therefore better look to their appearances; often this involves no more than an actress's keeping trim, taking care of herself, and showing some taste in hair style and clothes.

Of course, there is always the reader who fulminates, "What

right have you to decide who is or is not good-looking enough for a given part?" This is a perfectly otiose question, and makes no more sense than asking a critic what right he has to criticize plays, stagecraft or scenery. It is a question stemming from that benighted notion, which apparently will never die, that criticism can somehow be objective, factual, scientific—rather than subjective, impressionistic, artistic. Or it may be part of that even more defunct but, alas, unburiable delusion that criticism should be constructive—i.e., make everybody feel good. The truth is simply that a critic is a man or woman of good taste (whatever that means exactly), and such taste must be presumed to extend to physiognomies, bodies and limbs as much as to facial play, gestures, sound of voice, delivery of lines, and grace or gracelessness of movement.

A seemingly more sophisticated and cogent objection would have it that an actress cannot help being miscast: she needs work to make a living and cannot argue with the director about her suitability for the part she is offered. On closer inspection, this argument seldom holds water. The kind of part requiring good looks—say, Desdemona or Lydia Languish or Hilda Wangel—is rarely forced upon some deserving novice who has all the qualifications save the physical ones. Such roles are usually given to established actresses, popular favorites, producers' or directors' mistresses or wives (Zoë Caldwell, for instance, is married to Robert Whitehead, who produced *Colette*); occasionally they may also be given to talented newcomers. If a successful established actress is offered such a part, what prevents her from declining it and getting something else? And if a newcomer is to be chosen, why can't it be one who has the physical qualifications too? The supply of performers is far in excess of the demand, and a director can afford to be choosy. Still, if he picks an ill-favored countenance over a radiant one, should we not blame him rather than the owner of the unfortunate face? Perhaps, but will it make much difference if the review reads "Mr. X. is to be castigated for casting the homely Miss Y. as Juliet"? As soon stick to the simple statement of Miss Y.'s physical unsuitability; it is no more devastating and saves space.

I spoke earlier of two failures in the popular and critical

sensibilities that cause outcries against assessments of an actor's physique. So far I have discussed the sheer aesthetic failure of not responding adequately to beauty and ugliness. But there is also an ethical misconception: the notion that criticism is a social act—social in the sense of good manners in public behavior. If I would not consider going up to Miss Y. at a party and making some remark about her plainness, what gives me the right to do this in a published critique, where it must hurt even more? This is a gross confusion of party-going with theatergoing, of the drawing room with the playhouse, the coffee table with the critic's desk. "Discourteous" and "rude" are valid terms as they pertain to social behavior, but irrelevant and meaningless in criticism. There too tones vary, and some may be more felicitous or efficacious than others. But the critic who has, for example, a Barbra Streisand, Liza Minnelli, Sandy Dennis or Zohra Lampert to contend with may well be pushed beyond all endurance and retaliate in less than refined fashion. If the concept of manners is to be invoked at all, it might apply as much to the obnoxiously self-serving displays with which certain repellent actresses assault our sensibilities. The same goes for actors, too, but one is always more sensitive to the gracefulness or disgracefulness of the opposite sex, aesthetics and sexuality being more closely related than is commonly admitted.

The trouble, in large part, is open admissions. There have always been open admissions for performers in this country: no one ever had to undergo any sort of winnowing by a Royal Conservatory or State Academy of Dramatic Arts, where the Mrs. Worthingtons of this land would be told not to put their daughters on the stage, or the daughters themselves would be so informed. Obviously looks would not be the main criterion, but neither would they be completely overlooked. Failing beauty, of course, there is always the alternative of charm, but that most elusive of qualities is no less infrequent on the New York stage. It is perhaps best defined by Rilke, who wrote this about Duse to his patroness, Princess Marie von Thurn und Taxis: "She magnifies without a stage, without a play, quotidian, unrefined life; the small, hasty, temporary happen-

ing comes into its own in her bearing, goes beyond itself—
would be awed by seeing itself there and would stay, stand
still, and no longer pass by." This was in July of 1912, when
Eleonora was fifty-three, and we must discount a measure of
poet's and adorer's exaggeration, but can we imagine a contemporary American poet, however impassioned, writing anything like this about Maureen Stapleton?

This is an élitist notion: heroic parts only for the beautiful.
But then, in art everything is élitist: anybody (as we see) can
become President of the United States, but not everybody can
be a poet, writer or leading lady, though there is much in our
supposedly democratic but actually mass-oriented culture that
tries to subvert this truth. There is something particularly
horrible about an out-and-out plain woman carrying on onstage
as if she were a raving beauty: it is so utterly unconvincing,
presumptuous and dishonest that in a sensitive spectator it
produces not only aesthetic revulsion but also moral indignation.

I once took a very pretty actress to a production of *The
Seagull.* We were watching a gifted but plain woman play
Arkadina. My companion pointed out that Miss M. had no
idea of what it is like to be a beautiful woman, or even to
have been one when young: it is something no unattractive
woman really knows. For when a woman is beautiful or sexy,
it produces a kind of assurance—at best a calm, at worst a blasé
condescension—that no homely woman can fully experience,
comprehend and convey. A homely actress is always driven
to *act* beautiful, and this is precisely what no beautiful woman
ever does. But suppose the homely actress elects merely to
be herself; once again, beauty is not achieved.

The preceding remarks are, to an extent, occasioned by
Maureen Stapleton's appearance as Georgie in a revival of
Clifford Odets' *The Country Girl,* directed by John Houseman
for Washington's new Kennedy Center, then transferred to
New York for a "limited engagement." What possible reason
could there have been for reviving this poor and by now completely irrelevant play, which its own author considered a
potboiler? It was written at the end of Odets' career, when that

dubious wave of thirties leftist enthusiasm and passionate, sentimental overwriting had long since spent itself, and Odets stood revealed for what he was: a well-meaning, mildly skillful hack, like the rest of our thirties dramatists. A hack who had lost his verve: even in 1950 this play about the rehabilitation of an aging, drunken actor by a young director who believes in him and by a tough, long-suffering wife seemed an unrewarding subject clumsily handled. Neither all that stuff about the mystique of the theater, nor the backstage intrigues, nor the limp love triangle Odets perfunctorily threw in had much interest even then. We never find out what drove the actor to drink in the first place, and we do not come to like him sufficiently to care about whether he'll make it, or whether the wife he emotionally exploits and also maligns will choose to stay with him. Still less do we care about the unconvincing semblance of a nascent love between the wife and the director.

But the ultimate absurdity is the present casting of Miss Stapleton as Georgie, the wife. Though middle-aged, Georgie is supposed to be still attractive. Her husband passes her off as a former Miss America, a story for which the canny director, even before he becomes interested in her, readily falls. On several occasions various people comment on Georgie's good looks, and we are treated to a scene in which the young director passionately seizes and kisses her. With Maureen Stapleton in the role, this looks like the unbelievable turning into the perverted. For the actress is one of the homeliest—perhaps, in fact, *the* homeliest—on Broadway. She presents a large, amorphous body out of which protrude flipperlike limbs and a face without a single redeeming feature. Whereas classical proportions would have the head go seven to seven-and-a-half times into the length of the entire human being, some on-the-spot calculations with my pen as yardstick revealed Miss Stapleton's head (hairdo, I admit, included) to go only five or five-and-a-half times into her total extension. Add to this the posture of a Michel Simon, a gait more suited to the bowling alley than to the stage, a gin-soaked voice whose range may not exceed a cricket's, an accent that might wait on you at Woolworth's, and you have the portrait of one of America's leading stage actresses.

The scene in which George Grizzard, who looks young and handsome, grabs and kisses Miss Stapleton was, I write it advisedly, rough sailing for my stomach. No doubt women as unprepossessing get kissed in this world, but it happens among four walls and between two consenting adults. Remove the fourth wall, invite an audience, charge admission, and you have something halfway between a freak show and a public nuisance. The fact that it is all lauded by critics and applauded by audiences is to my mind only further proof of our cultural, artistic and aesthetic decadence—if further proof were needed.

Consider: the great shrine of culture for Washington and the nation, the Kennedy Center, opens with Leonard Bernstein's *Mass,* a piece whose eclectic, mindless vulgarity perfectly matches the building that houses it. In charge of the Center is Roger Stevens, a real-estate millionaire and heavy contributor to the Democratic Party; a former Broadway producer of no particular taste, he was put in charge of cultural affairs by L.B.J., and his public utterances were worthy of Dwight Eisenhower. The Kennedy Center was immediately up to its neck in labor trouble, the stagehands' union having squeezed out of Stevens a contract whose terms were a new height in chicanery—more like blackmail. Since then, the Center has housed a number of questionable cultural offerings designed especially for the needs of the uncommitted middlebrow. One of these is John Houseman's revival of *The Country Girl.*

The idea was to put on something hick-dazzling and burgher-approved. "Next only to *Golden Boy . . . The Country Girl* was Odets' most successful play," writes Gerald Weales in his Odets monograph. I suspect that the reason for this was the perfect casting of the original production. As the ex-star, Paul Kelly, an understated movie actor with an ascetic, tormented, Hibernian face, conveyed admirably both excessive consumption of liquids and insufficient ingestion of solids; as the director, Steven Hill, a fleshy, dark, Mediterranean type, was voluble, mercurial, boyishly ardent—the perfect antithesis of Kelly's desiccation. In the middle stood Uta Hagen: quiet, repressed but smoldering, with a strength that seemed to surface after traveling a great internal distance, but then bursting out in triumph and, above all, with style. She was a handsome woman, a trifle too masculine perhaps to be beautiful (Michelangelo would have painted her with pleasure), with a solidity of build and forcefulness of gaze that were commanding and would be irresistible to such weaker men as the actor and director in the play. The performing of this trio was real ensemble work, the whole appreciably greater than the sum of the parts Odets had written.

For the play is poorly structured, pedestrian, trivial, unsurprising; moreover, its language is banal even for Odets. Cliché jostles cliché, the simplest observations are peddled as insights, the theater is presented in that irritatingly phony light of yes-what-grubby-hustling-but-oh-what-glory-too, and the minor characters are stereotypes, while the major ones are fuzzy and uncompelling. Yet John Houseman (whose recent volume of theatrical reminiscences, *Run-through,* shows an attitude toward theater not unlike that of the play) evidently perceived *The Country Girl* as a middle-class classic ripe for revival with suitably crowd-pleasing stars. Well, Jason Robards is boring as the actor, repeating for the umpteenth time his combination of cuddlesomeness and bluster. Twice in his career Robards has been impressive: in *The Iceman Cometh* and in *Long Day's Journey into Night;* the rest of the time he has merely rehashed bits and pieces from those two performances with ever-decreasing returns. As the director, George Grizzard fares equally unwell; he is a fascinating actor when his agile, somewhat femininely insinuating personality can wiggle into an appropriately oblique and various role. His voice, for instance, has a slightly querulous tone, but can also slither with a sinisterly serpentine grace, and he looks like a slightly depraved matinee idol. All this is wasted on or misplaced in the part of the director. And then there is Maureen Stapleton, droning, lumbering, fishwifing on. Time and again she even misinterprets her lines, usually turning something serious into farce, and sabotaging what little pathos the play might have.

(Here, of course, the director is equally to blame.) But the audience, at least on opening night, chortled, whooped and bravoed as if witnessing the première of a masterpiece whose last performance would coincide with Judgment Day.

The reviews were commensurate and predictable. Clive Barnes in the *Times* danced his famous eggshell minuet, having it, as usual, both ways with "a great theatrical melodrama . . . I exulted in its sheer vulgar theatricality." There was "grand-slam virtuoso acting" in this "splendid, no-holds-barred, no-bars-held [???] performance" in which the "superb" Miss Stapleton "alone would justify Odets." We were informed that "Broadway is illuminated with these obvious but thrilling fireworks." In his Sunday column, Walter Kerr wrote, "Thank God someone remembers—or once did—what the shape of a dramatic tug-of-war looks like." "The eruptions," he concluded, "are face-to-face, hand-to-hand, honest enough as psychology, tub-thumpingly gratifying as showmanship." With all those unbarred holds, unheld bars, tugged ropes and thumped tubs, here clearly was the ultimate cross between Barnum & Bailey and Spike Jones. But my favorite comments, as usual, came from Richard Watts of the *Post:* ". . . lessons in what acting at its best can be," Watts warbled; "the American theatre has no players of loftier distinction." If the latter remark be true—and it just may be—God pity the American theater: so much loftiness can lift it right off the map into oblivion.

HOW PERSONAL
CAN A CRITIC GET?

(1971)

The other day a painter friend of mine called to complain about a review he had just received. "I don't mind his disliking my pictures—that's his privilege—but what do you think of the personal attack?" I had read the review in question, and said that it might be unfair (I had not seen the show), but that I had not noticed anything personal in it. "He called me a dull artist!" the painter recited with rancorous emphasis. And I marveled at the fact that my friend, an intelligent man and by no means ungifted painter, should have so lost his sense of proportion and, worse yet, humor.

Last night I was reading Tyrone Guthrie's posthumously published book *On Acting*. In it, among other things, he votes for Bernard Shaw as the greatest dramatic critic in the English language; he then proceeds to quote Shaw at length on the subject of Sudermann's Magda as played consecutively and contrastingly by Bernhardt and Duse. Now, Shaw much preferred Duse the actress to Bernhardt the star, and from Sir Tyrone's comments on stars like Gary Cooper and Barbra Streisand, it is clear that he too valued good acting more highly than stardom. Yet after reproducing what seem to me Shaw's delightfully ironic but by no means offensive comments on Madame Sarah (e.g., "Her lips are like a newly-painted pillar-box; her cheeks, right up to the languid lashes, have the bloom and surface of a peach . . ."), Guthrie observes that this "marvelous description of star acting" is "rather too cruel, too subjectively coloured by the writer's personal antipathy to Bernhardt." There's that word again: *personal*. Guthrie considers references like the one to the newly painted pillar-box "gratuitously insulting." "But perhaps," he continues, "it is rather comforting that a critic so pre-eminent and a man so kind and fastidious as Bernard Shaw should, now and then, like the rest of us, sink to cheapness and vulgarity . . . to making his column more readable by personal ribaldry [there it is again!] at the expense of those who cannot answer back."

I had always thought of Sir Tyrone as a director, an often inspired one (his productions of Chekhov, for example, or his *Tamburlaine*), and a sometimes cheap and vulgar one (his updated *Troilus and Cressida*, for instance), but upon reading these comments, I guessed that he might have also been an actor. For only an actor who had felt the critics' sting could have so overreacted to Shaw. And sure enough, Guthrie's first five years in the theater were, I found, spent as an actor. "Cannot answer back," indeed (quite aside from the pleonasm)! Nowadays there is hardly a columnist who doesn't seize upon an actor's replies to his critics, and editors gleefully bustle to turn over space to the "maligned" actor—provided only that he pull no punches in getting even.

But this is not the only way in which an actor or director or playwright fights his critics. To be sure, if critic A attacks him, there are always critics B and C to defend him. But if A is more read and influential, yet in this case grossly unjust, surely the unfair attack will boomerang on the barbarian. The man who spits at Praxiteles' Venus is really spitting in his own face. The beauty and nobility of the statue, which does not spit back, remain unimpugned. "There lives a freshness deep down in me," writes the great Swedish poet Gunnar Ekelöf, "that no one can deny me, not even I myself—." True artistic talent is a marvelously unimpeachable thing, which not even some of the self-destructive things theater people do—far more deleterious than the most ill-considered review—can obliterate.

But "personal attacks"—what are these personal attacks? Does anyone really want criticism to be impersonal? Written by a computer? Of course, among the unenlightened, we still hear that old toothless saw "objective criticism," debunked though the notion has been by every critic worth his salt and pepper. Geometry perhaps can be objective and impersonal, as can xerography—but criticism? It is one of the most personal, most subjective arts—just like the arts of acting, directing or playwriting. Like them, it may fail to persuade, or it may sway only in a demagogic, public-besotting manner. But if a critic can play upon the public's vices to the point of making some vicious, undeserved attack stick, is this his fault only, or is the public just as guilty? And is the reviewer who likes everything *less* personal than he who carps? Is the man who gushes about Sandy Dennis or the genius of Neil Simon being impersonal and objective?

The real danger, as I see it, is the pursuit of an impossible *im*personality. For example, in the recent Central Park production of *Timon of Athens,* the churlish malcontent Apemantus was played by Michael Dunn, who is not only a good actor but also a dwarf. So afraid were most of our reviewers of becoming "personal" by merely mentioning the fact of Dunn's subnormal stature that the public could not be enlightened by them about the casting gaffe involved. For Apemantus is an antipathetic character whose misanthropic rantings should seem exaggerated and finally contemptible even to Timon, the true misanthrope. But when Dunn played the part, his bitterness seemed ipso facto justified, and a sizable portion of the play was warped.

"Still," someone will sputter, "insults! Has the critic the right to insult an actor?" It seems to me that a genuinely atrocious piece of acting—or, for that matter, writing or directing—is (in the critic's opinion, admittedly, but then everything he writes is in his opinion) an insult to God and man. To forgive may indeed be divine; to retaliate seems to me only human.

BLACK PLAYS,
WHITE REVIEWERS

(1971)

I HAVE NOT SEEN as much black theater as I would have liked to. My space here is limited, and Broadway and off-Broadway have the right to preempt it. Much of black theater stays in an area that could be called off-off-off-Broadway, except that black theater, quite rightly, does not see the theatrical world as a kind of Ptolemaic universe, with the Great White Sun of Broadway at the center, and everything else revolving around it. But I have a primary obligation in this non-avant-garde publication I write for to cover what is more accessible to the majority of its readers and, frankly, to me.

There are, moreover, many kinds of critics. There is, for example, the scout type, who is always out there at the frontier, looking for the new. There is another group—I shudder to call them the curators but I may have to—who are chiefly concerned with evaluating the more settled, established, classical theater. I may be one of these—though, I hasten to add, I much prefer serving the Establishment Theater as a gadfly—or if as a curator, at least as a more demanding, intransigent one than most. I prefer, then, to wait till playwrights and productions come to me, rather than to go ferreting them out at their remote sources. Doubtless I lose out on some good things, but I am also spared a good many bad ones. In the end, I suppose, it balances out, and the worthier drama does eventually reach at least off-Broadway, if not Broadway; this goes for black playwrights as much as for white ones.

What I absolutely do not hold with, however, is the opinion of at least two prominent white critics. According to this view, serious white critics should not be reviewing black theater at all. The reason is partly that whites are not supposed to share and understand the Negro experience, and partly that the white theater has evolved way beyond the fledgling black one. As a result, Negro playwrights are supposedly just beginning to discover things that white dramatists have long since outgrown. But for Negro playwrights and audiences this antediluvian stuff is a brave new world, and who are we, as one such white critic said to me, to spoil their fun by telling them how dreadfully old hat and feeble their theater is?

Now, whereas the black theater people would undoubtedly find the second argument offensive, they would, I am certain, applaud the first. I myself disagree with both and find them equally patronizing, parochial and reprehensible. Surely the world we live in is too large for any of us to have exactly the same experiences as others, or to know about them in detail. But equally surely, the world is too small for us not to recognize parallels, kinships and a common ground with all sorts of people, wherever they may be. And the world of art is both smaller and larger than the physical world: smaller, because it brings the tiniest details of any existence into microscopic focus and magnification; larger, because it enables our understanding of, and compassion for, others to soar to greater heights than a mere spaceship can attain. If black playwrights can reach only black audiences, they would not be able to survive even economically, let alone as universal artists, to which estate it is the right and duty of every true dramatist to aspire.

As for the other argument: shall there be one set of rules for white plays, and another for black ones? Shall white critics review only white plays (and possibly yellow ones; they are perfectly willing to discourse on Kabuki), while black critics review only black ones, and perhaps dark brown and red as well? Shall color barriers be abolished everywhere but in criticism? Shall the ghetto mentality be perpetuated in the theater? To all these questions, my answer is a resounding no. I reject equally the Sunday *Times*'s practice of having a Negro guest reviewer pronounce on black plays (aren't the two white ones good enough? and if the black man is good, why not have him review the white plays as well?) and that absurd letter the black theater people circulated and had printed in the *Times*, angrily protesting Mel Gussow's reference to a certain black theatrical enterprise as "parochial." I did not see it, and it may or may not have seemed parochial to me, but that is not the point. If a white reviewer perceives a black effort as parochial, it is his right to say so, and the high-handed and hate-filled (as well as hardly literate) letter of protest made poor sense. I am sorry that Gussow honored it with a reply—and not a very good one at that.

There can be only the same standard of excellence in the theater, however you choose to define it, for all plays and performances: white, black or purple. Though our black playwrights are starting from behind, they cannot ask for quarter from white critics; this would be as much beneath their dignity as beneath ours. There are talented men and women in the Negro theater, and they are moving fast. Their plays may come to resemble white drama more or less, but they will become better and better—they will be good and, in due time, great. Then there will be no more talk of black or white theater, only of theater—even if individual styles continue, I hope, to be vastly divergent.

CHARM: INDEFINABLE
BUT INDISPENSABLE

(1968)

As JUDGE for last year's Yale Festival of Undergraduate Drama, I mentioned a quality almost indispensable to an actor: charm. In the audience was a drama teacher and contributing editor to our leading drama review who jumped on me for giving students such fictitious and useless criteria as charm. Since he and his publication are signally deficient in this quality, there was no point in pursuing the matter, particularly as charm is even less definable than dispensable.

That charm is virtually impossible to define, or that its allocation gives rise to disagreement, does not make it illusory or mythical. Who can define poetry, as opposed to mere verse? Yet there is no doubt of its existence. Thus, hardly anyone would dispute that actors like Cary Grant, Henry Fonda, Albert Finney, and actresses like Anouk Aimée, Katharine Hepburn, Dorothy Tutin have charm—whatever else they may have or not have. It is an elusive, even perishable quality. Some, more often women, lose it as they grow older (Judy Garland, Margaret Sullavan, Joan Fontaine—but also James Stewart, Peter Sellers, Jean-Louis Barrault); others, more often men, develop it further with age (Pierre Brasseur, Marcello Mastroianni, Dirk Bogarde, Laurence Olivier—but also Edwige Feuillère, Sophia Loren, Laurette Taylor). Some actors have it much more onstage than on screen (Richard Burton, Jason Robards); with others (Olivia de Havilland, Richard Basehart), it is the reverse.

Good looks can help, but are by no means essential to it.

Think of the charm of Michel Simon, Celia Johnson, Peter Ustinov, Shirley Booth, Ray Bolger. Nor is it a question of age: what charm there is in Ethel Griffies, Cathleen Nesbitt, Alan Webb, Roland Culver. Some performers have managed quite nicely without a trace of it—Jack Palance, Joan Crawford, Barbara Stanwyck; others have capitalized on imitations or even travesties of it—Robert Goulet, Gregory Peck, Helen Hayes, Ruth Gordon.

Certain nationalities seem to abound in it. Think of British actors like Leslie Howard, Rex Harrison, Noël Coward, George Sanders, David Niven, Peter Finch, Peter O'Toole; and of all those French and Italian actresses too numerous to mention. I would guess that in a country where great culture is combined with repression of the female, women are forced to develop their charm to get ahead; I surmise also that a highly sophisticated upper class that sets the tone and that, at least tacitly, fosters homosexuality, elicits charm in men, even heterosexual ones. But there may be political or genetic factors involved; Germany and Russia have produced as little charm in the performing arts as in life.

Charm is a hidden ingredient. It is like that *je ne sais quoi* without which you are not a great chef even if you have committed the entire *Larousse gastronomique* to memory. It is an ease, poise, self-assurance; perhaps even a slight but unpremeditated eccentricity. It is the quality of pleasing without— at least noticeably—trying to. Though it may come from background, culture, sophistication, often this is not so: consider such essential nonsophisticates as Tracy, Bogart, Steve McQueen, Robert Redford, Godfrey Cambridge. Even the shyness and awkwardness of Barbara Harris or Gene Wilder are charming: openness and vulnerability will take the place of poise.

Movement and deportment have something to do with charm—if it is lithe, springy, rhythmical yet unselfconscious. Nevertheless, there is also a bumbling charm. Vocally, charm tends to lie in variety without affectation; yet here again, how charming the throaty, almost hoarse, monotone of a Joan Greenwood or Diane Cilento! What it comes down to, ultimately, is power of suggestion: in comic situations, a certain twinkle that suggests a smile without quite being one; in sad ones, conveying the tears inherent in things without having to resort to one's own.

One of the most charming gestures I have ever seen onstage took place when Olivier, as Astrov in *Uncle Vanya* some twenty years ago, broke the tragic mood of Elena's imminent departure by suddenly snapping his fingers. Seeing him do the part again quite recently, I could hardly wait for that diapason-changing snap. It didn't come. There was charm in that abstention, too: what was charming in a rather youthful Astrov would not have been so in a middle-aged one. For charm is also a sense of the appropriate.

New York culture, and with it the New York stage, are not greatly aware of, appreciative of, or conducive to charm. There may be ethnic explanations for this, as there certainly are others stemming from hard, desperate competitiveness, and the insecurity it generates. Though I am convinced that charm cannot be taught, I do believe that it can be encouraged, educed, nurtured. Unfortunately, Method acting, which still dominates our theater, emphasizes the very opposite of charm; and avant-garde acting techniques tend simply to ignore it. In last year's telecast of the Actors Studio *Three Sisters*, one saw Kim Stanley, Geraldine Page, Shelley Winters and Sandy Dennis rubbing shoulders and mannerisms: enough charmlessness to cause a short circuit, if only the TV tube were more cybernetically advanced.

But charm exists even here. In fact, a number of our actors subsist on charm alone. I could name some, but that would be ungracious—indeed, uncharming.

IN PRAISE OF
PROFESSIONALISM

(1972)

I DO NOT OFTEN AGREE with Peter Brook, but I subscribe wholeheartedly to this passage from his *The Empty Space:* "Incompetence is the vice, the condition and the tragedy of the world's theater on any level: for every good [work] there are scores of others . . . betrayed by a lack of elementary skills. The techniques of staging, designing, speaking, walking across the stage, sitting—even listening—just aren't sufficiently known; compare the little it takes—except luck—to get work in many of the theaters of the world with the minimum level of skill demanded say in piano playing: think of how many thousands of music teachers in thousands of small cities can play all the notes of the most difficult passages of Liszt or sight-read Scriabin. Compared with the simple ability of musicians, most of our work is at amateur level most of the time. A critic will see far more incompetence than competence in his theatergoing."

True, and still more horribly so if the critics themselves cannot distinguish between competence and incompetence. Take an awesome recent example: the raves heaped on Susan Tyrrell for her performance as Oma in John Huston's barely mediocre film, *Fat City.* Vincent Canby declared this one of the best portrayals of a drunk on screen; other reviewers were scarcely thriftier with their superlatives. Yet what Miss Tyrrell does in her first major film role is exactly what she has been doing for years onstage: sheer self-indulgence; a slight exaggeration of what is (cf. an interview in the *Times*, August 13) apparently her offstage personality (if she is ever offstage); and an exact replica of all her stage work from *Futz* to *The Time of Your Life*.

What this proves about our film reviewers—some of whom also go to the theater—is, at the very least, their forgetfulness; otherwise, they would have to remember this actress performing the same ritual grossnesses from role to role. Some reviewers, however, are so unprofessional themselves that they would hail a crass routine—or exhibition—precisely for its sameness, just as Radio City Music Hall patrons daily applaud the identical artless high kicks of the Rockettes. Any sharp observer should be able to tell on first exposure that what Miss Tyrrell does is not acting but acting out, not drama but psychodrama. As long ago as in 1773, Diderot's *Paradoxe sur le comédien* clarified the difference between mere displays of derailment and its artistic enactment.

Of course it is the reviewers and the public that must bear the blame even more than the unhappy performer, as often as not perverted by Lee Strasberg or some other Method mentor into spewing forth "private moments" rather than learning how to move or develop his voice. In the eighteenth century, let me once again remind the reader, one of the fashionable entertainments was visiting madhouses. Thus, in that 1771 best seller, Henry Mackenzie's *The Man of Feeling*, we read, "Of those things called Sights, in London, which every stranger is supposed desirous to see, Bedlam is one." And it is thither that someone takes the protagonist "after having accompanied him to several other shows." Do not, however, hasten to condemn an age that considered the madhouse a "show"; it may be no worse than one whose shows can often be considered madhouses.

The trouble with hysterical performing, still very much in vogue, is its sheer amateurish inefficiency. A fine piece of acting offers us not merely a character but also a glass partition from behind which we can study and evaluate that character. Call this, if you like, the alienation effect; I prefer calling it professionalism. It means either not pulling us into the part so deep that we drown in it, or pulling us in even deeper so that we emerge on the other side, the glass partition becoming, in this case, a glass tunnel. Whichever, it means not allowing us to fall sloppily in love with the character or, worse yet, performer to the extent of becoming blind to the author's intentions concerning that character. In no case should the performer's wallowing drag us down to similarly dehumanizing behavior.

This would not be the case if the performer depended on adequate technique rather than on regurgitating his inner chaos, as the Method and some of its derivatives urge him to do. And here Brook's musical analogy is particularly helpful. It is virtually impossible to encounter in the concert hall the amateurishness that hounds one in the theater. First, because without hard study there is no playing an instrument plausibly, whereas ignorant spectators will always be taken in by an actor's spilling out his guts—by which standard real murders or suicides onstage would be the ultimate in acting. Secondly, in the concert hall at least a sizable part of the audience has come because it has survived a process of elimination: it has achieved the maturity, attentiveness and subtlety required to put, say, Bartók and Mahler above Presley and The Stones. It is no ready prey for amateurishness and animalism.

True all-around acting needs the sort of learning and instruction for both of which our society has progressively less patience, culture and understanding. Here, though essentially I agree with that marvelous poet and Ibsen translator, Christian Morgenstern—"One cannot reform the theater without simultaneously reforming the entire spirit of the age"—I must also insist that without small, specific improvements there can be no universal amelioration. Just imagine the gain for the theater if passing some examinations were a prerequisite for becoming an actor. There would be no hordes of starving, unemployed and unemployable actors gumming up the works, and the rest could expect not occasional typecasting, but steady and stimulatingly diversified careers.

A CRITICAL NEED OR TWO

(1969)

THE BASIC PROBLEM with criticism is that it needs a common language. Reviewing needs no such thing. That is why there is so much reviewing and so little criticism. The by now widely recognized difference between a reviewer and a critic is that a reviewer turns out a rapid review for a paper, TV or radio; whereas a critic has time to put a thought or two into his weekly, monthly or quarterly article. But this is a fictitious difference. A man who has standards can uphold them—though probably less cogently and eloquently—even on short notice; a man who hasn't any standards will not excogitate them in a week or in a year. Walter Kerr's distinction—that a reviewer writes for those who don't know the work reviewed, a critic for those who do—merely accounts for differences in tone and strategy, but not for height or lowness of critical demands. My own quip to Brendan Gill, that a critic is any reviewer who does not feel obligated to like at least one thing in ten, describes only the effects, not the essence of criticism.

"In art," wrote Friedrich Dürrenmatt, "one sees, or one is blind; but the proofs of the seeing man *cannot* be valid for the blind one." Now, a common language is a shared way of seeing, just as a common culture and shared frame of reference are a common, universal language. It was relatively easy for men like Pope and Dr. Johnson to be critics, because educated society—and there was only educated society, the rest did not matter—had a common stock of knowledge, common backgrounds, and even, to a large extent, common aspirations.

But if today's critic faults a novel for coming not even within striking distance of, say, Proust, Kafka or Joyce, can he be sure that his readers really know those authors? If he criticizes poetry, what can he assume them to know about metrics and prosody? And if he is a drama critic, dare he suppose that they know their Hazlitt and Shaw, that they have some knowledge of the work of such great actors as Gielgud and Olivier, Jouvet and Barrault, Gustaf Gründgens and Helene Weigel? Can he expect his readers to be familiar with the theories of stage design of Gordon Craig and Adolph Appia, or with the theories of directing of Brecht and Grotowski? No.

But without such a common language, he who writes about theater has, by and large, only this choice: to be a snobbish, impossibly demanding, esoteric and generally unread critic, or a mundane and ultimately useless reviewer.

I would prefer to posit the difference this way: a reviewer is someone who has no expertise, standards or vision beyond those of his readers—or, in the rare case that he has them, keeps them well hidden; a critic is someone who knows, demands and envisions more than most of his readers. A critic, in short, is an artist, a teacher, a philosopher. He writes as well, or nearly, as a novelist, playwright or scriptwriter. He tries to teach his readers all that they have not learned even in college, even in most of their reading, even in most of their humdrum exposure to the art in question. He is enough of a thinker to perceive connections between this play, film, opera, ballet, painting or whatnot and the world and life in general. For all of these reasons he wants his subject to be a work of art, which is to say entertaining but also significant, penetrating and somehow revitalizing—and not *only* a piece of entertainment, which is to say a weapon for killing time.

But the expectation, indeed the demand, at newspapers and magazines is for reviewers, not critics. The reviewer is not to upset the readership with his superior knowledge and standards; more important yet, he is not to upset his editors and publishers. Thus, for example, *The New York Times* has had, in its entire history, only two men whose criteria, background style, and vision qualified them as drama *critics:* Stark

Young and Stanley Kauffmann. Neither of them lasted longer
than a year. Who, after all, *is* the drama reviewer to pan things
that make the editor and his wife, the publisher and his
mother-in-law happy? In his book *The Season: A Candid Look
at Broadway*, William Goldman observes (it is one of the few
pertinent points in a generally questionable work): "Being a
drama critic on Broadway wouldn't keep a decent mind oc-
cupied 10 per cent of the time. So you don't even get sec-
ond-raters." Actually, Goldman, who is himself a bit of a
Broadway playwright, rather embellishes the situation: no-
where near ten per cent of plays and productions could, in
themselves, seriously occupy the mind of a first-rate critic. But
there is the surrounding non-Broadway theater; there are general problems and issues. Even the worst plays can provide
the rare critic with pretexts for brilliant and absorbing speculation.

A publication like the *Times*, however, is terrified by the
thought that its critic might kill nine or more plays out of ten;
it would mean the end of Broadway theater, the demise of
one of New York's chief entertainment industries and tourist
attractions. The fact that a new and better theater might rise
from the ashes of the old, a phoenix from a lot of turkeys, does
not occur to these people; and from an ultraconservative point
of view, and a very middle-class one, they are probably right.
Yet when a commercial, Broadway-oriented writer like Goldman has to reject out of hand so much of what pops up on the
New York stage, things have to change.

Why is it that so much newspaper and magazine reviewing
is not at least a little more efficacious in cleaning up the worst
of the mess? Once again, it is partly because the American
public does not understand what criticism is. First of all,
everybody thinks himself qualified to pass judgment on theater, movies, books and such. Not on music, mind you. That
is a more arcane art, resembling mathematics—and no ordinary citizen would dare tell the scientists what to do. Of
course, a play is not comparable to nuclear physics; nevertheless, in viewing drama, too, there are considerations, such as
quantity of knowledge, sophisticated discrimination, diversi-

fied experience, time spent on meditating about problems of
the theater, that should make the self-appointed critic espouse
a little modesty. Not humility, certainly not silence; just cau-
tion.

Look at all the misconceptions about criticism that are still
flourishing among the public. First, that there is such a thing
as "objective" criticism. You stick a piece of litmus paper into
the play or movie, and if it flushes with delight, the work is
good; if it turns blue with chill, the work is bad. Clearly,
there is no such thing—only the elusive taste and intelligence
of the critic, which, when presented with lucidity and style,
may make an opinion persuasive and therefore authoritative.

Next, the notion that there is such a thing as criticism by
consensus. If the majority of reviewers, or the plurality of
viewers, or all the people at a party agree that this play or
film or piece of sculpture is marvelous, then it is surely worth
seeing. Certainly it may be worth seeing *then,* but that still
does not make it good. Consumer research has no bearing on
art: you cannot buy a play as you would a refrigerator because
the majority of purchasers have found it noiseless, efficient,
easy to clean, and durable. But durability is the clue. The
only test of a work of art is time: will it still be important
twenty-five, fifty, a hundred years from now? Unfortunately,
neither you nor I will be around to verify this. The next-
best alternative is a critic who thinks in long-range terms—if
you can find one; he may be wrong, but at least he will be
wrong on the right track. In any case, you do not read a critic
the way you carry a light in a mine shaft: if the light goes out,
the air is unbreathable. No, you read a critic as a whetstone:
something to sharpen your own understanding on, either by
agreement or disagreement, in a dialogue.

Worst of all is the ancient fallacy that there are such things
as destructive and constructive criticism. Most often this merely
means praise or dispraise of me, agreement or disagreement
with me. Of this attitude, no refutation is possible—or needed.
But there is always the decent, well-meaning soul who would
like you to tell the artist how he should have done it. This is
usually impossible. If the critic could do so, he would have

written the play, or acted that part. And even then, the critic would be his own kind of playwright, his own kind of actor, and the artist under review would justly resent being forced into the critic's mold. But if the critic frankly and aptly expresses what he found wrong or right, he is teaching the intelligent artist quite enough.

Yet whatever the faults of publications and readers may be, the largest part of the blame still must fall on the reviewer. The typical reviewer has a Willy Loman complex: he wants to be liked. Or, to translate that great American disease onto the plane of reviewing, he wants to be known. How? By being quoted in advertisements, on marquees, everywhere. Beware of the "critic" whom you find quoted left and right: "Best show I've seen in years!" "I loved it!" "A masterpiece!" *This* is the way reviewers make names for themselves; do not believe the pretty fiction that it is done by knocking things. Now and then, no doubt, but whereas a specific, spectacular attack may call temporary attention to a critic, in the long run the public feels more comfortable in the heartwarming company of approvers. Just as long as they are also clever enough to throw in a stern word here and there. Recently a reviewer congratulated me for walking out after three minutes on *Whores, Wars and Tin Pan Alley.* "After that," he said, "it gets even worse." A few days later, I saw a highly laudatory quotation from him in the show's advertisements. This incident is far from unique.

The most serious damage of overpraise is not that it may keep a piece of nonsense running longer than it deserves. The real danger is that Crying Wonder can become just as self-defeating as Crying Wolf. There is hardly a reviewer left who hasn't used up and devaluated his entire stock of superlatives. There have been so many miracles, masterworks and unique experiences that the public, duped a thousand times too often, has lost faith in all those workaday wonders. Then what happens when a truly wonderful play or film or composition comes along? It has been discovered that though a single powerful reviewer or a large body of ordinary reviewers in negative agreement can scuttle a show, they are less and less able to sell and save one.

At this point a few readers may be thinking, "This is all good and well, but must everything be art? Is there no room for plain, unpretentious entertainment?" Of course there is, and any responsible critic will try to make allowances for it. But two important considerations present themselves. Much of what is genuinely, generously entertaining is so precisely because it is art: the farces of Courteline and Feydeau, the comedies of Goldoni and Chaplin, the witty critiques of Oscar Wilde and Max Beerbohm. Secondly, art *is* entertaining, as well as something else besides. If you enjoy *As You Like It* and *The Way of the World* more than *Plaza Suite* or *The Front Page*, you will end up with every bit as much entertainment *and* something beyond it. Once you learn to be entertained by brilliant pursuit of truth more than by clever pursuit of success, you will be entertained by *Waiting for Godot* and *Danton's Death* even if they are not conventionally (or at all) cheerful. And you will be entertained less by *Promises, Promises* or *Forty Carats*. Because once the laughter and the tumult of the popular hit are over, you will realize that you have spent your time and money on something that does not linger in and continue to work on your awareness, and does not tell you anything about yourself, your world and the perilous business of living.

YET WHAT THE FUTURE of the theater will be I cannot tell; I know only what I would want it to be. It seems to me that the time has come for the theater to make use of the fact that some (though, alas, not all) hoi polloi have irretrievably defected to the movies and television, and so there is no need to keep wooing them. Instead, the theater can become an aristocratic art. This is not quite the same as a minority art—it does not mean pleasing only ideal readers—but it does mean aiming at the more cultivated and earnest people whom at present the commercial theater has all but lost. It also means accepting on one's own terms those who come along for no better reason than curiosity or snob value. Even snobs may be capable of learning something. But as crowd-pleasers, Broadway and the rest have failed; they must accept this failure and try for something else.

How could this change come about? By having fewer theaters rather than more; by subsidizing only ventures which, because of their seriousness, are apt to lose money (and not expect, as foundations now do, the subsidized theater to become self-supporting in a couple of years); by establishing a National Theater with government support but no strings attached; by instituting further training programs, especially for directors. Whatever else the present American theater may need, it needs directors more. Therefore, any conceivable program for the development of directors—however expensive or slow or hard to come by—should be given top priority. In the end, these directors may even act as midwives for the new drama and, if no such parturition is in sight, give birth themselves.

One other thing. We need critics. Critics with high enough standards to squash Broadway if it is necessary—and I suspect it is. (I don't wish it; I just fear that it may be unavoidable.) Critics who will thus make room for something better—and, inevitably, less profitable at first—to take its place. Let it come from the best of the new and the best of the old. Let it come from the repertory companies and Broadway, from off- and off-off-Broadway, from the university and the regional theater. Let it be lovingly and sternly watched over by critics.

And to hell with mere reviewers.

INDEX

ABOUT THE AUTHOR

JOHN SIMON was born in Yugoslavia in 1925, attended schools there, in England and in the United States, and received his B.A., M.A. and Ph.D. in comparative literature from Harvard. Since then he has taught at Harvard, the University of Washington, M.I.T., Bard and the University of Pittsburgh.

Mr. Simon has been the drama critic for a number of magazines and for Public Broadcasting, and currently appears in that role in *The Hudson Review* and *The New Leader*. He has also been a film critic for the latter, as well as for *Esquire,* and at present reviews the medium for *New York*. His book reviews, articles on the cultural scene, and film, drama and art criticism have appeared in a score of magazines, among them *The New York Times Sunday Magazine, Harper's, Horizon, The Reporter, Time, Vogue, The Saturday Review* and *The National Review*.

Mr. Simon lives in New York City and is the author of four previous books.